Discourse and the Two Cultures

Science, Religion and the Humanities

Volume 19

Exxon Education Foundation Series
on Rhetoric and Political Discourse

Series Editor

Kenneth W. Thompson

White Burkett Miller Center of Public Affairs
University of Virginia

University Press of America

Lanham • New York • London

The Miller Center

University of Virginia

Copyright © 1988 by

University Press of America,® Inc.

4720 Boston Way
Lanham, MD 20706

3 Henrietta Street
London WC2E 8LU England

British Cataloging in Publication Information Available

Library of Congress Cataloging-in-Publication Data

Discourse and the two cultures : science, religion, and the humanities
/ edited by Kenneth W. Thompson.
p. cm.—Exxon Education Foundation series on rhetoric and
political discourse ; v. 19)
1. Religion and the humanities. 2. Science and the humanities.
3. Religion and politics. I. Thompson, Kenneth W., 1921–
II. White Burkett Miller Center. III. Series.
BL65.H8D57   1988
001.1—dc 19   88–17157 CIP
ISBN 0–8191–7058–5 (alk. paper)
ISBN 0–8191–7059–3 (pbk. : alk. paper)

The views expressed by the author(s) of this publication do not necessarily
represent the opinions of the Miller Center. We hold to Jefferson's dictum that:
"Truth is the proper and sufficient antagonist to error, and has nothing
to fear from the conflict, unless by human interposition, disarmed
of her natural weapons, free argument and debate."

Co-published by arrangement with
The White Burkett Miller Center of Public Affairs,
University of Virginia

Discourse and the Two Cultures

Dedicated

to

Mr. and Mrs. William Odell

Table of Contents

TABLE OF CONTENTS

PART THREE: THE TWO CULTURES, RELIGION AND POLITICS

Preface

Thousands of books offer competing explanations of the problems of communication between peoples. If there is any consensus amidst a vast diversity of views, it is that the assumptions and presuppositions of the communicators shape and mold their conclusions. Even in a television age, the "message" continues to rival the "medium" in importance and the "message" is determined in significant ways by underlying philosophies, values and conceptual frameworks.

The British writer and statesman, Lord Snow's most important legacy may be his concept of "the two cultures." As Snow viewed contemporary approaches to society's problems he identified at least two fundamentally different perspectives. The one is the frame of reference to the scientist and the other the approach of the humanities, broadly defined and including religion. Some challenge Snow's division into two distinct conceptual approaches. For example, it is argued that scientists make use substantially of the humanist's concepts and thinking. A good scientist, it is argued, has recourse to hunches, imagination and sheer guesswork. Scientific breakthroughs follow bold new paradigms that share the characteristics of a new literary form or a social invention such as a new constitution forged by the Founding Fathers. It is uncertainty and indeterminism in science that demands insights and imagination. The more or less mechanical process suggested by the steps of the scientist in stating an hypothesis, testing it through experimentation and arriving at scientific laws is a misreading of the actual task of the scientist. Instead science at its best is a human endeavor that requires demystication.

For their part, humanists and even theologians find that thought and creativity has its scientific component. Father Malloy in the opening paper of this volume offers numerous examples of theological inquiries depending on scientific confirmation of the truth about complex biomedical and social problems. History is an empirical science with its own forms of testing and validation. Malloy speaks of theological science as something apart from mere religious speculation.

Yet these arguments for the unity of all human inquiry having been made, the examples of the differences about which Lord Snow wrote remain persuasive. Humanists speak of the limits of science in the qualitative dimensions of human experience. Also humanists and most notably theologians undertake to transcend scientific experience. Science for its part, at least in its formulation by some respected scientists, leaves open the possibility of faith and spirit and what the philosopher Max Otto defined as reflection on the *mysterium tremendum*. We are impressed with the number and variety of scientists who acknowledge the reality of the two cultures.

Moreover, when scientists or humanists depart from the recognized and accepted distinctions, they confront problems that they themselves had predicted. Thus the world renowned physicist, Robert Oppenheimer, wrote that the scientist who seeks to be both scientist and politician will fail in both. Yet Oppenheimer fell prey to the toils of "atomic politics." The problems of crossing the line separating the two cultures is well described in the essays that follow.

However, the controversy about the alleged differences between the two cultures and conflicting approaches to coping with the differences will continue. Obviously, the publication of this little volume will not resolve the debate. Our purpose in a series of publications on political and social discourse is not to resolve that debate once and for all. Rather the aim is to pose the issue through the thoughtful reflections of some of the nation's best minds. Their analysis helps to illuminate a basic problem with which society will continue to grapple for years to come.

Introduction

A colleague once had a phrase to describe the organization of meaningful discourse that applies to the preparation of this volume. Whenever we discussed how to arrange consultations on an important topic, he would say: "Who are the half dozen persons you would most like to have sitting around a table and discussing that subject?" Who are the thinkers most likely to further conversation and understanding?

With that injunction in mind, we at the Miller Center invited ten wise and thoughtful Americans to consider with us a subject that undergirds the most urgent question that men and nations confront. In one sense, it is the fundamental question "What is man?" or "How are we to understand human nature?" In another respect, it is how do we approach and assess the most difficult and perplexing questions that stem from recurrent questions about the nature of man. Shall we approach such questions through science or through religion and the humanities? Is understanding to be pursued through qualitative or quantitative methods? Can "science save us," as one writer asks, or must we turn to other avenues in the search for truth? Lord Snow posed the question in terms of what he described as the two cultures, the one being the scientific culture with its emphasis on precision, experimentation and the quest for scientific laws, with the other being the humanities, which he saw as the search for justice, beauty and truth through history, philosophy and sometimes theology.

INTRODUCTION

The Miller Center is fortunate that, not long after his election as the President of the University of Notre Dame, Father Edward A. Malloy consented to speak at the University of Virginia in its famed Dome Room. For anyone of lesser moral and intellectual distinction, the succession at Notre Dame would have presented an awesome if not impossible challenge. Father Theodore Hesburgh's service as president exceeded that of any other American university president. The dramatic emergence of Notre Dame as a world class university is associated in almost everyone's mind with Father Hesburgh. Yet a wise and good friend, the late Stephen Kertesz, who headed the University's Center of International Relations in its halcyon days, prophesied that Father Malloy would prove equal to the challenge. He noted that Malloy was in process of developing a profound understanding of ethics through testing his views in seminars and lectures. Kertesz prophesied that Father Malloy gave evidence of becoming a profound theological and ethical thinker eclipsing even his brilliant predecessor at Notre Dame.

Perhaps this is the best way to introduce Father Malloy. We who have heard him feel that we were listening to a theologian and educator standing on the threshold of greatness in theology and ethics. William James described philosophy as "an unusually stubborn attempt to think clearly." Because Father Malloy approaches the two cultures in this spirit, his is the first essay in this volume.

Professor Roger Shinn has been a major figure in theology and ethics over several generations. Through the turbulent 1960s and 1970s, he occupied the Reinhold Niebuhr chair at Union Theological Seminary in New York City. He kept a steady hand on his subject when others were transforming ethics into various forms of political activism. His students are today important contributors to the literature of ethics and society. Throughout, Shinn maintained an interest in science and participated in groups that sought to bridge the two cultures. If Father Malloy can be viewed as one of the leaders in Catholic approaches to the study of ethics, Professor Shinn has a well-deserved reputation as a leader of Protestant thought.

Dr. Joseph Fletcher is considered by many the father of "situation ethics." His essay is especially appropriate to this volume because he examines the relationship between theology and the humanities and, more particularly, between theism and humanism. Therefore, he carries the analysis of Father Malloy and Professor Shinn into areas such as biomedical ethics which they touch but toward which he directs his full attention. Dr. Fletcher also provides a bridge between the two cultures through his discussion of pragmatism, defined in his words: "Ethical theory, like all kinds of theory, must be born out of experiences with actual problems. It is experimental, empirical, and data based, *a posteriori*, not *a priori*." Or again: "Value judgments to be valid have to be inductive, not deductive." If these axioms contain elements of science, as some would define science, Dr. Fletcher discovers a link in pragmatism and he writes that "the logic of pragmatism in ethics leads to humanism. He concludes "pragmatism determines the validity of ideas in both science and ethics by looking at the consequences, and it weighs consequences in the scale of human benefits."

Professor E.D. Hirsch is the author of the best-selling book, *Cultural Literacy*. He is also the founder and organizer of an educational movement seeking to establish criteria and tests for determining and advancing cultural literacy in the American elementary and secondary school system. It would appear that Hirsch in his efforts was seeking connections between the humanities (he is a distinguished professor of English and literary theory) and science. On the one hand, he argues that true literacy is dependent on students and citizens appropriating and mastering their society's cultural traditions. Without such understanding, they lack the tools and concepts needed for literacy. On the other hand, science and the humanities are both part of the wider cultural legacy necessary to achieving literacy. Finally, Hirsch and his colleague, a physicist James Trefil, set about the discovery of the elements of literacy making use of the scientific method for determining a list of concepts and facts essential for literacy. Those who have criticized Hirsch argue that he gives too much weight to determining "scientifically" the essentials of literacy and is optimistic if not utopian in imagining that such literacy can assure progress toward an ideal society.

Richard Rorty is a University Professor at the University of Virginia associated with the Department of English. More than seven hundred people undertook to attend his lecture entitled "That Old-Time Philosophy" in the Dome Room of the Rotunda sponsored by the Miller Center. In the lecture, Rorty focused on the best-selling book, *The Closing of the American Mind* by Alan Bloom criticizing its anti-democratic tendencies. However, the main target of the criticism was Bloom's mentor, the University of Chicago political philosopher, the late Leo Strauss. It was Strauss who rekindled interest in the classical political philosophers and it is Strauss whom the followers of John Dewey have singled out as a major antagonist. If Strauss is seen as the representative of classical philosophy and therefore the humanities, Dewey and Rorty may be viewed as the champions of trial and error, experimentation, pragmatism and empiricism. Since these aspects of modern thought are in part derived from science, Dewey and those who follow him have been identified with the scientific approach.

Edward Teller is a scientist, sometimes called "the father of the hydrogen bomb." He also is considered the scientist who early on influenced Ronald Reagan's thinking on the Strategic Defense Initiative. Although Teller has denied that he inspired Reagan, his frequent appearances with the President suggest otherwise. In the presentation from which we have drawn excerpts for this volume, he analyzes the problematic role of the president's science adviser. He concludes that the problem that is inherent in science advising stems from the fact that the scientist and the politician live in two different worlds. They belong to two different cultures.

Ian Graig is the author of a forthcoming work on physicists and politicians. He received his Ph.D. from the University of Virginia's Government and Foreign Affairs Department and is one of the rising young scholars concentrating on theories of international relations.

Professor Martin Marty of the University of Chicago is one of the foremost scholars on the history of religion. His contributions have been enormous both in some twenty books and in several thousand articles and numerous reports and papers. His studies of religion and politics include inquiries into the religion of American presidents. He discussed this subject with a group of political scientists, historians and theologians at the Miller Center.

Harold J. Berman is Woodruff Professor of Law at the Emory University School of Law. Earlier he was James Barr Ames Professor of Law at the Harvard Law School. His analysis of religion and law in relation to the First Amendment touches directly on problems of the two cultures. Professor Berman argues that a reasonable perspective on the first amendment must view it through the eyes of the founders and as revealed in ongoing historical interpretations to the present. Drawing on a distinction by Professor Jaroslav Pellikan of Yale University, Berman distinguishes between tradition and traditionalism. Tradition is the living faith of the dead. Traditionalism is the dead faith of the living. Traditionalism becomes historicism whereas tradition is a belief in history. Thus while legal interpreters must look to original understandings or intent, they also need to understand the present and the circumstances and problems it presents. Through his analysis, Berman helps restore the proper role of history and thereby of the humanities in the context of the two cultures. His paper is an adaption of a law journal article entitled, "The Interaction of Law and Religion," which appeared in the *Capital Law Review*, vol. 8 (1979), pp. 345-56.

Professor Robert Benne is a leading scholar of religion and society at Roanoke College who has written on religion and economics and religion and politics. He was formerly a professor of religion at the University of Chicago. He examines the various alternatives and options available to religious groups in the policies they espouse in national and international politics.

In conclusion, I have added my own paper, "Religion and Politics in the United States: An Overview," which appeared in *The Annals of the American Academy*, vol. 483 (January 1986), pp. 12-24. The four papers on the two cultures and on religion and politics illustrate the interaction of the cultural setting and of approaches to politics in four major areas. They serve to make concrete some of the broader principles set forth concerning the two cultures.

PART ONE

THEOLOGY AND HUMANITIES

CHAPTER I

Discourse Between the Two Cultures

PRESIDENT EDWARD A. MALLOY
UNIVERSITY OF NOTRE DAME

NARRATOR: The subject for today is "Discourse Between the Two Cultures: Science, Religion and Humanities." It is very appropriate that Father Edward Malloy, who has established himself through his scholarly work and teaching in the area of our subject speak to us. Father Malloy is known and respected for his research and teaching in the broad field of ethics. He holds a Ph.D. from Vanderbilt University in Christian Ethics and holds Master's degrees in both English and Theology from Notre Dame. He has been the number two academic officer of the University of Notre Dame for a number of years and in the spring of 1987 became its president. We are pleased that, early in his career as president-elect, he visited this University. Father Malloy.

FATHER MALLOY: I understand that I came to engage in a conversation with all of you. I would like to speak as I think the context demands for about thirty or forty minutes and then to allow you to question me. I would take that as part of the process by which I can clarify my own ideas more effectively and also hear from some things that you might have to offer.

It is clear to me that many of us who live in multiple worlds sometimes suffer from a narrowness of vision. I am a priest and live as a Catholic Christian person who belongs to a particular religious denomination and tradition. I am also a teacher and a practitioner of the science of theology in the subspeciality of Christian ethics, and a university administrator; yet I'm sometimes embarrassed by those who claim to represent any of those worlds. It is possible for religious people to be very narrow-minded and unaware of what's going on around them and of the changes that are demanded by our culture and our time in history. It is possible for theologians to be so self-satisfied and convinced that they have risen above the human condition that they really fail to take concrete human experience into account or to see their responsibility for the ramifications of their theoretical conclusions. In addition, it is possible for university administrators and all of those who would speak on behalf of the intellectual life to have such a restricted notion of the nature of a university that religion would have no place there. We would have such a parochial understanding of a university that it would cease to be a university in any real sense of the term.

I'd like to begin my presentation by establishing some presuppositions, each of which would demand whole books. I am simply going to assert them here, however, and give some indication of why I say what I do. In addition, I'd like to make reference to some obstacles or problems in the relationship between science, religion and the humanities. Then I'd like to reflect upon some issues which allow us to see the sometimes precarious relationship in the discussion and rhetoric that come forth from the various institutions that are represented by science, religion and the humanities.

Let me begin with my presuppositions. I believe that there is no such thing as a value-free science.

There are all kinds of epistemological presuppositions built into that not very original claim. Max Weber, one of the founders of what we know as sociology, Thomas Kuhn, and others have reflected for all of our benefit upon the kind of relativity built into the questions that are asked and the resulting answers that might be obtained from scientific research. We all would like to make some kind of claim for objectivity in our search for the truth. We would like, as much as we can, to free ourselves of bias, prejudice and ideology in the sense of false consciousness, but in order to achieve that state, it seems to me, we would have to become so ethereal that we would resemble the angels about whom we speak in theological speculation. Human beings who practice the various sciences are always going to bring their humanness to the endeavor. Part of what they bring are various kinds of value identifications and commitments. Whether those values come out of the Enlightenment, or a specific religious tradition, or Marxist perspectives on reality, or from other sources, they are, in fact, full of values in some sense of that term. The questions that we ask at least partially determine the answers that we are able to obtain. The so-called scientific method, with its attempts to get at data so as to develop and test hypotheses and regular explanations of why things are the way they are, is a function of the curiosity and inquisitiveness of human beings. Even within the context of graduate education, one can see that, because of the financial support structures that often come from the federal government or private institutions to underwrite the costs of that education, we are lead in certain directions.

As an ethicist, it is interesting to me that in the last twenty to twenty-five years there has been a burgeoning of interest in the area of biomedical ethics. It has not occurred because everybody is innately interested in that area. It's taken place

5

simply because the money has been there; one has seen the establishment of groups like the Hastings Center in New York, the Kennedy Center affiliated with Georgetown University and many other think tanks. There has also been an interest in the question of nuclear strategizing and so we now have a series of think tanks like the Hudson Institute. Scholars have been led in a direction that might have been different had money been available elsewhere. The same thing is true more recently in issues in business ethics. We have become focused on the economy today, at least with regard to ethical considerations, in a way that was not true two or three decades ago.

My second presupposition is that science is, or can be, a vocation. The language of "Vocation", which was employed in a very interesting way by Martin Luther in describing what it meant to be a Christian in the world, often is employed only for commitments of life relating to ministry. I think in the times since the second Vatican Council we have rediscovered a more broadly based notion of what it means to say that one has a vocation or calling to a particular form of life. We have rediscovered all the discipline and rigor that a commitment like that demands. We've also been reminded of the exaltation that can result from giving one's self over to that type of endeavor, the sense of commitment to the pursuit of the truth. Science is and can be a vocation in that sense of the term. Additionally, from my vantage point, any search for the truth can be a route to God, whether it is for a given individual or for a community of scholars. Science can be a calling, a rich and fruitful way of trying to arrive at a greater approximation of the truth. If that is the case, I see it as something to which a person from my particular tradition can well be called and give himself or herself entirely.

6

My third presupposition is that the study of nature, including human nature, strives toward a unified theory. We are too fragmented and stratified today. In a sense we have become much like a physician who looks only at bones and not at the whole person. To a great extent, we are people who are only interested in one dimension of human experience. It may be that the best way we can mobilize a particular group of people is to have some fruitful breakthrough in terms of our knowledge and understanding; however, it seems to me that another case presents itself. That is, only when we try to incorporate that knowledge and understanding into some broader view of nature, including human nature, can we really satisfy our curiosity about why things are the way they are and what it means to have some kind of creative interaction with the "givenness," with the status quo all around us.

Connected to the lack of an appreciation for the desire for a unified theory is a kind of disavowal of the results of our quest to understand. So what if my theory leads to certain results? So what if we can make some kind of connection between Hegel and Hitler? So what if somebody's theory about the worthwhileness of a certain component of the human family leads us to practices which are detrimental to the whole of civilization? It seems to me that built into the particular study of some phenomenon, including the human phenomenon or part of it, is the demand that we try to see the connection between that specific piece of knowledge and the way we perceive and understand all of reality around us.

A fourth presupposition is that reason counts. The weakest form of argument, even though a legitimate form, is the appeal to authority. Arguments do count. I believe that one of the richest parts of the particular philosophical and theological tradition that is my own—a broad western tradition which is specifically Roman Catholic—is a

7

respect for reason. It is not the case that our hearts, our experiences and our feelings don't speak to us as well; it is a confidence that, given sufficient time and effort and goodwill, people can arrive at a working and effective consensus about matters of public dispute and disagreement. Only if we trust in that process, only if we believe that words and pictorial representation and symbols can allow us to get at the truth and to communicate effectively, can we have some kind of handle that will allow us to make progress toward mutual understanding. One of the things that I most greatly fear in our particular time—perhaps it has always been present—is that people will simply categorize those who disagree as irrational or oblivious to the truth, that they will cease to try to communicate and will cease to arrive at some kind of consensus about troubling issues, especially in the public forum.

Finally, I believe as an ethicist that one of the most difficult and perplexing things about the relationship between science and religion and the humanities is to figure out how we move from value language to normative, principled, rule-oriented language. How do we go from the most general claims about where our heart is, symbolically or metaphorically, from where we stand as unique human being with what makes sense to us, with values that attract us or give a power and a beauty and a kind of resonant spirit to our lives, to the more difficult description of normative kinds of claims which require precision of language? How do we take the step to a principled language and do we think principles will enable us to make universal claims or are they just roughly useful? When it comes to public policy matters, most of us would like to be able to move at least to the level of principle, because if we can show the transition from values which may be widely held to principles, we can make at least some progress on matters of public conversation.

When we come to the level of rules, of course, we will always allow for a greater range of disagreement and for exception making. That shouldn't surprise us, however. The stuff of everyday life is never entirely amenable to being subsumed under our categories of thought. I think, however, we can make progress at this particular moment of our collective history by trying to describe the transition from values to principles, if not always to rules.

The second part of my presentation has to do with problems. What are the problems we can identify as we try to find some bridges across the bounds of science, religion and the humanities? From the vantage point of the religiously committed person, the first problem is what might be called the "scientific imperative." Is it true to say that whatever we can do by way of research or exploration, we ought to do? Beyond that, should we fund such projects if we have an opportunity to commit our resources for that purpose? The federal government and major institutions, including the business community, are responsible for subsidizing most of the research that goes on in the broader American community. There are choices to be made about where we should put our resources. It seems to me that the bald claim that there is such a thing as the "scientific imperative" and that all research that can be done ought to be done are misguided. I think we need to make some correlation between the value commitments of our lives, i.e., the kind of information or knowledge we believe to have the highest priority, and what kind of obfuscation might come from the wholesale support of every possible route of exploration. We have the Dr. Frankenstein phenomenon which suggests that some isolated researcher, privately supported, can well do anything that he or she would like and afterwards come back for approbation from the broader scientific community.

9

I believe that one of the more important notions of any profession is that there be some code; it could be self-generated but at least should conform with the broader society. There should also be some procedures of adjudication of the code. This notion ought to apply to the scientific community in both the natural sciences and the social sciences. I reject the untrammeled view that the scientific imperative ought to reign supreme. I think the scientific imperative, i.e., scientific research and the support for such, needs to be determined on the basis of the values of a given group or culture and that some hard choices need to be made along the way.

A second problem has to do more with religion than science. That is, religions—whatever religious tradition—are inherently conservative, for they are communities which try to preserve the memories of certain great events of the past, including those relevant to their own foundations, and to reinterpret ancient traditions for the present generation. There will always be a certain amount of suspicion about the new, about the radical, and about the breakthrough possibility. One sees that attitude in every religious tradition. You might find some areas in which there is less of an attempt to preserve, but generally, every religious tradition will have some area of life or behavior with which it will concern itself; the effort is to guard the quality or the integrity of the past.

We can look to some obvious phenomena in western history: the Inquisition, the rack, the ordeal, and torture to obtain the truth (supposedly to obtain the truth). Those practices were given approbation by theologians and religious leaders. In retrospect that tradition seems to be seriously misguided, just as from my vantage point in ethical theory I take the crusades to be a great aberration. Yet for a period of time these were considered to be the appropriate responses to the new, the challenging, and the revolutionary. We can see the same thing in the responses to the thought of Galileo, Darwin, Marx, Freud, and so on. Every great revolutionary thinker of the nineteenth and twentieth century was suspected by the religious leaders of the day. That doesn't mean there weren't any good reasons for that suspicion, but I think it reveals to us that religion is resistant, to some extent, especially in its official statements, to the breakthrough of new knowledge. One of the challenges, then, for the intellectual representatives of those traditions, including the Christian one, is to find an effective way to mediate the new knowledge and show that it is not totally incompatible with the tradition of the past. As we will recognize looking at some of the issues, it is not always so easy to pull that off.

The third problem is fundamentalism. What I mean by fundamentalism is not simply the certain kind of biblical fundamentalism that is present notably in the Protestant world but also to some extent in the Catholic world, the Islamic world, and the Jewish world; rather, fundamentalism is a belief that control of the sacred text is control of the thought processes of the adherents. It is an attempt to disallow any recognition of the history of ideas in the evolution of understanding, or the importance of what is called "hermeneutics," the science of interpretation. Coming to grips with that very complex methodological question is as important as anything else in trying to promote greater cooperation among science, religion and the humanities.

There is a kind of authoritarian fundamentalism which regards authority in much the same way that the first fundamentalism that I described regards the text. This authoritarian fundamentalism exists because people feel threatened and picture the modern world in dire, apocalyptic terms. Everybody is going to hell in a handbasket. If you want to, you can write a cynical book at any given time of human history. We are always looking to the future for fulfillment in this world, and one of the tasks of religion is somehow to interpret this world as something other than the be-all and end-all of existence. Perhaps we would have a transformative role within it and should not see it as, in a sense, heaven or earth. We cannot live merely for the dictatorship of the proletariat or some other utopian promise in this world. Fundamentalism addresses a very basic human need for stability, order and assurance, a need which all of us possess to some extent. Yet I think it errs because it addresses this need in the wrong way; it tries to assure or guarantee access to the truth by controlling the text or controlling the process of communication within a religious tradition.

All of those assertions are open to demur and disagreement. Let me list some issues. I want to quickly give you a series of issues that I believe highlight the tension between science, religion and the humanities.

The first issue is criminal behavior. I've done a little writing in this area so I'm somewhat familiar with the key ideas. We know from the history of criminology that there have been various attempts by scientists to explain why people act the way they do, not simply violating the fifty-five mile an hour speed limit, but why they steal, wreak physical harm on one another, and refuse to abide by the claims for the common good. One theory at a particular moment of history was that our forehead shape could determine whether we had criminal tendencies. This method of phrenology was taken quite seriously. In old criminological textbooks you see the side view and the front view, and they black out the eyes so you can't tell who it is. They show gigantic foreheads among the criminals in prison but, of course, that was due to very selective sampling.

Another attempt was body shape, ectomorphs and endomorphs. All that you see here are these somewhat nude shapes with appropriate things blacked out; some are big and others thin. All kinds of suggestions were taken seriously as a kind of scientific explanation. More recently we have had the xyy or the super male chromosome claim that one could tell by doing certain kinds of genetic checks who had a propensity to be a sociopath. That had the potential of being a self-fulfilling prophesy, and fortunately it was never borne out. In short, you find attempts by science, whether on natural grounds or social scientific grounds, to try to account for why we do evil. From the vantage point of a theoretician of religion, claims about original sin or temptation seem to have as much credibility as the accounts that have been provided entirely on scientific grounds.

Is it nature or nurture that leads us to perform evil deeds against one another? On the basis of our theory we might or might not provide an account of moral accountability. Are criminals simply sick? Are criminals so environmentally determined that they have no freedom left to control their behavior? Or is it in fact true that people can be held morally accountable for their deeds? It seems to me that there are partial explanations available on the basis of scientific evidence, but I have seen no persuasive or even plausible explanation for criminal behavior that does not take into account human freedom and the context within which human freedom is properly exercised.

Derivative from all of that is what we do about criminals to shape them up. We have a great debate in our culture about whether deterrence, retribution and rehabilitation, or even isolation is the proper strategy of response. For a period of time, the explanation behind our criminal justice system was that we could rehabilitate criminals by putting them in jail but there is no evidence that I believe conclusively shows that it works that way. I wrote an article one time that simply said "If you are going to put somebody in prison, the only reason for doing it is to isolate them for the common good." While it doesn't *necessarily* deter, it might; it is hard to prove. One might believe in theories of retribution or righting the wrong; one might think we can rehabilitate, though I doubt it; one thing we surely can do is isolate. Thus, we should only put people in prison who we think need to be isolated. We face a great crisis in our society today over building more prisons and incarcerating an ever-growing proportion of the population. We can see the connection between the account we give of why people perform criminal deeds in the first place, why they are malefactors, and what we do in response to that later on. Moral accountability ties very much into value systems that stem from religious traditions and adherence to codes that come out of religious commitments.

A second question is alcoholism. Why are some people alcoholics and other people are not? Is alcoholism a disease? I think there is good reason to believe that it is a disease, at least partially, and that we should treat people with all of the respect that goes along with that acknowledgment. Yet it also seems to be a function of social conditioning. If you live in a society where nobody drinks, you are liable never to discover that you are an alcoholic or could be. The availability of alcohol opens up the possibility for somebody who is predisposed, like Irish people or American Indians, to become alcoholic. I don't know of any Irish family of any size that doesn't have at least one alcoholic member, including my own. The availability of alcohol and the social support structures for drinking a lot accentuate the possibility that alcoholism might be a problem for a given individual.

What about moral blame? We have a very curious phenomenon in that the most successful therapy available for alcoholism is provided by Alcoholics Anonymous. Alcoholics Anonymous claims to be a

14

nondenominational, nonreligiously affiliated group, but in its twelve steps one must appeal to a higher power, some source outside of one's self to whom one is accountable. One makes amends by going to all the people that one has harmed along the way and asking for their forgiveness. Each member tries to be open and confessional; that is interesting isn't it? One is confessional in front of the group in saying "I am an alcoholic."

Religion has had a place. Drunkenness is morally blameable conduct, but is it only that? Science has forced religion to take into account a dimension of the experience of alcohol abuse that religion on its own grounds might never have had to do. We now find a boundary point where we have redescribed, even on religious grounds, alcoholism as a disease but we have simultaneously tried to preserve the notion of moral accountability.

Venereal disease and AIDS raise somewhat similar questions. Every day and in every paper in America there are at least two articles on AIDS. There has been a consciousness-raising for many reasons. It is possible, of course, to see venereal disease and/or AIDS, especially sexually related AIDS transmission, as punishment from God and there are certain religious representatives that use that language. I think such a position is reprehensible myself, but it happens. It is surely the case that the more promiscuous one is in sexual habits, the higher the chance of getting venereal disease and AIDS. There is a connection. It seems as if "condom morality"—give everybody a condom and we'll solve all our problems—is fallacious in the sense that it fails to give any accounting for discipline or control over one's behavior. One can debate whether one ought to do this for other reasons, but as a solitary strategy it seems fated not to work.

Is AIDS or venereal disease a merely medical problem? The prediction is that 100,000 people will die of AIDS by 1991. There are half a million people infected in various parts of the country; it's heterosexually transmitted in Africa and Haiti. Even if we controlled the homosexual experience and the drug experience, we still wouldn't prevent the transmission of AIDS. Is it a social problem? Is it an educational problem? If so, doesn't education presume a certain configuration of values? Or is it a moral problem? Is it God's punishment? Is that adequate language to talk about what is a very complex experience? I don't think so, but it surely is used—another area where science and religion come together.

Let me raise an even more controversial social question: race and ethnicity. Is there any correlation between race or ethnicity and intelligence? Do IQ tests or SAT scores, which are variable and predictable almost by race and ethnic background, have anything to do with truth, with worthiness or with a right to education? Is the continuation of a divided society, even on college campuses a satisfactory state? When we integrate college campuses, and blacks hang together, whites hang together, Hispanics hang together and so on, what does that reveal? Is the support structure in the primary and secondary schools sufficient to allow people to prepare for the kind of highly rationalized tests (with certain verbal presuppositions) or not?

What about athletic ability and musical talent and race? Why do so many blacks have an ability to jump higher and run faster than whites? "White man's disease," we call it—those of us who play basketball. I can't jump worth a darn; I'm not very fast either so I had to make up for it in playing basketball by being a good shooter and having a certain amount of finesse. I played against blacks my whole life and many of my best friends are blacks. Yet I really haven't seen any scientist take on the issue of black predominance in the Olympics or in certain other sporting activities. What does that mean? Does that have a moral quality to it or not? Does that mean that every team ought to have affirmative action for whites? If you want to turn it around, reverse the intelligence quotient question. There are many theories which have to do with notions of social justice, the influence of religion and the question of competency that come out of notions like race or ethnicity. The resolution of problems in those theories is not simple but I think the healthy interplay of science, religion, the social sciences and the humanities force us not to settle for cheap answers to those questions. Rather, we must keep going back for a more adequate description and an even better analysis.

There are a couple more obvious questions: nuclear power and nuclear deterrent strategy. The American Catholic bishops wrote a letter several years ago which I think employed an excellent process. They went out on the highways and byways, they brought in experts from all sides, they put a draft out, they asked for criticism of the draft, they put out another draft, and they asked for further criticism. Finally, when the third draft was approved, they had distinguished in their document between different levels of teaching. You can disagree with it or not—and they encourage actual disagreement about the concrete particulars—but the process itself is interesting because it respects the intelligence and the rights of those who make up the Catholic religious tradition, and even people outside of it, to speak in an informed way on a controversial issue.

The bishops used a similar process in drafting the letter on the economy. It is interesting that before both letters and the final draft came out, a group of more conservative Catholics released their own letter saying, in effect, "Thank you, bishops, but we think we know more about this than you do." I think that's an interesting process and very American in a sense. Probably only in America, at least in the Catholic tradition, could we have pulled that off. Maybe one of the things the American Catholic experience has to teach the rest of the Church is that internal debate is possible and desirable. This is something that I would want to argue.

Organ transplantation is another issue with moral implications. I'm on the Indiana Governor's Commission on Organ Donation and we have to recommend public policy with regard to many sensitive normative issues. The questions we face include determining the criteria for patient selection. How are we going to foster the giving of organs? Should we take them? Should we presume consent unless proven the opposite? Or should we have a process for giving consent for organ donation? At one time that was a very controversial issue. Most people I know agree that organ donation is a good thing, but there are questions over how we do it and who gets access to it. Should the president be going on television arguing the case for a particular recipient—some little girl somewhere—when there are fifty or a hundred or a thousand other people who have equal claim to the same organ or to comparable organs? That's a matter where religion and the motivation people have for donating organs is very much related to the amelioration of a significant, social, biomedical problem.

Finally, there is death and dying technology. We all know that we'd rather die with our boots on; that we'd rather be relatively in control rather than completely dependent upon those around us, strapped up, connected to all kinds of intensive care equipment and separated from emotional and personalized support. We have the hospice alternative and various ways of counteracting what is perhaps an over-dependence on technology. We are going through some continual discussions about the right to die, about the definition of death, and about the kind of resources that we can afford to make available to people in the dying process. Again, this is a very emotional and difficult issue that involves religious affiliation, scientific research (and the technology that emerges from it), and a public debate about where the money ought to go. It is not clear that we can continue to go in the direction in which we have been going up to this point. The notion of Diagnosis Related Groups (DRG), with all that it has done to hospitals, to competition for economic support, and to medical plants is redefining the nature of American medicine, for better or worse. I think that religion, science and the humanities all have a role to play in this debate.

We live in a pluralistic culture. Therefore, public debate on the matters I have mentioned is crucial. The work of the Miller Center and of other similar institutions—to help people become informed and recognize the connection between the values that they have (whether religiously inspired or not) and the kind of civil responsibilities that they bear—is particularly important at this moment in our history. Otherwise, the decisions may be made by the few so-called experts or may be made by default by those less qualified than ourselves to exercise our options.

In addition, we need to try to persuade rather than to coerce. Yet the temptation of the elite in religion, in intellectual life, and in the body politic is always to act on behalf of everybody else. We say on the one hand that we trust the common lot of humanity, that this is a democracy and republican form of government and that popular rule is deeply rooted in our traditions, and yet we all think that "the masses are asses and the elite are effete". We suspect elitism and yet we really don't have a great confidence in the mass of humanity. We struggle from the desire to be coercive, especially if we are gifted with words or with knowledge of the political process. We want to skip the steps that are necessary for people to know what they are doing and to give common assent to it.

Finally, we will continue to live, I think, in an interdependent world in which neither science nor religion nor the humanities can go it alone. Therefore, whether a scientist or a humanist is also a religious adherent or not, he or she must take into account the rights of religious people to have a say in the decisions of the government, university life, and in the kinds of priorities that we establish for ourselves as a people in doing his work. I believe a university is the most fruitful place to promote that kind of interaction. It is my honor to have been chosen the president of a major university. It is even more of an honor to be chosen to come and to give a presentation at a great university like Virginia. I only hope that Notre Dame, Virginia, and all the other great universities and colleges of this country can serve not only the scientific community but also the Church to keep us all honest and to keep us all in conversation. Thank you.

NARRATOR: Who would like to begin our conversation?

QUESTION: Regarding your earlier statement about the Church's responsibility to maintain the dogmatic principles in teaching, can you comment on the Catholic Church's recent statements over the surrogate mother question?

FATHER MALLOY: The question is about the recent statement that came from a congregation in Rome under the Pope's authority, a statement which the Pope read and approved. There are several levels on which I can answer that. One is to identify the status of the document. It is not a papal statement or an encyclical nor is it like a document of an ecumenical council. However, those who put it forth would necessarily like it to be taken at the ultimate level of significance. It seems to me that the process that was used was not entirely adequate for the level of significance internally proposed for the document. There was a very limited contribution by the range of theological opinion and the range of scientific and medical experience. This affects the quality of the arguments and the information that is built into the document as I read it. In fact, the conclusions of the document are stronger than the methods used to argue the case because the methods employed in the document could have been used a hundred and fifty years ago or a hundred years ago or fifty years ago. I do not think that the notions built into it—which are completely consistent internally—are as persuasive as I would like them to be.

Most of the disagreement within the Catholic community among ethicists about the elements taken up in the statement revolves around whether a married couple could legitimately and morally employ *in vitro* fertilization, for example, in order to have a child. I think there are at least plausible cases made for assenting to that which the document overlooks. However, I would say, at least within my own religious community—and I'm pretty familiar with the range of at least Christian and Jewish responses to the biotechnology field—that there is a greater consensus of a negative sort about some of the procedures than there is about others. Many people intuitively, and maybe experientially as well, are suspicious of surrogate motherhood to a greater extent that they are of *in vitro* fertilization for a married couple, although there is some resemblance in the kind of arguments you could make against each.

In sum, I would say the document intended to clarify, from an official Church standpoint, what the prevailing teaching (and *perpetual* teaching for the authors of the document) would be concerning matters of biomedical technology. I think it gives a clear answer; there is no quibbling. Yet in my opinion, it is excessively clear about some matters that are still, and have been open to debate for quite a while. I really think it would be better for the dialogue to continue with that as a starting point, perhaps, and see what areas of disagreement still exist. If you broaden the debate to the larger community, it is clear that American medicine is the most advanced. The technology started in England which has supplied other nations with the techniques. Australia has done a lot of work and so has India, ironically, but the United States is one of those nations that I think probably has as much to say from our experience in the medical community and the ethical community as anyone. I do not think, personally, that American opinion was sufficiently taken into account.

One can agree or disagree with the particular conclusions. If you ask me as an ethicist what I think of the methodology, I don't think it was as good as it should have been.

QUESTION: I believe you used the term the "science of theology." Were you speaking in an empirical sense or in a disciplinary sense?

FATHER MALLOY: In a disciplinary sense. I think theology is a science, a legitimate science, in the sense that it has its own procedures, accepted methods of exploration, standards of argumentation and historical tradition with which one can become familiar, for example, in doctoral studies. Then there are journals; there are recognized outstanding theologians whom one can study; and there are some people who wield a greater influence by virtue of their expertise at a particular moment. One needs to display sufficient acquaintance with that tradition and the ability to employ its language in methodology in order to win acceptance as a qualified practitioner. I don't mean theology is simply an empirical study, but rather, theology is a recognized discipline, comparable in its own way to chemistry or history or law.

QUESTION: What do you think of the importance of teaching creationism in schools and of the recent court ruling in Alabama on secular humanism?

FATHER MALLOY: I don't think the recent ruling in Alabama will stand the test of the Appeals Court, so the decision in itself is not going to last in terms of the judication process. Creationism is an interesting thing but as a Catholic I feel a certain distance from it. There was a time in Catholic theology when you could easily have had a creationist-evolution controversy, but that is not where the main stream of Catholic thought led. The Catholic tradition has absorbed modern biblical criticism. Once one has done that—even if you have to make some decisions about how far to push the methodology—there is room for an interpretation of the text that acknowledges the problem of evolution. We are not seeing anything incompatible between certain basic notions of evolution and elements of the Christian belief system such as the stories in the Book of Genesis or various parts of the Old Testament.

I do think, however, that those who object to certain notions of evolution (such as either Darwinian survival of the fittest or a kind of embedded, enlightenment, anti-theistic position) are well taken. It is also possible, for example, that somebody could do a history of America and not take into account the history of religion in America or the role of the churches. It seems to me that this is very poor history because it does not recognize how the churches have, in many ways, been the most important element in influencing the value system of the people of this country. Churches were not as important in the earliest stages of our history because very little of America was religious at the time of the

Revolutionary War, but after the Second Great Awakening one could describe America as a religious country. The notions of the Bible Belt of the South, the preachers out on horseback and the tent meetings represent how democratized religion has become in the American experience.

I would say that it is possible to give a fair accounting of evolution in any textbook. It is a theoretical position which seems to account for a lot of phenomena in a way that nothing else does. One can push it too far, however, as an utter or a complete explanation which would be exaggerated or inappropriate. So I think the critics are forcing certain elements of the scientific community to be more humble and limited in the way they present scientific theory. Nonetheless the evolutionists can say to the creationists, "You cannot give as full an explanation of the world as we can and until you can, you should not represent yourself as equal and adequate scientific (theorists)." Those are my thoughts about it anyway.

QUESTION: I'd like you to address the problem of society that nearly everybody is educated in only one of three streams of thought: religious, scientific or humanistic. They don't speak on the same terms with one another, thus limiting their interaction. How do you deal with the problem of those three groups communicating with each other since they each have a kind of distinct personality?

FATHER MALLOY: The easiest answer is for the same person to be in all three groups. Is it possible for a scientist to be a believer? Some could imagine that it isn't, yet I know people whom I consider excellent scientists who are believers and are also very well educated so as to be open to the arts and to the broader notion of human well-being. If you don't find it in the same person, then human

24

mechanisms like friendship, working on common projects, looking for areas of consensus and minimizing areas of conflict have to suffice. Just as you do with any other group with which you have to start out on a different wavelength, there are problems. There is a skill in bringing that off, but what I fear most is the case of individuals who represent different strata of society sitting back and hurling diatribes at one another. As a result they don't increase the communication at all, but rather increase the level of suspicion and antagonism and elicit from the other side something comparable. That's not my style and it is not at all productive in the long run.

Let me give you an example of a productive way to overcome these problems. There is a man who graduated from Notre Dame named Jim Muller who teaches at the Harvard Medical School. He was one of the co-founders of the Physicians for Nuclear Responsibility which won the Nobel Prize. He learned Russian when he was at Notre Dame and he became concerned about the whole question of nuclear deterrence and the possibility of nuclear holocaust. When he went to Russia he was able to speak the language of the people on some research projects. When the possibility came along of trying to bring Russian and American scientists together, he had a head start because he had already established a rapport with people on medical grounds. That led to the broader concern about the survival of our two cultures which for him was linked to his religious convictions as a Catholic. It so happened that when he went to the Nobel Peace Prize ceremony, another Russian physician there had a heart attack on the stage. He came up to the stage where some people were working on the physician—many were cardiologists—and the medical people from Sweden examined him and said, "He's dead; it is too late for him." But Jim said, "No, I think there is still a chance to save him." Jim stuck with him and did therapy on him until they got to the hospital and the physician lived. So in the very ceremony at which they all received the Nobel Prize together, he saved the life of a Russian physician who has subsequently been very instrumental in getting greater cooperation from the Russians to make this project have some success. That's an example that nobody could have predicted, of how getting involved in one project can lead to a higher level of communication and mutual trust. It then led to the possibility of getting other people involved in the same kind of conversation.

Beyond that, I don't have any magic scheme. Father Hesburgh has as his number one priority to work from within the Institute for International Peace Studies on bringing people together. He has focused on scientists first of all because he believes that the scientists are most in touch with the potential for ill that goes along with the use of nuclear weapons, and because of that they can have an influence on their cultures that nobody else can have. Therefore, we brought together at Notre Dame a group of retired Russian generals and a group of retired American generals to talk for a period of time about their experience of war and what they think of the nuclear question. We brought three people from the U.S.S.R., three from China, three from the United States, one each from Japan, France, England and Germany, all under twenty-five years of age, to spend a year doing a Master's degree in Peace Studies together, to try to prepare the next generation of leaders to know each other, to speak the same language and to have some common concerns on which they can cooperate. I think what we are doing is great. It's the kind of thing that can work better than simply sitting back and thinking that the scientists are all merely absorbed in their own work and have no sense of humanity or that the humanists are out of it or that the religious people are Neanderthals.

QUESTION: What are your views on research in the area of *in vitro* fertilization?

FATHER MALLOY: The main objections to *in vitro* fertilization that appeared early on in the literature were classic ones. Is it a threat to the notions that we have presumed about sexuality and the relationship between genital intercourse and the bearing of children? Is there something very unique about blood bonding and the way that one identifies with a child as wholly one's own? I think that's a legitimate question.

A second concern has to do with what has been called "playing God." Are we presuming a kind of wisdom that can only be tested by time? Will we discover after the fact that we regret having promoted this kind of step?

A third concern (in the Steptoe and Edwards research in England) revolved around the rejection of some of the fertilized eggs that we could see as an abortive process. If you believe, as I do, that you have human life from the moment of fertilization and therefore, a protectable human life—all things being equal—and you deliberately reject some of the fertilized eggs, then perhaps this is the case.

Another objection that appears in this document, which I don't find very persuasive, has to do with the way that the sperm is obtained. The same problem applies, to some extent, to obtaining the eggs from the woman. In the end the real debate is whether this is an excessive mechanization under the guise of doing good for infertile couples. Is it an excessive mechanization of what is or is taken to be a natural process on other grounds? Will the results in the end destroy the delicate fabric of the family concept and parental bonding as we have known it throughout human history? I don't think the answers are yet available to those questions. I think one needs to be wary and at least concerned about the significance of *in vitro* fertilization, even if restricted to a couple. Still, I think one can at least entertain the possibility that it can be a moral procedure and that one can look at the arguments for and against it.

Once it extends past the marital bond, then I think we have a different situation, one that I would find morally objectionable because of what it does to the notion of family. It is possible now to have five parents: the donor of the egg and the sperm, a host mother, and the nurturing couple. It is possible in the same way to have lesbian parents, homosexual male parents, single parents, elderly parents or juvenile parents. You could reconstruct the whole understanding of parenting on the basis of what is already available, no less the frozen embryos which brings to mind the idea of hatcheries that goes along with the Brave New World image. All of that is good reason, if not for alarm, then at least for deep and consistent concern. To that extent I'm glad that a document came out that tries to force people to come to grips with this reality.

In saying that I have quibbles about some elements of it, particularly the methodology, I don't want to discount the importance of trying to focus moral attention on these questions. Those are at least some of the issues that I have seen and would believe are important as far as ethical analysis goes.

QUESTION: There is a great new debate about papal teachings. As an ethicist and an academician, what is your view on that question? Does papal proclamation completely and finally end debate and what is your view on the Church's quick, decisive reaction when dissent has been repeatedly vocal?

FATHER MALLOY: Well, it's hard to know where to begin on that question. I think if you've ever studied church history, whether Catholic, Protestant or any other, you know that there are certain periods that are more marked by conflict than others. Certain issues rise to prominence and become a kind of test of orthodoxy. It's lamentable from my point of view that so much of the discussion about authentic teaching and orthodoxy has revolved around sexual morality. It seems to me that there is a wide sweep of concerns (of which sexuality is only one) which we might employ to see where somebody is within the broader context of the Catholic community or any other community.

For instance, Michael Novak, William Simon, William O'Brien and others came out with a letter about the nuclear question in which they pushed the matter of the criteria of just war past its traditional interpretations. William O'Brien said in his response to the Bishop's letter—this is from a conservative perspective—that the principle of noncombatant immunity or discrimination was not an overarching moral principle that should stand behind any judgment about war. Rather, it was a beginning point or a *prima facie* duty, and that the evil of the Soviet system with its threat to all the freedoms that we know, was sufficient to override the immorality of deterrence as a nuclear strategy. Hence we should be prepared to fight a limited nuclear war. He argued the case that we should start by limited targeting but be prepared, if necessary, to implement targeting for total devastation.

That goes against the grain of all that I know in just war thought as it evolved out of the Catholic tradition. O'Brien is a dissenter. Michael Novak argues the case for an extension of the notion of right intention, which is way beyond what I think has been true in much of the discussion in the Catholic community and even in the broader Christian community about right intention as a criterion of just war.

I don't say that they shouldn't be able to voice their dissent because it depends on what issue you are pointing to, on where dissent lies, and on how much freedom of discussion people wish to tolerate. I'm on the progressive end of the spectrum when it comes to the range of the exploration of ideas and allowance for disagreement, especially in a university setting. I think that's the proper context within which to do it.

It doesn't mean that individuals shouldn't have to acknowledge that they are at odds with the inherited traditional position. I think that needs to be part of the good teaching and good writing. Yet in the Catholic intellectual world today, the great hope is in this country where we have more qualified and committed scholars than in any other part of the world. The European tradition is much more suspicious of what goes on here than it ought to be, especially if you look at the quality of life and worship with regard to the Catholic community in general. I wish Europeans could spend more time here and learn firsthand the kinds of things that are going on and see the wide range of issues that are being taken up. They should see what the American political tradition has done to the notions that Catholics have and what ought to happen in the life of the Church. I think the university community needs to try to preserve the discourse as much as possible. That doesn't mean that we should be centers of some kind of hostile opposition although there are always going to be individual celebrated cases of opposition. Sometimes the people foster public opposition for their own reasons and sometimes not.

At my institution, the most conservative Catholics, fairly liberal Catholics, and all the range in between are represented. We have very few really radical types on our faculty. I like the diversity; I think it is healthier than just being identifiable as one kind of Catholic university. Whether or not

Rome will like that is not for me to say. It is for me to try to represent it well and to build bridges rather than try to breed conflict.

NARRATOR: Whatever our differences on some of the issues that were mentioned, it seems to me that on one issue we can be in full accord; that is, intellectually, morally, and scientifically, Notre Dame is in good hands for the years ahead. Thank you very much, Father Malloy.

CHAPTER II

The Two Cultures and Public Policy

ROGER SHINN

NARRATOR: We thought today we'd move toward the completion of this discussion of the two cultures with a presentation by Roger Shinn, who has had a very distinguished career in the field of social ethics. He was Reinhold Niebuhr Professor of Social Ethics at Union Theological Seminary for almost two decades and was simultaneously a professor at Columbia University. He has been a professor at Jewish Theological Seminary as well.

Roger was born in Germantown, Ohio. He did his undergraduate work at Heidelberg and later graduated *summa cum laude* from Union Theological Seminary. Then he went off to war. He rose from private to major in the Armored Infantry, was awarded the Silver Star medal, was inducted into the Infantry Hall of Fame, and has been recognized in other ways for his combat service in the European theater of operations. Following his return, he got his Ph.D. from Columbia University and then taught, first as professor, then as Dodge professor, and then as Reinhold Niebuhr professor at Union Theological Seminary. He has also served as acting president of that institution. He is the associate editor of the *Bulletin of Science, Technology and Society* which suggests continuing interest in our topic today. He is also the author, most recently, of a book called

Forced Options: Social Decisions for the 21st Century, and his earlier works include *Search for Identity: Essays on the American Character; Faith and Science in an Unjust World; Man: The New Humanism*; and an earlier work *Restless Adventure: Essays on Contemporary Expressions of Existentialism*.

Over the years and through turbulent times as well as more tranquil ones at Union, Roger Shinn was always, it seemed to me, profoundly concerned about ethics and moral issues while also seeking to maintain the continuity of that institution. It is a great personal pleasure to have him visit the Miller Center and speak to you on two cultures and public policy.

PROFESSOR SHINN: Thank you, Ken. I've known and appreciated Ken Thompson for many years, and I'm fascinated by the outflow of activities and publications from this Miller Center. It is good to be here.

When Ken proposed the topic, "the two cultures," I ran back to C.P. Snow's book of 1959 to refresh my mind on just how he put it. You may be familiar with this, but I'll just remind you of his language. His thesis is that Western society is "being split into two polar groups," represented on the one hand by literary intellectuals and on the other by scientists, particularly physical scientists. These groups have "almost ceased to communicate at all," and this is an international phenomenon. So, he says, you can move from Chelsea to Greenwich Village and scarcely lose a breath, but neither of these places can talk with MIT—it is as though MIT were speaking the Tibetan language.

Now my own opinion is that this thesis is quite inadequate to describe our culture in many ways, but still it is very important for certain purposes. As to its inadequacy, it seems to me quite obvious that most people in American society are neither literary intellectuals nor scientists. If you are to listen, for

34

instance, to what are flatteringly called the debates among presidential candidates today, you could obviously see that there is no literary intellectual running for president; there is no scientist running for president.

Snow has picked a very peculiar phenomenon, and he heightens its importance. If Snow had never used the phrase and I heard the phrase the "two cultures," I would think immediately of Disraeli's description of England as developing into two nations, and the United States Commission on Civil Rights picking that up. Those are the cultures I might think of. I might think of the culture of poverty because of the apparently increasing number of Americans who are just "out of it," with none of the motivations that seem to operate throughout much of society. This is related to but not identical with a racial culture. Or I might think of several emerging ethnic cultures, of the drug culture, in some cities of the gay culture, or of the youth culture (although the generation gap is not nearly so prominent now as it was). I think of all these things.

I might also ask where the social scientists— neither physical scientists nor literary intellectuals—fit into C.P. Snow's scheme. So as a general description of the culture, I say I find it quite inadequate. Yet it is very important in the respect that science and technology has become increasingly critical for public decisions. However, decision-makers and the general public usually aren't scientists. I'll try and show why I think that is important.

Let me just say a bit about the way I come at this. My career has been in social ethics. I have found myself, since 1966, increasingly interacting with scientists, partly through a number of projects of the World Council of Churches and partly in Columbia University Seminars, which by definition are interdisciplinary in nature. These are not seminars in the catalog that people take for credit; these are primarily gatherings of faculty and other scholars from the Northeast, always on interdisciplinary subjects and almost always involving the interaction of scientists and humanists. To this I would add my peripheral work with governmental agencies, especially the National Institutes of Health (NIH) and an occasional congressional committee. At this moment I'm involved with the New York City Board of Health, where issues come up that require some bringing together of scientific and ethical understandings with some possible influence on the course of government.

Now let me give some examples of problem areas that I think illustrate the issue. The most obvious one, I suppose, is national defense and military policy. The general opinion, which I'm inclined to think is right, though I'm no expert on this, is that Casper Weinberger spent more and more money to get less and less national defense. This is because he was trying to buy a set of technologies that came with the endorsements of people with great professional competence, who lured others to buy one technology after another. With every military situation that comes up, it turns out that those particular sets of tools aren't especially helpful. The big debate about the Strategic Defense Initiative (SDI) is a current example. While there are many debatable things about it, one aspect of it is simply the question of whether it can do what it purports to do. The answer to that is primarily a scientific, technological answer. Ideology gets into it in all kinds of ways. But will the computer technology work? Will other aspects of it work? A public official wants some answer to that question if he or she is to make any judgment as to whether a policy should go in that direction. I will come back to that a little later.

Another example would be the progress in genetics and the legal and political issues that it raises. There is a national organization that has annual meetings on genetics and law. Not many geneticists know a lot about law; not many lawyers know much about genetics. But you'd be surprised at the number of people who are highly competent in the very precise discipline of the relation between the two—people who can stand up and say that on this particular issue twenty-seven states have legislation that goes this way, in thirteen it goes another way, and the rest have none at all. How has the career of a state legislator prepared that person for a considered vote on what the law ought to be in this area? Yet issues keep coming up in courts and public agencies all the time.

The wider issues of health are involved here also. AIDS is an example very much on the public mind right now. The whole business of the financing of health care is immensely intricate. It is a decision of public policy. Medical and biological scientists cannot make it; the public must make it. Yet we can't make it without some accurate sense of what is going on in scientific areas.

Still another example is energy policy. We've gone in recent years from a situation called energy crisis to one called energy glut, and we respond to these situations in all kinds of ways with no intelligible public policy that I can see. But apart from the blips that produce momentary crisis and momentary glut, to think intelligibly about policy requires at least some awareness of whether it is possible that a fusion reactor will be developed that will solve one set of problems. What really are the prospects for appropriating solar energy? How will superconductivity affect this? There is a whole bunch of scientific issues that bear on public policy.

Now the implications here are that any senator or representative has to vote on many issues on which that person has no personal training or competence. For that matter, any citizen who'd like to be reasonably responsive in participating in the democratic process has to do the same thing.

37

Everybody who votes on the President's budget is going to vote on appropriations for projects which that person doesn't really understand very much.

I said that I'd come back to the issue of SDI, a particularly interesting issue because it has a history. Sometime around 1970, a proposal for the antiballistic missile was very much in public debate. At that time, a group organized itself called Computer Specialists Against the ABM. It happened for a variety of reasons that the head of the group, the one who organized it, was a student of mine. His name is Dan McCracken. He spent a career in computer technology, wrote ten textbooks on the subject, and at a certain stage got interested in the ethics of it and decided to do a degree in theological ethics. He organized a committee of very diverse people—it was one of these ad hoc committees that survives for a year or so, buys some ads in the paper, and then goes out of existence. It was a committee of computer specialists organized on one shared belief that the computer technology proposed for the ABM would not work. It could conceivably work in a laboratory; but in space, with all the jolts, temperature, and other problems, it just wouldn't work. They made their representations to political decision-makers.

Senator Fulbright was chairing a Senate committee that had some hearings on this. The Defense Department produced a set of witnesses who said the technology would work. Senator Fulbright, at a certain stage in the hearings, pointed out that every witness who had declared it would work was either an employee of the Pentagon or an employee of a corporation that had a contract with the Pentagon. He asked whether they could get any neutral witnesses. The Deputy Secretary of Defense, at that time David Packard, replied, "That is irrelevant. Scientists are objective about such matters."

That raises the question of what is the objectivity of science. Much of the success and esteem of science in our society is due to the fact that it does have certain processes of verifiability. There are some things you don't argue about forever as people in many walks of life may do. You define the crucial experiment and settle it. However, you can't quite perform the crucial experiment on an ABM or an SDI; you can perform a lot of experiments that may point you one way or another. If we perform the crucial experiment, we may not survive to find out how it works. You can't do that, so you do the best you can. Thus, Packard claimed objectivity. Fulbright's reply was quite interesting. He said approximately this: "I'm the senator from Arkansas, and I just want everybody to know I am pro cotton and pro poultry. And if anybody wants to get an expert witness on these subjects, don't call me; I know where I stand on this." It was very clear he was not impugning the honesty of witnesses. He was not saying they had been bought to say something they didn't believe. It was rather that when you get caught up in an experiment, you invest a lot of energy in it. The enthusiasm will get you; you've almost got to believe in it, or why would you bother to do all the work?

The fact that it's well funded had something to do with it too—though again, not in a cheap sense. Since C.P. Snow used MIT as an example, I'll say that I've spent some time on the MIT campus in recent years. I've talked to a lot of students, who are wondering about their careers and who are finding that the big money is in projects on which they would rather not work. It's not simply the salary, it's the funding for research. You can't do exciting research unless you get it funded. If the funding is drawing them into certain types of military or commercial research that are not their real interest, what do they do?

The controversy between Fulbright and some of the witnesses continued in the interesting way I've

39

described it. The point in it that bothered me most was that one person testifying said that it is not simply chance that all the witnesses are employed by the Pentagon or by corporations with contracts; this is necessarily the case because nobody else knows enough about the subject to have a judgment. Now if that becomes the case, it leads one almost to despair about the democratic process. That is, if nobody can be competent without being enlisted on one side of an argument, what do you do? Now I prefer not to believe that, but I'm not sure I could verify my belief.

This has led one team of authors writing on the place of scientists in the political arena to say this: "The common man has never been less in control of his life and livelihood than he is today. Whether confronted by the threat of atomic annihilation or something as trivial as a balky home appliance, almost all of us must place our trust in the hands of the relevant specialists. . . . As our common pool of scientific knowledge increases, the ignorance and powerlessness of each individual increases correspondingly."[*]

I believe it was Ken Bolding, the economist, who coined the phrase, "the ignorance explosion." The knowledge explosion is very real in our time, but the ignorance explosion simply means that of the available human knowledge, each of us progressively knows a smaller and smaller segment. In one sense we are not ignorant compared with Aristotle: we know a lot that he didn't. But of the available knowledge that is shaping the world, we know a lesser and lesser proportion.

---

[*]   Joel Primack and Frank von Hippel, *Advice and Dissent: Scientists in the Political Arena* (New York: Basic Books, 1974), p. ix.

This led to some proposals that what we really need is a new "social invention" comparable to the past invention of parliamentary democracy. But where we are going to get it, nobody is sure. One characteristic of inventions is that you don't quite know what they will do until you have them or are on the verge of having them. But this leads to some interesting reflections, I should think.

The rationale of parliamentary democracy was that citizens can elect representatives who can make decisions in the public interest. The rationale of representative government is that it is quite important to have diverse interests represented in the parliamentary process. Madisonian democracy, to a very great extent, is built on that idea. Now the assumption is that the representatives, deliberately chosen to assure a diversity of interests, most obviously geographic but with other kinds of diversity too, are competent to interact with each other and make decisions.

Thomas Jefferson referred to what he called a natural *aristoi* among human beings. This is interesting, coming not from Hamilton but from Jefferson, who was the most democratic among the Founders. Jefferson did not want a hereditary or a monetary aristocracy. But we would like to have the best people as the representatives of diverse interests—people who can interact and produce policies that are fairly likely to serve the common good. That assumption of competence, though you can never really prove that it worked in the history of American legislative processes, was still a plausible assumption.

I've already suggested that nobody in the Congress is personally competent to vote on all the issues that come before that person. This, of course, is one of many reasons for the multiplication of congressional staff. You get specialists who share your interests and who advise you.

The same issue comes up increasingly in jury trials on issues of medical malpractice. What ordinary juror is really competent to know what constitutes malpractice? What I assumed as a child was that when you go to a doctor, maybe you'll get help and maybe you won't. They don't know everything. Now if you don't get help you tend to blame the doctor. My wife was on such a jury recently, and it became very complex knowing whether the doctor and hospital who failed had performed the best that could be expected in the light of available knowledge or whether they had performed malpractice.

If you start toying with the idea of social inventions, what can we do? I've already said we don't quite know, and if we did know, we might invent it. But some interesting processes are developing. One example would be in the area of bioethics and biopolitics.

President Carter, at one point, appointed a President's Commission for the Study of Ethical Problems in Medicine and Biomedical and Behavioral Research. After it was underway, he added to its agenda a study on genetics and politics—gene splicing, as it is often called. That commission produced a book called *Splicing Life: The Social and Ethical Issues of Genetic Engineering with Human Beings.* The committee included a variety of people with various professional competencies. It was staffed by Alex Capron, a very able lawyer who knows a lot about biology and genetics. He had a professional staff of research assistants, consultants, and so on, representing a variety of scholarly competence and a variety of interests. They produced what I think is a good book. Now that does not produce legislation, but it becomes available to legislators who may have to propose laws or vote on these issues.

Representative Gore, now Senator Gore, presidential candidate Gore, chaired a House subcommittee that held hearings, just after the book came out, on proposed legislation. He invited me among others to give testimony at that time. Many of the people invited were scientists, as I make no claim to be, but here was an effort to get the testimony of people with various skills that might inform a legislative process. So far as I know, no actual legislation has come out of that, but one thing it quite probably decided was that we really don't know enough to legislate right now.

The National Institutes of Health used similar processes. I got involved in one that involved medical experimentation on infants. One of the usual ethical guidelines for medical experimentation is that the subject must give informed consent. An infant cannot give informed consent to an experiment. What do you do? Do the parents become surrogates for the infant? One popular device among experimenters is to work in an orphanage where the director of the orphanage can give the informed consent for maybe a hundred subjects. It's a lot less trouble than hunting out a hundred families, and the subjects live in a controlled environment. You've got a much better chance in knowing whether the experiment produced certain effects or whether a whole number of extraneous factors did. But is the administrator of the institution the person rightly entitled to speak for a hundred infants?

I don't know if the NIH would want me to say this, but I get the impression that they know that if something goes wrong, Congress is likely to legislate. They are afraid of blunderbuss legislation. It seems to me that they would like to get a set of rubrics to guide their work that is good enough that Congress will have to look at it and say, "Yes, this is fair. It is a good way to do it, we don't have to legislate." I have a hunch that if the pressure of possible legislation was not on, they might be a little less eager to get those careful rubrics. But that is one way they work at it.

In the same area, the Supreme Court ruling on patents of genetically engineered products was a very interesting one, in that the Court said, in effect: "It is not a constitutional issue. As we look at present laws, it looks as though it is legal to patent these. We're not saying that's good; that's for the Congress to decide, and the Congress has access to information and research facilities that the Court doesn't." The Congress can appoint a committee and get all kinds of commissions, and so on. I never read a Supreme Court decision that came so close to begging Congress to do something here. Again, here is a situation in which the legislative and judicial process, if it has any wisdom, depends on a kind of knowledge that is esoteric.

If you move on to the question of armaments, which I've already mentioned, you get exactly the same problem. I would not want to give the impression that a lay person is totally helpless here. I know many lay people who don't claim any competence on the science and technology of antiballistic missiles, strategic defense initiatives, and so on, but who can at least see that initially the program was presented as a way of keeping attacking missiles out in space and as therefore ethically better than mutually assured deterrence. They can see that by this time, there is apparently no public figure, with the possible exception of the President, who thinks it will be that, and that the defenders of it now say that it will work to protect launching sites. Some people think it won't even work to do that, but if it does that is a very different game. It gets you back to protection of retaliatory missiles, and that is mutually assured deterrence. So you don't have to be an expert physicist or weapons specialist to follow the debate, here to some extent. But there are still many aspects of it that are in the area of scientific expertise.

44

I've mentioned some examples of the way in which government is trying, in fumbling and halting ways, to deal with this sort of thing. What can we say about what the churches are doing here? For a little over twenty years I've been involved in some of the processes of the World Council of Churches (WCC). It has no authority; it doesn't tell anybody what to believe. It produces educational documents to guide people who want to be guided by them. Its processes are more complex than those of Congress because it is international. They are more inadequate, in the sense that it would be extremely expensive to bring together people in these international panels for long sustained activities. So they meet, they go home and do some work, they meet again, and they produce something. They always try to get a representation of many parts of the earth and of many technical skills. Some of the world's ablest scientists, many of whom are not in the least bit Christian, have gladly cooperated as sources of information and judgment. The WCC also tries to get ideological diversity. My own opinion is that many church documents, whether of denominations in this country or of the World Council of Churches, are not very competent. That is, they don't subject themselves to a sufficient intellectual discipline, and like all legislative processes (even though these are not legislative), there are trade-offs going on. You try to reach consensus and say, I'll give you this point if you give me this point, and they end up with inconsistencies. But they still do give the reader a notion of where some of the tension points are and why a Brazilian, for instance, might react so differently from the average North American or West German to a certain public issue.

In the development of these panels, whether by a government group or a church group or even a university, I think it quite important to give attention to the composition of the panel. You definitely want a variety of technical skills. If you are going to talk about ethics, politics, and genetics, you want skilled geneticists who can tell you the state of the art: what is happening and what are some of the consequences of what is happening. You also want a diversity of ideology and social situations. These two often come very close together. Fulbright's comment on coming from Arkansas and being pro cotton and pro poultry is one example of what I mean.

This is quite important for medical issues. There have been some crimes committed in the name of medical research. The Tuskegee syphilis experiments are a good example. Now the NIH, if it wants a panel to set up guidelines for research, wants some black people on the panel. You might say, science is science whether you are black or white; but the practice of science affects different people in different ways. One important medical issue of public policy in relation to medicine is how much we as a society should spend on the afflictions of the aged. If you are going to get a panel together, you want some old people on it and you want some people who are not old on it because, increasingly, the larger share of the money is going to the old. You really don't want a society in which half of your medical budget goes to people in the last five years of their life. On the other hand, you don't ruthlessly want to wipe them off the slate and say, let's not treat people past seventy. But we do have a rule of no heart transplants past a certain age. I don't mean Congress passed a law on it, but it is a standard practice now.

Regarding the technical aspects we ask, will this work? Will more money help us toward a solution? What are the possibly horrible side effects? The technical interrelates with interests and values, so you need both kinds of diversity.

Lester Thurow, the economist at MIT, has made an interesting observation on this. He was writing on the question of why economists disagree so much

46

among themselves. I've occasionally gotten into situations with theologians and economists in which the economists sometimes comment that they can't get any help from theologians because theologians never agree on anything. Usually I reply, "If that's the test of economics, how much help will we get from you?" Thurow says that there are certain purely technical points on which all economists will agree. Pump a lot of money into an economy without pumping in consumer products and you get inflation. When it comes to recommending policies, there is not much agreement. And Thurow says the reason for this is that there is no economic policy so good that everybody will benefit from it, and it is hard to find one that is so bad that nobody will benefit from it.

So the moment you move from the purely technical into policy-making, you've got conflicts of interest. Consider the question: what are the causes and cures of inflation? There is another question: what are the benefits and costs of inflation? These are different kinds of questions. So you need the interaction of the scientific and the political and ethical in all these issues. The problem has been with us through all human history, but it has become increasingly important in our time. I don't know where it is going to lead, but my guess is that competent public policy will increasingly depend on certain scientific judgments: judgments of that one culture, which Snow describes, to which most of the public doesn't belong.

COMMENT: Perhaps on the theme of inventing something like parliamentary democracy you might want to say something about the role of the National Academy of Sciences. I take it that Congress thought that that was what it was inventing when it set up the Academy. I assume that this hasn't in fact proved to be the case.

you ought to look at this problem, not from the vantage point of the scientist but from the way it looks to the president. How does the president see his need? What kind of science advising is needed, where you put it, what kind of structure and organization should you have, what should be the relation of the adviser to the Office of Science and Technology Policy (OSTP)? All of these things ought to be considered.

Both of these examples illustrate what you have been talking about, and yet there is real tension. In this first report we say that we need more of a role for medical scientists, and in the second report, Harold Brown and others are saying that the scientists are demanding too much of a role in science advising, one which lacks a clear reference to the view of the President. I don't know if you think that illustrates what you've said or whether you would care to comment on it.

PROFESSOR SHINN: It does illustrate my point. Part of the problem, as you've suggested, is that you are going to have a finite budget for scientific research. It is all right for scientists to say we should put more into that. However, no matter how much you put in it, it is going to be a finite budget. There are points at which funding (A) means you don't fund (B). Who makes that kind of judgment? The scientists involved in the projects think they are important; they are going to push for more. They are not the ones to decide, but the politician who must decide had better know something of what the scientists are thinking.

In medical science this gets quite interesting. We are up to about 11 percent of the gross national product (GNP) now going into health. By health, I don't mean adequate nutrition, and so on, but rather health in the more technical sense. The professional health advocates say we are putting 6 percent of the

GNP into military defense; why not take 2 percent of that and add it to health? Well, you could, but there is still going to be a finite health budget. I don't say 11 percent is too much; maybe 15 percent is not too much. There does come a point at which it is too much. You've got to settle the priorities, and unless a dictator is to do it or a platonic wise man or somebody like that, the political process must decide that. We aren't very well tooled up to do so.

QUESTION: I have a question about humanitarian work and technology. We've all been brought up with the idea of millions of people around the world being undernourished if not starving. Recently a couple of Albemarle County farmers have told me we've not just been exporting U.S. food, we've also been exporting our agricultural technology. All these areas of the world that we thought were so hungry now have surplus food, and gluts of food. Is this true, and if so, how must we rethink our public and private humanitarian work?

PROFESSOR SHINN: The food issue, which I've had some opportunity to study in an international context, is a very interesting one. The world is producing enough food to give everybody an adequate diet. I don't mean the world can give everybody the number of steaks that Americans eat, but it can give everybody an adequate diet. That does not mean, as some folks say, that if we were just morally sensitive enough, we'd feed everybody. Feeding people is a very complex process—just physically it would involve extensive transportation of food. Economically, many projects designed to feed hungry people have undercut the agricultural market in the recipient country so that the farmers couldn't afford to produce. The projects made the situation worse.

In recent years, on every continent except Africa, there has been a growth of food production that more

PROFESSOR SHINN: It is a very pointed question. I find a usefulness in the distinction between technical reason and whatever you want to call the other, though I do not absolutize that. I think science contributes to our revision of goals as well as to our reasoning on the means to get to those goals. Here I follow in part John Dewey's means-ends continuum. You don't start out with a set of clearly defined goals and then turn to scientists and ask them how we get to these.

Certain scientific and technical achievements open up new possibilities. (For our purposes, I've lumped science and technology together, though for other purposes I wouldn't.) For one thing, the high culture of some ancient societies was built on a class society, a slave substratum, and a group of workers that were not expected to participate in the political process. The elimination of slavery was not only a moral achievement, but it was in part a scientific achievement to the extent that you could make machines the equivalent of slaves. I think that science contributes to visions of new moral goals though science, qua science, does not have processes of verifiability for settling those issues. At that point, the insights of poets and prophets and sages become very important. As I work with a scientist such as Garrett Hardin on some of these issues, I disagree with almost all of his conclusions. But I agree with his point that there are problems with "no technical fix." This refers to problems that be solved only by a revision of goals, ends, and values. How do you build up that world of goals, ends, and values? This is accomplished partly out of traditions, whether Platonic, Judeo-Christian, Confucian, etc. There is a heritage here, but scientific, technological progress tends to loosen up past definitions of human good.

The notion of a society in which you expect most infants to grow to adulthood is fairly modern. High infant mortality has been an assumption of most human history. You might say, that the essential value, the worth of personality, may be virtually eternal. The feeling that infant mortality is a calamity that we can almost eliminate and ought almost to eliminate really comes out of the scientific revolution. So I see more interaction between the two.

QUESTION: You've talked about food aid, medical assistance, infant mortality, and so forth. What are the ethical issues that a nation faces—and how are they handled in various parts of the world—in viewing all of those things in the context of world population growth. What are the long term ethical issues involved in this?

PROFESSOR SHINN: I certainly think population is a very authentic issue, but I disagree with the "population monomaniacs." Actually the strain on the resources of the world has increased more in the affluent, low reproductive parts of the world than in the highly populated, poor parts because every American child grows up to consume so much more than most children in India. Even though our population is fairly stable, we contribute to that problem. But the world cannot support an infinite number of people.

Just to do the old numbers game of projections, which never works in reality but which gives you the theoretical framework, there comes a time in which present rates of population growth would mean that the number of human beings would outweigh the earth itself. You know it is not going to happen. Why is it not going to happen? The reasons for high reproductivity are very complex. Starvation can be one reason to lower productivity; the Irish potato famine could be a good example of that. More often prosperity does it.

Roger Revelle, the Harvard population specialist, said that the first thing to do if you want to reduce population growth is reduce infant mortality. One would think that this would mean a surge in population. However the motivation of people is to have children that survive. If you have high infant mortality, you want a lot of babies so that some of them will grow up. In a society in which children are your old-age insurance, as is certainly the case in India and in rural China, you want male survivors. That's for social reasons, not biological ones. You want at least two sons, and in the process maybe you get two daughters. The incentive to reproduce is very high.

Something is going to slow down population growth. Partly it will be voluntary. Most of Europe and North America have done it voluntarily. In China there are great elements of compulsion, which I think is quite understandable. We ask is there compulsory abortion? The government answers, no. However, the difference between compulsion and very strong economic incentives and very strong peer pressure is a very thin difference sometimes. If everybody in your group is telling you that this is not your turn to have a child, you may get the abortion.

QUESTION: I think you are saying that there isn't going to be a problem, so therefore there are no ethical issues?

PROFESSOR SHINN: No, it is a very real problem, and one aspect of it is how you relate freedom to compulsion, which is an aspect of all political living. I'm free to do some things, and a whole lot of things the law tells me I can't do. In this country it would be almost incredible to have a government enforcement policy on the size of families. Some people would like to do it with certain minorities, but a government policy would be almost incredible. In China it is very understandable.

When I asked a prominent Protestant leader in China what the Roman Catholic Church is doing there about the population problem, including abortion, he said that they don't approve it, but they understand the reasons for it. There may be a justification for inhibiting personal freedom in some societies that there is not in others, but I think it is a serious ethical problem. How do you relate freedom to compulsion there? Above all, how do you stop American sermonizing to the rest of the world that we've found the answer and now you should adopt it?

At the United Nations population conference in Bucharest in 1974 the United States and Western Europe were all reading lectures to the Third World on the importance of restraining population. The other countries were replying, no, your over-consumption is the problem, not our overproduction of children. Ten years later at the U.N. conference in Mexico City, the process was reversed. The American delegation, appointed by the President, was presenting the argument that if you would adopt a market economy you could feed an almost infinite number of children. The Third World, looking at China, was saying, "Population is a problem; it is a public issue and not solely a family issue. Will you in the industrialized world give us help in methods?" At this point the means-ends distinction comes in. The Americans replied that they wouldn't; they wouldn't fund anything that might by any conceivable device contribute to abortions. Now I don't think abortion is the best method for population control. I just use it as an example. But it illustrates a very curious ideological change in ten years.

COMMENT: Several years after FDR's spectacular saving of the economy at the beginning of his term, the economy began to slip again. He asked his aides what to do about it and said we've got to get an expert here. He asked them what economist in the country knows most about money, and they told him Wesley Mitchell, with the National Bureau of Economic Research. So Mitchell was summoned to the White House and the President asked him whether or not to lower the gold content of the dollar. Professor Mitchell said, "I'm very sorry, Mr. President, I can't answer that question. I can tell you what will happen if you do lower the gold content of the dollar, and I can tell you what will happen if you don't. But I can't tell you what to do, that's your job." Do you agree with Wesley Mitchell?

PROFESSOR SHINN: For the most part, I agree. The President or whoever is determining policy, needs the most accurate information possible on what will happen. I don't think the economists know entirely, because economic prediction is always prediction of human behavior. They cannot be absolutely sure, but there are a lot of things of which they are fairly sure. Whether you'd rather risk inflation or unemployment is not a decision for an economist to make; it's the decision for the body politic to make in the light of the best information it can get.

QUESTION: How does ethics relate to the issue of cloning? They are now cloning cattle, and they say this may be used with human beings.

PROFESSOR SHINN: The commotion about cloning human beings has subsided somewhat in recent years. At first there was great trepidation, and I think most people don't want it. So the commotion has died down, but it is still a possibility. I'll just say, very subjectively, I'm against it. I can't really conceive what kind of monstrous ego would want this exact genetic duplication of the self. The Pharaohs developed the whole economy of a nation to assure their personal immortality. Here is a new form of immortality with a genetic replica living on. The fact that this is happening with cattle is a pretty good sign it can be done with human beings. One common belief is that if it can be done, it will be done. I'm not convinced of that. Whether we need a law against it, I don't know. I would have a little trouble formulating my reasons for a law against it; that is to say, I'm against a lot of things that I don't want to forbid everybody to do. I have some belief in freedom too. On what grounds would I make a case that this is of sufficient public concern that we should have a law against it, I don't quite know. But I'm giving you my opinion whatever it's worth.

NARRATOR: Maybe the highest tribute one can pay to our speaker today is that he has spoken on crucial issues in the same manner and within the same tradition of the man whose chair he occupied for nearly two decades. I remember that my chairman when I taught at the University of Chicago, a very distinguished, public administrator, said to me when Reinhold Niebuhr came to lecture at Rockefeller Chapel, "Why should I go to hear a mere preacher?" He went to hear him once, and thereafter he heard him every time he came—if he could get into the Rockefeller Chapel. It is that kind of breadth and virtuosity, I think, which Roger Shinn brings to our subject. That's why we are terribly grateful to him for coming to Virginia.

CHAPTER III

Humanism and Theism in Biomedical Ethics*

JOSEPH FLETCHER

I have a twofold purpose. First, I want to take a look at some of the differences between humanism and theism, comparing humanly centered values as a basis for biomedical ethics, and, on the other side, an ethics based on divine commands and supernatural sanctions. The second purpose is to consider ethics in general, but especially biomedical ethics, in relation to the principles of pragmatism as it has been expounded and acted out in the American tradition.

In the past quarter of a century, ethics or moral philosophy as a discipline has gone through a marked change, venturing from its classical preoccupation with metaphysics or linguistic analysis to the critical examination of very down-to-earth problems, especially with those being faced by responsible professionals in medicine, law, government, and the social services. As the Australian philosopher Peter Singer once put it, "Philosophers are back on the job"—the job, that is, of trying to sort our practical

---

* Reprinted by permission of "Perspectives in Biology and Medicine," Vol. 31, No. 1 (Autumn 1987), pp. 106-16.

problems of right and wrong, good and evil, in which actual human beings stand to gain or lose something when moral choices are made.[1]   This is a shift of attention from metaethics, so-called, to normative ethics.

This move from theory to practice is by no means treason or a sellout of "high" philosophy.   Sound theory is the most important tool in the practitioner's kit.   Nonetheless, some of us are convinced that, as a matter of *cognition*, we cannot establish a theory first and then proceed to cases.   G. E. Moore said, "Casuistry is the goal of ethical investigation," the goal of getting down to cases—to what lawyers might call case law ethics and physicians might call clinical ethics.[2]   Principles or guidelines, however, have to be formulated out of cases to begin with, not prior to cases.

To be sound, ethical theory, like all other kinds of theory, must be born out of experiences with actual problems.   It is experimental, empirical, and data based; a posteriori, not a priori.   Moral rules and principles ought to be empirical generalizations, changeable when experience changes; not rigid laws but more like the prima facie guidelines that W.D. Ross expounded—at first sight obliging but sometimes not always so on a second look.[3]

In short, the process of ethics runs from practice to theory and then back to practice again.   Moore certainly never supposed that, while casuistry or case ethics is the goal, its general principles come unempirically from a transcendent source in metaphysical reasoning or religious revelation.   The shift in ethics recently to actual problems promises, therefore, not only some help in practice but further gains in theory as well.

In medical research and treatment both we are more likely to find good answers to value questions by consulting the scientists and clinicians than in syllogistic reasoning by armchair intellectuals, no matter how brilliantly the latter hop from premises to conclusions. Notoriously, the conclusion of a syllogism is already present in its first or major premise. Divorced from the hospital or the laboratory, all abstract and generalized talk about ethics can too easily be impersonal or unhuman and therefore unethical. Value judgments to be valid have to be inductive, not deductive. Theories cannot reproduce themselves; they are, as Aristotle said, *sterios*: beautiful, perhaps, but sterile.

MEDICAL ETHICS GROWS UP

One very welcome result of the new normative focus in ethics is that what was for a long time called medical ethics has now grown up. Now it is "biomedical" ethics, taking into account the whole range of the life sciences, with medicine at their center. It has been converted from a concern with merely the etiquette and the deportment of physicians into quite a serious value analysis of significant practices and innovations—at both research and clinical levels.

Until fairly recently, what physicians called medical ethics was little more than a body of moralistic advice about (a) medical manners and (b) the physician's guild or association rules. It consisted of paternalistic advice about not sitting on the patient's bed; not smelling of tobacco or pungent beverages such as Madeira (or maybe something even stronger); how to practice the art of touching—which is what medicine is—with Victorian propriety; and what one owed to one's professional brothers in the way of respect and discretion. "Don't criticize other doctors," they said. "You belong to a fraternity, a guild. Recite the Hippocratic oath, then go ye forth and practice." In the annual George Washington Gay lectures in medical ethics at the Harvard Medical

School, which are classical, most of the speakers unfortunately treated the subject with this kind of superficial moralism.

Now that is all changed. The subject has grown up philosophically and biologically. Books and journals, including the American medical bible, *The New England Journal of Medicine*, often have articles and editorials probing moral issues and value choices as they are posed to physicians and patients—and also, we should add, to public officials and the law.

In 1976, Dr. Howard Brody of Michigan State published his book *Ethical Decisions on Medicine*, the first one in modern times written by a physician for medical students, and it contains not one single word on etiquette or guild rules. Instead it copes with such problems as allocating clinical resources (not just clinical triage), elective death, proxy consent powers, quality-of-life judgments, tissue and organ transplants, guidelines for animal and human experimentation, resuscitation, artificial modes of human reproduction, psychosurgery, fetal interventions, transmission of genetic (not only infectious) diseases, and patients' rights.

This coming of age of biomedical ethics, sometimes known as bioethics, is for the most part an American story. It has developed more vigorously and fully in America than in Europe or elsewhere. Scientific research and its effect on clinical practices are not, of course, a product solely of Americans, but biomedical *ethics* is nearly so; it still lags comparatively in other countries, if we are to judge by the number of people, publications, and teachers devoted to it.

Van Rensselaer Potter, an oncologist professionally, first used the term bioethics, a carefully coined one to connote the ethical aspects of all of the life sciences including ecology and population problems, not just medicine and its base, biology. Biomedical ethics has had the deepest and widest development thus far, but Potter's own focus on the ethics of environmental and ecological studies, such as overpopulation and toxic wastes, along with the ethics of land use, will almost certainly find fuller or equivalent development.[4]

Of some interest, historically, is the further fact that much of the credit for this American pioneering goes to people in theological ethics as distinct from philosophical ethics. Religiously motivated or religiously sponsored moralists were the first to tackle right-wrong, good-evil problems in medicine and medical care.

Catholic moral theology had faithfully sustained a continuous system of medical ethics, based on the church fathers and occasional papal decrees and allocutions, but other religious moralists had not been dealing with medicine's problems in any serious way. Catholic manuals of moral theology, including special treatises on medical ethics, had much greater sophistication than Protestant ethics. The latter tended to be more hortatory and pious, and not too much on the mark.

My own *Morals and Medicine* in 1954,[5] and then in 1959 Immanuel Jacobovitz's *Jewish Medical Ethics*,[6] opened up and widened the field of biomedical ethics as nobody else had done for centuries. At that time I was a theologian and Jacobovitz an exponent of orthodox Jewish thinking. Philosophers doing biomedical ethics are, in a real sense, Johnnies-come-lately.

What needs to be pointed out here, however, is that more and more since that beginning the religionists have tended to keep their religion hidden and cryptic. They rarely ever use religious language anymore; they never avow whatever theological propositions underlie their reasoning. They try to sound just like philosophers. They know that theological doctrines are inescapably controversial, and, therefore, to keep in touch acceptably with the world of medicine, which has a humanistic raison d'être and abhors religious discourse like the plague, they find it prudent to keep their bottom line religious beliefs in the closet.

What I have just been saying leads us at once to the first of my purposes, namely, to discuss the differences between humanism and theism as foundations for ethics as such and for biomedical ethics in particular.

Most historians and philosophers, both abroad and here in America, are agreed that the major contribution of Americans to philosophy is pragmatism. I am speaking here not of America's pragmatic politics and culture but of the theory itself. Its founding fathers were Charles Sanders Peirce and William James. It was nurtured further by Chicago's George Herbert Mead and, above all, by John Dewey and Sidney Hook. In Europe the work of F.C.S. Schiller at Oxford, Giovanni Papini in Italy, and Hans Vaihinger in Germany was valuable by any accounting, but the credit (or blame, as some see it) goes primarily to the Americans.[7] The phrase "American pragmatism" is practically all one word.

Like most other primary conceptual theories, pragmatism has had a number of variants. Arthur Lovejoy, a student of James's at Harvard, believed he could distinguish 13 different ways of expounding it.[8] Nevertheless, the core of the pragmatist method is, as Dewey made abundantly clear, that the pragmatist shies away from abstract principles and arbitrary categories and looks to consequences—to what follows in actual practice form any proposition or statement. This provides both a cognition test, for example, the physicist Bridgman's "operationalism," and an ethical test, for example, John Stuart Mill's "utilitarianism." Pragmatic philosophers are "consequentialists," and some of those engaged in ethics actually call themselves that.

While American pragmatists and British empiricists have always trained their sights on Pilate's question, "What is truth?" they have never neglected Socrates' question, "What is the good?" As James puts it, "The truth, to put it briefly, is only the expedient in our way of behaving." (Dewey's term was "satisfactory" rather than expedient, perhaps because for many people "expedient" carries a flavor of cheap or unprincipled self-seeking: words are important psychologically.)

Scientists, physicians, lawyers, public officials—anybody in a responsible role—will quickly grasp the crucial importance of consequences, testing by results. This is certainly the name of the game in both the laboratory and the clinic. As we shall see, the pragmatic criterion for satisfaction or "good" consequences is human benefit and well-being—that is to say, humanism's standard, and nowhere is this humanistic test used more pragmatically than in the world of medicine. At this point, however, what I want to stress is the two-headedness of pragmatism: that it is both a theory about cognition and a theory of ethics or moral judgment.

Let me summarize what I have said up to now in William James's own words: "A pragmatist turns his back resolutely and once and for all upon a lot of inveterate habits dear to professional philosophers. He turns away from abstraction and insufficiency, from verbal solution, from bad *a priori* reasons, from fixed principles, closed systems, and pretended absolutes and origins. He turns toward concreteness and adequacy, toward facts, toward actions, and toward power."[9] (By power he meant effectiveness, desirable consequences; the "acting out" of our ideas as the only way to judge what they mean and whether they are valid.)

A final word is in order about this American philosophy, pragmatism. When James and the others say they want nothing to do with "fixed principles, closed systems, and pretended absolutes," they are following their own logic. They are embracing relativism in their conception of truth and their conception of value. In effect, they decline to speak of the truth and recognize only truths (in the plural), and likewise they accept the changeability and relativity of value and speak of values only in the plural. This relativity, as you will understand, is opposed consciously to the notion of fixed or absolute facts, a notion that was typical of prescientific thinking, and to the notion, as well, of fixed or absolute values and moral norms of conduct—as in medieval thinking.

HUMANISM AND THEISM

It is obvious that if we believe or claim to know there is a God, and even to know (through revelation in some form) what God wills and wishes us to do, then the kind of relativity of moral judgment that pragmatism favors is logically impossible. The religious world is one in which the groundwork consists of absolute and eternal verities; in that world there are definitive truths and absolute moral rules, given *de rerum natura* by the Absolute itself—or Himself, as some would say. In ethics, this would mean that our human problem is merely to discover what are the correct moral principles, not to formulate or choose among them.

Over against such a posture, we may say with Alexander Pope, "Know thyself, presume not God to scan/the proper study of mankind is man." Long ago Protagoras of Thrace said that man is the measure of all things. Likewise, the African slave and philosopher Publius Terentius was, he declared, a man, and would therefore let nothing human be alien to him. We should promptly acknowledge that religion itself is, after all, believed in by human beings. This, however, only makes religion a matter of proper interest to the humanities—not to humanism.

Humanism is intellectually much humbler, of course, than God-talk and God-thought, but it is also—for many people—too little supportive in the face of life's difficulties. Faced with their own finitude, some personalities turn to religion, hoping for comfort and sometimes apparently finding it. They hope to reach an ultimate and final reality that is not to be had in the finite or relative parameters of a man-centered outlook. Thus humanism and theism represent a genuine antinomy of worldviews.

(I can feel some sympathy with "personalists" who like to think their person-centered view of life and values is a truly middle ground between theism and humanism. But the heavy metaphysical baggage personalism carries—owing in the final analysis to its theistic substrate—makes it untenable for the secular humanist no matter how much else he shares with the personalist. At most he might call himself a "personist," since the humanist really centers on personal beings, not on the merely biological human. This question arises, e.g., in the debate over the status of fetal life.)

In the age of Pericles there was an explosion of humanism in Democritus, Euripides, Hippocrates, and Socrates, only to be extinguished after a while by the oriental religions that came in following Alexander's military adventures. Socrates, in the Protagoras dialogue (actually Plato, of course) laid out a countervailing and plainspoken humanist ethics based on human happiness and well-being. The European Middle Ages, in their turn, became thoroughly an age of theism and religious dominance, this time with Christian doctrines.

Just as Hippocrates had to repudiate the Dogmatist cults of Empedocles and Pythagoras, which based medicine on religious and metaphysical grounds rather than on empirical evidence, so postmedieval medicine has had to win its way by a stubborn insistence on empirical principles rather than metaphysics or religion. In our own times Albert Camus expressed it all quite coherently; he found he was content simply to live with what he knows.

My purpose is not to make a case for either humanism or theism but to remark on the significance of their differences, especially for ethics. The negative role of most religionists is familiar to physicians and workers in the life sciences; it is manifest in such matters, to mention only a few, as autopsies, abortion, fetal interventions, tissue transplants, contraception, and medical genetics. There are, be it noted, those who argue that this religious obstructionism is due more to one brand or another of theology than to theism, as such; that nondoctrinaire theism can by comparison be quite open to scientific discovery.

In any case, at all times a great many people have been humanists and not theists, and in our own times humanism is plainly increasing in strength—consciously or unconsciously—on the quite pragmatic ground, perhaps, that "by their fruits ye shall know them" (as Jesus remarked—in full agreement, it so happens, with pragmatism).

Pragmatism is not always well enough understood. For many people the word itself is pejorative and almost an epithet because they suppose that "being pragmatic" means to sacrifice high ideals for the sake of convenience. That is, of course, a canard. Pragmatists say what moralists of all schools have always said, that we ought so to act that we maximize (or optimize) the good. As to what that good is, pragmatism makes no stipulation. It only stipulates how, not what.

I would like to remark, in this connection, that since pragmatism as such yields no substantive value theory, no standard, so to speak, by which to measure or define the consequences which it focuses on, some such standard must be had from somewhere. Though pragmatism says the true and the good are what works, there must be some answer to the entailed question, "Work to what end?"—some criteria with which to distinguish those consequences that indicate success and those that indicate failure. What is that criterion to be?

Humanism's answer is, "Whatever helps people is good, whatever hurts them is evil." Theism's answer is, "Whatever does the will of God is good, what ignores or flouts God is evil." There is a fairly obvious way to bring the two answers together: Christian situation ethics does it by the simple proposition that loving concern or whatever helps people is God's will, but most Christians condemn that kind of ethics.[10] They turn instead to the ethical rules and universal negatives of traditional theology.

One version of theistic ethics is to quote sacred texts, such as the New Testament or the Old Testament or the Koran. Another is to set "the law of nature" as the standard, nature being God's ordering and creation. This doctrine of the divine will revealed in nature is still theism—although perhaps at one remove from the religious ethics of sacred texts. One leading religious ethicist has argued in a treatise on genetic control that God and not man is the creator; that to meddle with human genes is impious; and that even if we or our offspring suffer in this world because we submit to the divine will, we shall be justified in the next. The same pundit has denounced in vitro fertilization for patients with blocked tubes, calling it unnatural and therefore immoral; he also condemns artificial insemination from an anonymous donor in cases of sterility, calling it "adultery."

This is one example, but only one, of how theistic morality functions. Some of its expounders are more obstructive to rational initiatives, others less. It is obvious, in any case, that theism can and does have logical consequences that bring it into conflict with humanism. I suggest, therefore, that humanism is pragmatic and pragmatism is humanistic.

Honesty compels me, nonetheless, to add a footnote. There are at least two distinguished pragmatists, William James in American and Hans Vaihinger of Tübingen, who have contended that religion or religiosity (though not doctrine or theology) has a motivating role in the moral life, and that people need it over and above their human motives. In the eighth lecture of his *Pragmatism*, James explained that there are appreciable reasons why some people make the leap of faith in God, and, in his essay on "The Moral Philosopher and the Moral Life," he suggested that what mystics call the *visio dei*, yearning after God, drives our human ethical concern, in what he calls the "strenuous mood," to greater efforts. Most pragmatists—for example, Peirce, Dewey, Hook, Schiller, Papini—have never accepted this idea about religion's consequences; they do not find that it stands up on the record. Even in my own theological days of the past I never accepted this religious motivation theory and still do not to this day.

Let it not be said I cast aside this notion about the utility of religion in a cavalier fashion. Apparently there is a paradox in pragmatism from the humanist point of view. It runs this way. If the pragmatic principle is accepted, that consequences validate ideas and moral norms, then supernaturalism is valid if it gives believers an added strength and moral fiber. This is what James suggested. As in all syllogistic reasoning, however, his conclusion is valid only if his premise is—the assertion, namely, that believers actually get "an added strength and moral fiber." Those who read the data of religious behavior differently, however, will logically come to the opposite conclusion.

This pseudopragmatism is used in the appeals of mass conversionists such as Billy Sunday and Billy Graham. They urge people to "accept Jesus" as their "savior" on the ground that this is the way to be "saved" and enter into "eternal life." First, however, they have to believe that what is asserted about both Jesus and resurrection is true; otherwise the pragmatic case for accepting it falls to the ground. Psychologists point out that the reverse is the case; because they want to believe in eternal life they believe in Jesus—or, in other cultures, Buddha or Jehovah or Vishnu or Zoroaster or whatever.

In any case we can imagine how appalled William James would be were he alive now and confronted by the self-styled Moral Majority of the Bible Belt. Spokesmen for fundamentalist religion and evangelical Christians, who constitute the right wing of conservative politics in America, are making a hard push to eliminate the teaching of evolution to schoolchildren or, at least, to offset it by getting "equal time" for their biblical doctrine of instant creation. The Catholic church is openly in politics in its condemnation of voluntary abortion and sterilization. These theistic forces make it stridently clear that in common what they fear is secular humanism, that is, the humanism of John Dewey, not the religious version of William James—to express the issue in terms of the American ethical tradition. Humanism rejects absolutistic morality based on supernatural claims; it relies on science and reason to solve human problems.

CAN ETHICS STAND ALONE?

America's distinctive contribution is pragmatism not only politically and culturally but philosophically, and the logic of pragmatism in ethics leads to humanism. In other words, pragmatism determines the validity of ideas in both science and ethics by looking at the consequences, and it weighs consequences in the scales of human benefit.

Let me be quite blunt. This course of reasoning means that ethics is autonomous, that as a discipline ethics stands on its own feet. The claim of autonomy for ethics always has been a bone in the throat of religionists. Once upon a time, I confess, I too denied ethics its autonomy. There had to be some source and sanction behind any standard of right and wrong, I supposed, and I decided that it must lie in the will and power of God. This amounted to saying that we ought to be moral—ought to do the right thing—because God commanded it. (I did not assert, however, that we could catch hell if we ignored morality's imperatives or reach heaven if we did. My stomach was always too weak for that kind of carrot theology.) Without the divine will to reinforce the human will, I contended, we would not act morally, and Nietzsche's warning, and Dostoyevski's, was correct—if God was dead, then anything goes, ethically speaking. Morality, I felt, depended essentially on a commandment ethic.

Then I started to wonder. Did I accept the commandment because of the commander, or the commander because of the commandment? If the commander commanded inhumane behavior or showed indifference to human need, I realized, I would have to repudiate the command and therefore the commander too. Thus, on second thought and reflection, I came to see that human values are primary. There is an old saw to the effect that "theology stands at the bar of ethics," meaning that religious doctrines have to square with our moral values; in short, that religion depends on morality, *not* vice versa.

This, of course, upsets the theological claim that ethics needs a superhuman basis. People do not "believe in" a god whose ethics and morality are offensive. With me the principle of autonomy of ethics won out; ethics had escaped the *odium theologicum.* (There are, by the way, a few serious theologians who are willing to concede ethical autonomy, but the god they claim exists tends to become a "vague oblong blur" intellectually posited but hardly worshiped.)

Moral standards are thus validated humanly, not theistically. There are good gods and bad gods and we have to choose among them ethically, according to whether they can pass moral tests. We approve or disapprove alleged divine commandments by a prereligious criterion. The ancient maxim is vindicated, *conscientia semper sequenda est*—conscience is always to be followed, but it is our human conscience, not God's that decides.

Theologians have occasionally admitted, reluctantly, that God wills this or that because it is right; that it is not right just because he wills it. Thomas Aquinas was one such. They do not, however, accept fully all that is logically implied, though at least they admit that much—that morality has an antecedent status, so that even God is subject to it. The primary datum, therefore, is moral, not religious; right and wrong are humanly perceived, not religiously revealed. In a word, humanism. Whether God is dead or not in other respects, he is dead as far as ethics is concerned.

To conclude: moral philosophers or ethicists are only, after all, people who happen to know more than most people about the history of ethics and think more than most about the different ways we make morally significant decisions. And this is all they are. As a profession they have a special knowledge but no special skill. In fact, they are if anything less competent at making practical decisions about actual problems than the professional decision-makers involved in medical, legal, or governmental functions.

Imagine, if you will, the members of a pediatrics service gathered to decide whether to continue treatment of an infant with spina bifida (or myelomeningocele) associated with mental retardation, neuromuscular disturbances, and incontinence. The parents, two physicians plus a neuropathologist, a specialty nurse, and a surgeon have all explained what each one thinks. If an ethicist were then to speak, what could he add to diagnosis and prognosis? In the ethics of pragmatism, he or she could add nothing to the balance of probable consequences and the alternatives available. In such a case the logic of pragmatism calls for the most humane choice—and that depends on medical knowledge, not on moral philosophy.

To some it may seem there is a contradiction between my having spoken of bioethics as a professional activity, only at the end to say that a humane decision clinically "depends on medical knowledge, not on moral philosophy." Actually, there is no contradiction, unless it is assumed (wrongly, I think) that moral philosophy as such has a special knowledge of what to do in cases of conscience. It has been my contention, to the contrary, that while ethicists may have a better understanding of different ways to make moral judgments, as used in the past or the present, the factual knowledge that determines what ought to be done pragmatically is provided by others.

The distinctive American contribution to ethics in general, and therefore to particular specialties such as biomedical ethics or legal jurisprudence, is the marriage of pragmatism and humanism. The consequence of this marriage is that moral judgment ceases to be a matter of expertise or of some arcane knowledge held by ethicists. Moral or value judgments are the business of any and all of us, according to our knowledge of the facts in decision-making situations. As William James said, "There is no such thing possible as an ethical philosophy dogmatically made up in advance."

Joseph Fletcher

ENDNOTES

1. Singer, P. Philosophers are back on the job. *New York Times Magazine*, pp. 6-7, 17-20, July 7, 1974.

2. Moore, G. E. *Principia Ethics*. London: Cambridge Univ. Press, 1960.

3. Ross, W. D. *The Right and the Good*. Oxford: Clarendon, 1930.

4. Potter, V.R. *Bioethics, Bridge to the Future*. Englewood Cliffs, N.J.: Prentice-Hall, 1971.

5. Fletcher, J. *Morals and Medicine*, Princeton, N.J.: Princeton Univ. Press, 1954.

6. Jacobovitz, I. *Jewish Medical Ethics*. New York: Bloch, 1959.

7. See James's *Pragmatism* [8]; Dewey's *The Quest for Certainty* (New York: Minton, Balch, 1929), and, with J. H. Tufts, *Ethics* (New York: Henry Holt, 1932); Mead, *Mind, Self and Society* (Chicago: Univ. Chicago Press, 1934) and *The Philosophy of the Act* (Chicago: Univ. Chicago Press, 1938); F.C.S. Schiller, *Studies in Humanism* (London: Macmillan, 1907); for Papini and others, Antonio Santucci, *Il Pragmatismo in Italia* (Bologna: 1963).

8. Lovejoy, A. O. The thirteen pragmatisms. *J. Philos.* 3:1-12, 29-39, 1908.

9. James. W. *Pragmatism.* New York: Longmans, Green, 1907.

10. Cox, H. (ed.) *The Situation Ethics Debate.* Philadelphia: Westminster, 1968.

PART TWO

HUMANITIES AND SCIENCE

CHAPTER IV

Cultural Literacy

E.D. HIRSCH

NARRATOR: We are very pleased to welcome you to a forum this morning with Professor E.D. Hirsch, Kenan Professor of English since 1973 at the University of Virginia. Some of you may have heard that he also is the author of the best-selling book, *Cultural Literacy.* What makes this in many respects a unique achievement is that Don Hirsch's credentials in the field of scholarship and English literary theory are enormous. He is the author of *Wordsworth and Schelling: A Topological Study of Romanticism* (1960), *Innocence and Experience: An Introduction to Blake* (1964), *Validity in Interpretation* (1967), *The Aims of Interpretation* (1976), and getting a little closer to the current subject, *The Philosophy of Composition.*

One generally doesn't think of best-selling authors as people with Hirsch's kind of scholarly background. The interest he has shown in the subject, however, does go back to work that he undertook with support from the National Endowment for the Humanities in the field of composition and as director of the composition program in his own department. He also served as chairman of that distinguished department. He has been adviser to various groups in the field of education including the National Council on Educational Research and the advisory council for the New York Regent's Competency Tests in Writing.

His book, as all of us know, has attracted wide attention and a broad range of media discussion. Even those of us who teach normative theory and political theory have managed to find sentences around which to build a seminar such as the concluding sentence on page 145:

> I hope that in our future debates about the extensive curriculum, the participants will keep clearly in view the high stakes involved in their deliberations: breaking the cycle of illiteracy for deprived children; raising the living standard of families who have been illiterate; making our country more competitive in international markets; achieving greater social justice; enabling all citizens to participate in the political process; bringing us closer to the Ciceronian ideal of universal public discourse—in short, achieving fundamental goals of the Founders at the birth of the republic.

This kind of audacious statement about the purpose of an undertaking in the intellectual, educational arena may be one of the reasons why such wide-ranging discussion has greeted his contribution. We at the Miller Center feel privileged, with the interest we've had in relation between culture and the presidency and politics, to welcome Don Hirsch to this discussion. He will talk briefly and then invite your questions.

PROFESSOR HIRSCH: Thank you Ken, very much, and thank you all for showing up. This is a forum I thought I might use not just to sketch some of the main points of my book, but I also thought that this group would, in the discussion which will ensue, be able to give me some advice. I am now in the arena of practical affairs, trying to put some of these ideas into practice, and many of you are experts in putting ideas into practice.

First, I thought I would bring in a book which looks a bit like mine on the cover but which has come out more recently, *What Do Our 17-Year-Olds Know?*. Actually, there is an interesting connection between these two projects. This book is authored by Diane Ravitch and Chester Finn, and it is the result of a National Assessment of Educational Progress. For the first time in that survey, there was an assessment of what our children know about literature and history. The survey had never undertaken to probe those subjects in a systematic way before. Why they hadn't undertaken it is rather interesting in itself, and it points to something about educational history, namely, the emphasis on skills rather than on content in American education. The results are somewhat dismaying for this year of the Constitution. I thought I would just mention one of the items that caught my eye in the history part of the assessment. I can tell you now that 40 percent of our 17-year-olds have no idea what the balance of powers is in U.S. government, and they can't come within fifty years of the date of the ratification of the Constitution. More than 50 percent can't come within fifty years of the dates of the Civil War.

One of the things that isn't mentioned in this book, which I think ought to be, is that when you have a multiple-choice questionnaire like the one on which these results are based, at least 25 percent of the positive answers may be pure chance because there are only four possibilities. So if you get a rate of 50 percent, it doesn't really mean that 50 percent of the kids necessarily know the right answers to these questions.

I want briefly to suggest, as I did in my book, that this knowledge gap has not been caused primarily by the TV culture of our times, nor was it caused by the movements of the 1960s—though it certainly was exacerbated by them. The '60s get blamed for a lot of our educational and social problems which starts much earlier. It is true that the SAT (Scholastic Aptitude Test) results show that the verbal aptitudes of our children plummet beginning in the '60s. In fact, Claude Kily couldn't negotiate the slope of the decline in the verbal SAT scores, so sharp were they between 1965 and 1985.

But you have to remember that in the early '60s, these children who are showing diminished verbal skills had been going to school for twelve years; their formative schooling took place in the '50s. So the causes go deeper than just the easily-blamed '60s for our educational failures. Again, I think those causes have to do neither with the social movements of the '60s, nor with the television age and too much television watching, nor with complex sociological factors like single-parent homes and all the other factors that are used to explain the decline of knowledge in our children.

Historically, those scapegoats not very credible because we know that the way literacy has been achieved in all the post-industrial nations—that is, in the nations that were created after the industrial revolution—has been through a national school system. The system which achieved literacy historically, as in France and Britain, can also fail to achieve literacy given enough time. That's the historical perspectives I think we have to keep in mind—particularly if it is clear that a change in what has been happening in the schools exactly coincides with the decline in the verbal SAT.

You should understand that the verbal SAT is a terribly important set of data. It is a consistent test that has been given for many decades. It is normed from one year to another so that the results are technically very accurate, and it is an advanced vocabulary test. That's all the verbal SAT is. It is billed as an aptitude test, but it is primarily an advanced vocabulary test. Therefore it correlates very highly with literacy.

As I mentioned before, the number of students with top scores on the verbal SAT—that is, of those scoring over 600—has declined by some 52 percent. Those scoring over 650 have declined in the last fifteen years by 72 percent. So there has been a decline not just in the general level of literacy but also in the communication skills of our very best students.

I said we should blame the schools primarily for this, and the reason is that the schools haven't understood the connection between literacy and traditional information. A point I stress in the third chapter of my book is that literacy has a very conservative influence on language and culture. It exercises a conservative influence because it is spread out so widely over space and over time, and it is recorded in so many books in the library. One of the examples you can use easily to illustrate the conservatism of literacy is the conservatism of literate spellings. As you know, there have been many efforts towards spelling reform in English, which has such anomalies as "enough," and "light" spelled with "ght," and "doubt," which never had a "b" sound, and so on. Yet those absurd spellings persist because of the innate conservatism of literacy.

Another point that needs to be stressed is that literacy is not just the ability to decode words. Literacy depends on having the traditionally understood background information that is taken for granted in all of those hundreds of thousands of books in the library and on the front page of the newspaper. When our schools ceased teaching that taken-for-granted information, the traditional vocabularies of our children inevitably declined. The traditional information that earlier students possessed as part of their intellectual baggage when they approached a newspaper or a serious article declined, and as a consequence, literacy and communication skills in the country at large also declined.

The schools began in the 1940s, after the Second World War, to introduce on a large scale ideas that had started back in the 1920s. There ideas stressed relevant rather than a traditional curriculum. The reforms that were being advocated at Columbia Teachers College in the 1920s, under the banner of Dewey but not necessarily under his approval, were reforms that flourished in the public schools only after the Second World War. Those reforms primarily involved the substitution of social studies for history, social studies being how do you deal with balancing the checkbook and how you get to the supermarket. The reforms introduced that kind of "real life" skills study instead of traditional history; they introduced basal readers, that is, contentless skills-oriented readers in the early grades, for the so-called language arts; and in later grades, they introduced up-to-date, relevant literary materials instead of traditional literary materials.

So there was a great increase in the amount of so-called imaginative literature, much of it ephemeral. Much of it was fragmented, not shared among the graduates even of one era; so, naturally the traditional information that could be taken for granted among school graduates declined as a consequence of this fragmentation of the school curriculum. That seems to me to be the main cause of decline in literacy in the country. The evidence is very strong that that curve of the literacy decline follows the fragmentation of American textbooks and of the American school curriculum.

I want to mention two significant points before I get into the practical reforms that the book advocates and that we are trying to put into effect. One point is that this fragmentation of the curriculum has had differential effects on different strata of our society. It has most deeply affected disadvantaged children. The reason for that is this: Starting in the early grades, from kindergarten through third grade, children from disadvantaged or illiterate homes learn how to decode language as well as children from middle-class and literate families do. So they are on par up to about grade three. That's because decoding print is a new task, and everybody starts on the same plateau. But when you move into fourth grade, the difference in reading skills between disadvantaged and advantaged children begins to show a marked separation, and this divergence continues to widen as they get to age seventeen. So far does the gap open up that it can't be closed very easily after about grade ten when the children are fifteen or sixteen years old.

Crucial information is not being taught in those early grades which if taught, could overcome that difference. The schools are not giving our children that needed information, with the students in the upper part of this divergent curve are getting some of that information from their homes. But, of course, they are getting it in decreasingly effective doses because *their* scores have declined too, as I mentioned at the opening of this talk. So, clearly, our focus on repairing the educational damage should be on the early grades, though it should continue all the way to the end of high school.

I mentioned that point about class divergence because it seems to me that it's not in anybody's best interest that this class structure should be enhanced and assisted by our public schools.

The last point I want to deal with in these introductory remarks is to mention the premature introduction of ideology into discussions of literacy. What hasn't been understood by either liberals or conservatives in relation to this issue—and this gets to the sorts of things that you talk about at the Miller Center—is that educational conservatism doesn't really have anything to do with political conservatism. In fact, French President Mitterrand is a socialist, and he is one of the biggest advocates of a return to educational conservatism in France. The reason there isn't a deep connection between the two is that it's not an ideological principle but a reality principle that's involved. You can't read, write, and communicate effectively without having the traditional, conservative information that literacy itself requires. Literacy itself exercises a conservative influence on language and is a highly conservative skill. It depends on traditional information.

Now that doesn't mean that new information isn't added to literate culture. It doesn't mean that everybody shouldn't learn now about Harriet Tubman, even though we didn't teach information about her in previous decades. Of course we should. But if you speak quantitatively about what literate culture consists of, what you are talking about in reforms like that is just a tiny tip of the iceberg or rather just the tip of the tip of the iceberg of literate culture. Literate culture is predominantly conservative, and there is nothing any of us can do about it. This is particularly true of literacy in English. Our decisions about the school curriculum can't be made independently of the requirements of literacy in English generally throughout the world. Every person who learns the English language, and who studies to speak and communicate effectively in English, learns about Shakespeare, Milton, Chaucer, and other traditional writers, and about some of the themes and myths that have gone along with traditional British literate culture.

Since ideology is out of place in this subject, I
see my own political job as trying to persuade people
that literacy isn't a liberal versus the conservative
issue (though it has been taken as such by some
reviewers of this book). The question is, how do you
institute a return to more traditional information in
the schools?

The first thing you do is persuade people, and as
I discover from many letters that I've been receiving,
particularly from school teachers; they want to be
persuaded. A lot of complaints have surrounded the
list at the end of my book, but obviously without the
list there wouldn't be anything concrete for people to
start working on or to begin improving. So I think,
from the standpoint of instituting reforms in the
schools, it was a good idea to include that list, and it
was one of the things that caused the book to receive
notice, whether favorable or unfavorable.

But the main device that we intend to use is to
try to popularize general knowledge tests of a
student's knowledge at the end of grades 3, 6, 9, and
12. These texts form an accountability principle from
the standpoint of content. The idea that you can test
for skills independently of content is really a myth
that has been disproved by cognitive psychology.
What we are trying to do now is to create a series of
general knowledge tests based on agreed-upon lists.
To do that we had to create an entity, a foundation
in this case, which will put out these lists and publish
these tests. The twelfth grade list and test will be
published in just a few months. The test has been
normed, and the statistics on it are very interesting.
Our hope is that if these tests catch on, that will
concentrate the minds of textbook publishers and of
school principals. Enough interest has already been
shown in this test project by schools and by school
superintendents for me to think that gradually those
tests will become popular and widely used. If they
do, they will drive the curriculum in a positive way

instead of in the way about which people often complain. After all, if you have a good test, it is probably the most useful bludgeon you can wield to drive the school curriculum. We want to drive the curriculum, and we want to have content accountability built into the educational system. Our prediction is that the positive results of making people more literate will become more and more apparent. In the not-too-distant future everybody will be making very good grades on the tests, and on surveys like this one by Lairtch and Finn there will be a much better score across the spectrum of students.

QUESTION: One of the things that concerns me most is that the Bible is probably *the* conservative document that everyone should know in detail. Yet do you find trouble getting the Bible taught in public schools, as presently structured, with the whole problem of the freedom of religion issue?

MR. HIRSCH: That is a very good question. The Bible is extremely well represented on our list, including the list of what every third grader should know. The way we hope to handle that touchy issue is through Bible stories, to take a Sunday School approach without religious doctrine. After all, the Bible exists in our culture in the form of certain phrases, stories, and characters, and as myth. I don't see how we can get away from introducing people to those materials. I think if there is a lobby, either from the so-called secular humanists on the one side or the Fundamentalists on the other, which wants to oppose the teaching of traditional information about the Bible, we tell them: "This isn't the same as teaching religion." After all, nobody complains, I suppose, about teaching about Confucianism or Taoism as something we can learn *about*. I don't see why we can't teach *about* the Bible or the stories in the Bible. Since it is in our general interest to have our children know that information, my hope is that there will be a kind of centrist lobby or common cause lobby that will prevail in seeing that this material does get taught to our children. They are being deprived of literacy. I hope there will be a strong enough centrist feeling about having that information available to our children that we will be able to introduce it into textbooks.

I don't know the disposition of the law suit, but there were a couple of suits brought against schools that graduated children who were illiterate. You may remember that they sued the schools for not making them literate. On those grounds our children have a right to literate knowledge, knowledge about the Bible.

NARRATOR: Do you want to say anything about the disposition of the suit?

COMMENT (from audience): I can't respond to that, but I do know that there is a giant task ahead to achieve the very laudable goal that you have because the positions have hardened to the extent that they have become sloganized. You also will have to do quite a job on selling the textbook idea to the textbook publishers who have practically denuded the textbooks of teaching about religion. The indexes are practically free of it; you can't even find the word religion in most of the textbooks. I don't think the court would stand in the way of any kind of exercise that is simply teaching about religion. In fact, they've made this very clear. But this has become one of the slogans that generate and have low-beam responses, and the task is a very difficult one.

DR. HIRSCH: Our idea about that generally is this: The strategy should be to mandate a result without mandating the way you achieve the result. That's the general principle of these tests. They say, "Okay, we don't care how you get there, but this is where you should get." In our lists of what every third grader should know and in what every sixth grader should know, there is a large dose of needed allusive material from the Bible.

COMMENT: We have the King James Bible, but it is being somewhat diluted to make it nice and easy to understand. I think that is a sad case.

DR. HIRSCH: There I think you are dealing with what grade level you start with first. Those who went to Sunday School didn't get the King James. In Sunday School we got little stories.

COMMENT: Go to any fundamentalist church now and they have these beautifully newly translated Bibles which are nice and easy.

DR. HIRSCH: I guess what I was getting at is that passages from the King James would come rather late in schooling, later anyway than the early grades in which you would want the materials first introduced. Actually—and I'm not dogmatic about this—since in earlier times we did teach the King James to very young children.

COMMENT: You give them stories of Shakespeare and then later on they read Shakespeare.

DR. HIRSCH: Yes. That's the plan. It's what Charles and Mary Lamb did back in the early 19th century.

QUESTION: In the realm of education in this country, don't you think the basis of other main religions should be taught as well and not just the Bible?

DR. HIRSCH: Yes, and they are on our list.

QUESTION: I think you partially answered the question in my mind in your latest comments. But let's assume for the moment that everybody agrees, the school systems agree, and we've got to follow your thoughts. Who is going to teach them?

DR. HIRSCH: The incompetence of teachers is a point that is often raised, and I defend the poor teachers—the younger ones—because they have had to go through this disastrous school system themselves. Then secondly they've gone to education schools where methods of pedagogy are taught instead of substance. What I say optimistically is that we can educate the teachers while we are educating the children. As a teacher, I have more than a few times taught material I didn't know until a few days before I had to teach it. The hope is that the textbooks would be so good that an older person would be able to teach younger persons materials about which he or she had little knowledge. Better textbooks will teach the teachers themselves. I don't see why this shouldn't be the case since it conforms to my own experience. It isn't as though you have to be perfectly formed before you go into the classroom. If that were so we would never get into the classroom.

COMMENT: I would like to say something quite different. You say that you do not agree with what most people say about the influence of television, and I would like to widen it to media. We have a child, and when he was four years old we disconnected the television and put it in the basement. Some of his teachers who do rely heavily on the help of the media to teach in school protested right away saying that we were cutting him off from the reference system of his peers. We knew that, and we didn't care. But what happened is that *we* became cut off from the reference system of our peers. But it is very important because, as I say, the schools are using heavily this media system, and I think we are really losing a tremendous amount.

DR. HIRSCH: First of all, let me tell you that the figures show that for young children, up to about ten hours of television watching per week enhanced reading and literacy. This is not surprising since television is actually a literate medium. Except for informal interviews, everything is written down. TV language usually comes from a teleprompter or from a written script. In the TV studio, word processors are going madly all the time. So certainly the people producing TV are literate. However, the background information that is sent out over the TV is widely dispersed in numerous channels. But I'm getting ahead of myself here. I should say that up to ten hours of watching will enhance literacy; over ten hours the correlation goes the other direction. That's also clear from a question in this book, *What Do Our 17-Year-Olds Know?*, "How much television do you watch per day?" The ratio between television watching and how well one did on this general knowledge test was an inverse relation which shows that indeed television is anti-literate. But suppose you have better television. Suppose television itself became more aware of its responsibilities. Now the schools are, after all, like a single TV channel that everybody has to sit and watch or participate in for twelve or thirteen years for several hours per week—more hours per week than people usually watch TV. This channel could provide the information that needs to be provided. My hunch is that the schools could do much better than they are doing, and if TV understood the importance of traditional information for the national welfare, I think that TV would also begin to help us out.

I think the main problem is that we haven't understood the problem well enough. My hope, my optimistic view of the matter, is that when this country is confronted with a problem, it tries to effect a solution. In the 1940s Hollywood made patriotic movies without any ministry of propaganda telling it that it had to make patriotic movies. So I hope that if the public wants more of educational value in TV that TV will oblige. I know that may be a pipe dream. There is no way that we are going to overcome the problem of thirty channels producing ephemeral materials. But since they are ephemeral, they are not really going to help your system of reference. For example, take "Starsky and Hutch"— who can refer to them anymore? Their shelf life is very short. That's really one of the inherent problems of TV culture. It is so ephemeral, whereas literate culture is intergenerational and brings people together. It has much more persistent systems of reference.

QUESTION: I'm interested in and agree with your assessment of the importance of SATs. Yet have we not, since I was a dean of admissions, gone through a denigration of the importance of SATs? Do you see those coming back in terms of being recognized as only a part but a very important part of assessment?

DR. HIRSCH: That's an important point—I have mixed feelings about the verbal SATs. They are not sailing under their true colors. That is the difficulty. Its objected that they are culturally biased; that's one mark against them, and it's objected also that they stress skills rather than content, which is another mark against them. Both of those complaints are valid.

There is, nonetheless, the maximum theoretical correlation between our general knowledge tests and scores on the PSATs and SATs. That is a result that's going to make people stand up and take notice of these general knowledge tests. The reason for that is that vocabulary is knowledge about *things*. Vocabulary is not just words; it's not just language. And so a vocabulary test is very important and useful. What makes SATs culturally biased is the fact that people aren't told in advance *what* is being tested. The interesting feature of our counterproposal or counter-test to the SATs is that everybody is told in advance the domain they are going to be tested on. You take away the issue of cultural bias because a general-knowledge test is like an achievement test. Once you reach some democratic agreement about what the knowledge domain should be, then, it seems to me, the issue of cultural bias can be removed because the schools can then try to teach the public culture.

So as you see I have mixed feelings. The verbal SAT is a very good test, a very good index to general literacy, but the two basic complaints about it are nonetheless valid.

QUESTION: I have worked with a number of Vietnamese in Charlottesville who have learned their English primarily in Washington, D.C., and there is a tremendous number of Vietnamese in the Arlington area. I'm wondering if, in future planning, there will be any sort of attempt to introduce into the school curriculum some of the hard languages such as Vietnamese, Japanese, etc.?

DR. HIRSCH: You are saying that your Vietnamese kids learned English well through television, and this, of course, fits in with the acculturative virtues and literacy of television as a general language medium.

Actually, I think we might be worse off in some respects if it weren't for television, given the recent fragmentation of the school curriculum. But then you ask whether we should teach Vietnamese or Japanese in the schools.

I've never been persuaded we should. We always make these pious bows to the importance of teaching foreign languages for various reasons, and I can certainly accept those good reasons. But I wouldn't want it taught at the expense of everyone becoming literate in English. We have such a distance to go to make everyone literate in our own language and culture. I think part of our own culture, though, ought to include knowledge of world cultures—the salient information about world cultures.

COMMENT: We are faced with the exploding economies, for instance of Japan and Korea, and yet we don't have a great number of people who can converse in those languages to those people, whereas so many of the Japanese coming over here know English.

DR. HIRSCH: That's true, but isn't that because English is increasingly becoming the lingua franca for international communications? I don't know whether you saw the Robin McNeil series on the Story of English. The series began with an Italian domestic flight; an Italian pilot was talking to an Italian control tower in Italy, but the pilot spoke English because it is the international language of air traffic. If we were speaking some other language besides English in this country then I would say, "Yes, we've all got to learn that lingua franca that everybody's using." We're just lucky that they are using our native language as the international one. Isn't that the basic reason the Japanese are doing so well learning English?

QUESTION: One of the questions I thought of when I read Russell Baker's criticism was, should I have been ashamed in the mid-1960s, when cities were burning and none of us knew what we could do that we in the private foundations supplied comic books and sports magazines at ghetto high schools because the educators, including some of the most enlightened ones, said this was the only thing that youngsters would read? At Locke High School in Watts test scores did go up, at least temporarily, as a result of reading that material.

Secondly, and both of these questions come from Bob Coles' discussion with you, what about the fact that in the 1930s we probably were more culturally literate in some regions than we are today and yet this was the time of lynch laws?

The third question is a time-honored one. Isn't it true that the most culturally literate and best educated people in the world were the German people who brought Adolph Hitler to power?

DR. HIRSCH: The last two questions are very similar, but let me address the question about the comic books first. My own sense is that I really don't care what the medium is through which this traditional and literate information is conveyed. For your example, though, it is important that it be *classic* comics not ephemeral comics. That's really the only point I'm making. One reason classic comics and classical TV might be a very important tool to use is that after you have the background information and the decoding skills that you need, reading becomes a much less painful task and much more interesting. I read comic books, and I think we all like picture books, movies, and TV. There is nothing inherently wrong with those media. It seems to me it's the content that is of primary concern, and that's really what my book is about.

E. D. Hirsch

As to what I would call the Robert Coles question, Goering was culturally literate, and Himmler was culturally literate. Just use those examples as encapsulating the question you are making about us and our lynch laws. But let's also put it the other way around. There are a number of evil people in the world who are illiterate. I detected in Coles a kind of noble savage principle implying that by being illiterate you would automatically be good. By being culturally literate and refined you would be more likely to be bad. I guess the reason I make this simple point is that there isn't any necessary relation of any kind between goodness and literacy, one way or the other. Perhaps you could say that without modern techniques and technology, the scale on which you could practice your evil would be reduced; therefore, if you have a greater capacity for positive action, you also have a greater capacity for evil action.

I see cultural literacy as simply a tool for literacy. That has to be understood first of all. Literacy is really what this is about. It's to enable communication in a democracy. That's really what cultural literacy, in both the idea and the book, is about. I thought that Coles question was a red herring, a kind of irrelevancy to the real issue. It is certainly a paradoxically true point that education or literacy doesn't necessarily make you good. It's true, but does that have any implications for educational policy? I don't think so. I think we have to go on to say that we made a decision early on that we need to have a literate citizenry. Then, a further question is, shouldn't we teach kids more than just techniques of communication? Yes, but that's in the realm of values and particularly what people now call consensus values in public schools.

NARRATOR: I talked with Coles a little, and the reason I read that passage is that he believes that passage suggests you have a moral vision as well as an educational purpose and that you hold out a kind of utopia in that concluding passage where you say that with your program good social developments will follow.

DR. HIRSCH: I see. I think certainly what will come about is more social justice, and that was my answer to Coles on the MacNeil-Lehrer show. Certainly increased literacy for everybody is going to produce greater economic equity in the country and therefore greater social justice. That isn't necessarily utopian, but it is at least an improvement over the severe, tremendous contrast now between rich and poor in this country.

QUESTION; It's perhaps too early for further encomia, but that's part of what I want to say and see whether Don agrees with the way I say it, and then I do have one question.

The expression of admiration I will put in this form. Thinking back before the 1950s or 1960s of these things that were written then, which I associate with what you are saying now, there was a book called *Educational Wasteland*. There was another book called *And Madly Teach*, and there were yet others of this kind. I was very sympathetic with those books which were criticisms of the cultural illiteracy then. The problem was, however, that they were heavily attacked for being culturally snobbish. Your friend who is a pastor at Harlem says, "These are snobs." They were taken as attacks on teachers. In some sense they were attacks. They attacked the educational establishment, e.g., the schools of education were the big focus of the attack. But these studies didn't have any empirical base. It seems to me you've bypassed all of those and put this whole discussion on a much better basis. I therefore admire very much what you are doing for coming back to the kind of thing that is not attacking. It's not the people who already have cultural literacy saying, with a bit of disdain, "Everybody ought to have it." You put it on a basis which is deeply egalitarian and worthy. That's my statement of admiration.

Now, I'd like to comment about your willingness to use television and the visual media. I just have a sense, without this kind of knowledge you have, that you are a little too soft on that and on comic books, movies, etc. There are those who are saying that with a radio, you've still got words. But when you get the habits of dealing with the world in images, that's a problem—even if they are images of King Arthur, Shakespeare, classic comics, and so on. A much less significant book than yours, *Amusing Ourselves to Death*, makes this point fairly strongly. If the habits of the world of content of communication are entertaining and visual, even if it is Shakespeare and even if it is material that would fit on your list—there is another kind of problem. I have a sense there was something in that. Radio is better than television even if you lose something. A single word is worth a thousand pictures.

DR. HIRSCH: I think that's right. I don't know enough about it, but I do wonder how we are going to do anything about it. There is no way that television can be put away in everybody's basement.

QUESTION: We have sort of an interesting experiment in our own family. We have two children, and one is an anthropologist who takes his two children with him, of course, to a small island where there are no media, no radio, nor anything but books. They have gone three times. The children are now eight and fifteen. For a whole year at a time, they have been cut off from the rest of the world. Those children are extremely great lovers of books. They are extremely well-read, extremely literate, and I suspect they are going to do extremely well on their SATs. Our other daughter lives outside of Boston and sends her children to a very fine public school. I notice there they are in front of the television a great deal. They do not want to read. I feel we are out to pamper the little darlings, and we think we are overtaxing them by giving them too much homework and so forth nowadays. It's an interesting experiment. Both of my children were brought up in the '50s and '60s along side of each other, but one has been forced to find means of entertainment other than movies, television, counter toys and so forth.

DR. HIRSCH: As I said, I don't want to whitewash television, but I think we've got to do the best we can in the television era by improving the schools. One of the factors that confuses the issue, when we are talking about television and schools, is that although the private and parochial schools do a lot better—as the breakdowns in this book show—in making children knowledgeable about the basic traditional literate information they need to have, these schools are now using the same textbooks that the public schools are using. There are no traditional textbooks anymore. Consequently, the marks that were made by kids from private and parochial schools, though higher, are only ten points higher than the average in public schools. That's not very many points on a scale of one hundred. There is a 10 percent difference, and that's not a very big difference. It used to be the case, say, twenty-five or thirty years ago, that you would get a superior education in parochial and private schools, and this just exacerbated the difference between private and public schools. Now I think there are no good textbooks.

QUESTION; I would like to ask you something about motivation. The motivation factor in the disadvantaged child, whose performance begins to decline in the fourth grade, apparently has to do with both the child's motivation to learn and the parent's motivation to have the child learn. The success of certain of the Asian immigrants in their children's learning somewhat balances previous generations of European immigrants with the motivation to have them learn to be literate in English. Currently, though, the motivation seems absent at least in a good share of these disadvantaged to the point where Diamond pointed out that these children aren't used to long-term goals; they need immediate goals. He recommended some system of paying children to learn and paying their parents to help them learn. How are you going to motivate kids and their families to participate in having them become literate with a new set of textbooks and so on?

DR. HIRSCH: What you are calling motivation can also be described as an anti-academic ethos (attitude). The positive side of the lack of motivation is that there is an anti-school point of view in both parents and children. I want to ask myself, what is the cause of that lack of motivation, the cause of the anti-school attitude that you find among black and disadvantaged white urban kids? The usual sociological reason given, I think, isn't right. It isn't endemic to the black family or the black culture. It's something that parents have because they got it themselves in school. The anti-school attitude seems to me to come basically from the fact that people tend not to do what is painful. After this third grade point at which everything is fairly equal, learning and reading become increasingly painful and humiliating for those kids. It seems to me that this is the origin of the anti-school attitude. You turn away from what's painful. My hunch is that their motivation would improve as enabling knowledge is imparted to those children. So, if the old sages are right that everybody desires to know and there is a natural curiosity in kids, that kind of attitude would change when learning became a more rewarding, less painful, less humiliating activity. I would think it is, in a way, psychologically very healthy to be against school if school is painful and unrewarding, particularly if you are doing so much worse than that other group. I think one can give, through various kinds of programs, the enabling information to kids that enables them to move from decoding to understanding and learning—and not just through words but also through images. You can't understand even comic books without the necessary background information. My hope would be that if that theory is right about why the anti-school ethic has evolved, you then could have a pro-school attitude evolving. I think parents want the best for their children. That is my impression, no matter what group you are dealing with. It is pretty well recognized that if they do well in school they will earn more money later on. I think the basis for motivation is there. But we need to make this differential process I described disappear. Then motivation will rise, I hope.

QUESTION: To revert to your point of departure, or at least something very close to that which had to do with the strategy, tactics, and realization of your project, I believe you said that the tests, in a sense, will serve to mandate a result rather than the means. This leads you, then, to materials and textbooks and so on. I wonder if someone shouldn't undertake to say something about or give some guidance concerning the textbooks that are required. The materials, the bank of information that you are interested in and have assembled, come from somewhere. Why not go back to the roots? Why not go back to the sources of that at least as one of the main thrusts in creating textbooks?

DR. HIRSCH: I agree. I haven't been advertising what the foundation is planning to do, but assuming it gets enough money and gets the tests actually made, the next step would be to have first-rate committees look at materials and say, "We don't care what ideological approach is being taken here. We are just going to say whether or not this basic information is being imparted effectively in a motivational, good, narrative way. Now textbooks get away with what is called "mentions," with a kind of checklist. So if the date of the Civil War is mentioned somewhere, they can say, "We fulfilled our obligations to all of these various interest groups that make up state checklists." The way state adoption committees work is too Byzantine for me to go into here at this last minute.

I'd like to come back now to two things. It would be good if the foundation were able, first of all, to give a seal of approval to materials that did a good job of this, just technically speaking, and secondly to have the sort of common cause effort in places like Texas where you have state-wide textbook adoptions. There could be a political force, a counter-force to the special interest lobbies that determine the adoption committees in a place like Texas. So yes, it would be marvelous once we got rich and effective. We already have a good board of trustees for the foundation: Boyer and Ravitch; of course the local trustees Jim Cooper, dean of the Education School and Harold Kolb; and Robert Payton; and Bernie Gifford who is dean of the Education School at Berkeley. The board is very good and carries credibility. The hope is that if we get the means to have some of these committees and go through some of these activities, yes, that would be the sort of thing we would do.

The Good Housekeeping seal of approval presumably became something people paid attention to because people accepted the fact that it was a disinterested activity, and so it could be believed. So we'll just give it a try.

NARRATOR: We said at the end of Richard Rorty's lecture that this kind of discussion was reminiscent of an earlier period when philosophers such as James and Santyana and Hocking in the Department of Philosophy at Harvard tackled not only abstract philosophical questions but very immediate, concrete, and specific problems. The best minds turned the power of their intellects to the most central issues, and I think that is what has happened with Don Hirsch. He is also the founder of something called the Committee on Humanities, which is intermittently active but which certainly is one of the most exciting groups at the university. We count it a high privilege that we've had this opportunity to discuss his work. Thank you very much.

CHAPTER V

That Old-Time Philosophy*

RICHARD RORTY

NARRATOR: The Miller Center is pleased to welcome those of you who were able to find your way into the Dome Room and also those who are on the floor below. Other than Dean Rusk and one other speaker, we've not had to use the advanced electronic equipment on the first floor, so either Professor Rorty or the subject has captured the interest of this University community to an extraordinary degree.

By way of introduction I might just say that we have invited Allen Bloom to offer whatever reflections he may have in this same subject. Richard Rorty is the University Professor of Humanities at the University of Virginia. He was Stuart Professor of Philosophy at Princeton. He has been a leading figure in the American philosophical profession and is president of the Eastern Branch of the American Philosophical Society. He is a graduate with a master's degree from the University of Chicago and holds a doctor of philosophy from Yale University. He's the author of *Philosophy and the Mirror of Nature* and of *Consequences of Pragmatism*. He received the MacArthur prize Fellow award for 1981-86 and a Guggenhiem Fellowship somewhat earlier. He has lectured and done research in Europe and in Israel recently and has also given the Northcliff lectures at the University of London on contingency

---

* This article originally appeared in *The New Republic*, April 4, 1988.

and lectures on Orwell and other thinkers at Cambridge University. He is Phi Beta Kappa Romanell Professor of Philosophy for 1988-89, an honor that only three or four American philosophers have received in this era. He will, as you know, address the question "Plato vs. Dewey: A Reply to Allan Bloom's *The Closing of the American Mind*." It's a great pleasure for the Miller Center to introduce Professor Richard Rorty.

PROFESSOR RORTY: Thank you very much, Mr. Thompson. Toward the end of his book, *The Closing of the American Mind*, Allan Bloom says:

> The real community of man in the midst of all the self-contradictory simulacra of community, is the community of those who seek the truth, of the potential knowers, that is, in principle, of all men to the extent that they desire to know. But in fact this includes only a few, the true friends, as Plato was to Aristotle at the very moment they were disagreeing about the nature of the good . . . This, according to Plato, is the only real friendship, the only real common good . . . The other kinds of relatedness are only imperfect reflections of this one trying to be self-subsisting, gaining their only justification from their ultimate relation to this one.[1]

This paragraph is an admirably frank expression of doubts about democracy which are shared by lots of intellectuals—usually with a bad conscience. These doubts are about whether the many non-intellectuals will ever want the sorts of things we intellectuals want, whether a democratic community can be built on the trash and the sleaze that they apparently *do* want, whether our allegiance to the idea of democracy is more than a cynical prudential strategy. You let

108

us have your gifted children for our universities, where we shall estrange them from you, and keep the best ones for ourselves. In return, we shall send the second-best back to keep you supplied with technology, entertainment, and soothing presidential lies.

One advantage of the Straussian school of political theory, to which Bloom belongs, is that Straussianism gives one a *good* conscience about these doubts. Straussians make no bones about saying that the allegiance of the "potential knowers" with the masses *is* just a prudential strategy. On their view, no one would accept the risks of being subject to the whims of an electorate dumb enough to have voted for Hitler (or to consider voting for Pat Robertson) if there were a better alternative. But there is not, so we make the best of a bad job. Straussians reject Emerson's and Dewey's attempt to find one's moral identity in one's membership in a democratic community. They see such an attempt—the attempt to pretend that a pluralistic democratic society can be *more* than an incoherent "simulacrum of community"—to be as childish as Marx's fantasy that an emancipated working class will read philosophy in the intervals of non-alienating labor.

Leo Strauss, the great emigre political philosopher who was Bloom's teacher, was relatively coy and guarded in his expression of such doubts. But his students have become increasingly open. Bloom sets out in cold print a story one might have thought should only be whispered to initiates. This story revolves around "the philosophers" (the Straussian name for the lovers of truth, the happy few capable of participating in "the real community of man"—people who must not be confused with the merely clever, the ones whom Straussians call, pejoratively, "intellectuals"). These philosophers have always been, of necessity, liars. (As Bloom puts it, "they have engaged in the gentle art of deceptions".) Strauss spoke, still more gently, of "the need for inexactness in moral and political matters." They lie because they are not, and probably never will be, the rulers. As an interest group whose interests can never be made intelligible to non-members, they must flatter and cozen whoever does hold power.

"In the days before the rise of democratic societies," Bloom says, the philosophers "allied themselves with the gentlemen, making themselves useful to them, strengthening their gentleness and openness by reforming their education. Why are the gentlemen more open than the people? Because they have money and hence leisure and can appreciate the beautiful and the useless."[2]

But then the mob rose and began cutting off heads, so the philosophers had to find a way of cozening the mob. Cleverly, they "switched parties from the aristocratic to the democratic,"[3] even though they "had no illusions about democracy." They "substituted one kind of misunderstanding for another":

> The gentlemen thought that philosophic equanimity in the face of death comes from gentlemanly or heroic courage exercised for the sake of the noble. The man of the people, on the other hand, takes the philosopher's reasonableness about avoiding death to be a product of the passionate fear of death that motivates him.[4]

Cultivating this latter misunderstanding, the "Machiavellian" philosophers of the Enlightenment realized that:

> If, instead of depending on the rare natures who have a noble attitude toward death, which goes against nature's grain, philosophy could without destroying itself play the demagogue's role—i.e., appeal to the passion

that all men have and that is most powerful—it could share in and make use of the power . . . In short, if philosophy should be revealed to man not as his moral preceptor but as his collaborator in his fondest dreams, the philosopher could supplant priest, politician and poet in the affection of the multitude.[5]

In other words, the mob came to believe that those nice, kind, hard-working Alphas were going to help them get the things they wanted—if not immortality, at least as prolonged a life as possible, lived in a brave new world of ever more exciting low pleasures (public executions, Rambo films, novel quiches and jeans—and always, in the background, ever more explicitly sexual forms of what Strauss liked to call "jungle music.") In exchange, the common people allowed the philosophers to live in well-funded universities—institutions which they naively thought of as "serving society." "The universities," Bloom says, "flourished because they were perceived to serve society as it wants to be served . . . Thus it is indeed true that there is a special kinship between the liberal university and liberal democracy, not because the professors are the running dogs of "the system", but because this is the only regime where the powerful are persuaded that letting the professors do what they want is good."[6]

What disgusts Bloom is that the vast majority of people in the social science and humanities departments of universities are, in his terms, intellectuals rather than philosophers. These intellectuals think that one can deal honestly with the public—if not by serving it as it wants to be served, at least by being open about how it ought to want to be served. They do not understand that the crucial function of the universities is to serve (and replenish the supply of) philosophers—the people who are not, and never will be, part of the "simulacrum of community" which is contemporary American life. Bloom's animus is not against the mob but against the intellectuals—the people who, following Emerson and Dewey, assume that the success of our "democratic experiment" has made us contemporary Americans wiser than the Greeks.

These are the local variety of the people whom Strauss call "historicists." Historicists believe that Plato and Aristotle are obsolete, as are Greek notions like "timeless truth" or "the nature of the good"—not to mention the philosopher-gentleman-mob way of dividing up society and the soul-body, or reason-passion, ways of dividing up human beings. Among the best examples of historicism—the clearest antitheses to Strauss—are Mill, Dewey and Rawls. About the first two, Bloom says:

> Liberalism without natural rights, the kind we knew from John Stuart Mill and John Dewey, taught us that the only danger confronting us is being closed to the emergent, the new, the manifestations of progress. No attention had to be paid to the fundamental principles or the moral virtues that inclined men to live according to them.[7]

But Bloom is harshest on Rawls, whom he describes as writing

> hundreds of pages to persuade men, and proposing a scheme of government that would force them not to despise anyone. In *A Theory of Justice*, he writes that the physicist or the poet should not look down on the man who spends his life counting blades of grass or performing any other frivolous or corrupt activity. Indeed, he should be esteemed, since esteem from others, as

opposed to self-esteem, is a basic need of all men. So indiscriminateness is a moral imperative, because its opposite is discrimination. This folly means that men are not permitted to seek for the natural human good and admire it when found, for such discovery is coeval with the discovery of the bad and contempt for it.[8]

In such passages as this, Bloom lumps books like *A Theory of Justice* with books like *One-Dimensional Man* (which he characterizes, with some justice, as "trashy culture criticism.") He sees no difference between the know-nothing campus-trashers of the 1960s, with their babble about "elitism", and writers who, like Rawls and Dewey, envisage a society in which, no batter how discriminating we are in private, we do not let the state or the institutions of society humiliate those whose tastes and habits we find contemptible. The difference which Bloom blurs is between saying, "Pushpin is as good as poetry," and saying, "In the interest of pluralist democratic community which encompasses both those who read poetry and those who never will, we must make our laws and institutions as indifferent as possible to the difference between pushpin and poetry." Bloom has no patience with the idea that such a purported community might be more than an "incoherent simulacrum." The idea that political thinking and social institutions should swing free from a hier-archical ordering of types of human being seems, to Straussians, *the* great mistake of the modern age.

Given his view about the special kind of friendship which bound Plato to Aristotle, despite their disagreements, one would expect Bloom somewhere in his book, to strike up conversations with theorists like Rawls, Michael Walzer, Charles Taylor, Roberto Unger, or Judith Shklar—the people who think about the same texts and problems as he does, though coming at them from different angles. One would expect him to treat them as fellow philosophers, fellow seekers for truth, good people to talk to. In theory, Bloom's view is that "error is indeed our enemy, but it alone points to the truth and therefore deserves our respectful treatment." [9] Yet in practice—and here Bloom is typically Straussian—he tends to take seriously only those who share most of his own views, only those who agree that philosophers must, perforce, be liars. He has no time for historicists who think that, as Rawls says:

> What justifies a conception of justice is not its being true to an order antecedent to and given to us, but its congruence with our deeper understanding of ourselves and our aspirations, and our realization that, given our history and the traditions embedded in our public lives, it is the most reasonable doctrine for us. [10]

For Bloom, anybody who could say *that* has already forfeited his candidacy for the only "real community of man"—has shown himself to be a mere "intellectual," rather than a "philosopher."

Bloom treats Dewey, who thought that notions like "the soul" and "timeless truth" belonged to the infancy of philosophy, to the period when we had not yet grown out of religious fear and awe, as himself infantile. Dewey was, Bloom says, "a big baby." Bloom is not interested in political thinkers who sincerely and un-Machiavellianly settle for what Isaiah Berlin calls "negative liberty" (being left alone, as opposed to the "positive liberty" of being aided in achieving the good). Such thinkers believe that (as Strauss put it) "what is needed in order to establish the right social order is not so much the formation of character as the right kinds of institutions." [11] But, Strauss thought, the latter idea will sooner or later bring one around to the claim "that the only legitimate regime is democracy"—to the mistaken idea that democracy is intellectually, not just prudentially, justifiable.

The result of this discrimination in admissions to Socratic discussion has been that the Straussians have become a sort of cult. Even though this cult includes some notably learned and genuinely thoughtful people, controversy between Straussians and non-Straussians tends quickly to become rancorous, and to bog down in questions about the correct exegesis either of Strauss himself, or of the texts (Plato, Aristotle, Locke, Rousseau) around which Strauss built his subtle and intricate account of our decline from antiquity into modernity. Toward the end of a review of *A Theory of Justice*, Bloom said that the "greatest weakness" of Rawls' book was "the lack of education it reveals," and that the "core of the book" was constituted of "misunderstandings" of Aristotle, Hobbes, Locke, Rousseau and Kant.[12] Straussians typically do not countenance alternative, debatable, interpretations of those writers, but rather distinguish between their own "authentic understandings" and others' "misunderstandings." In this respect they resemble the Marxists and the Catholics. The tone in which Bloom writes about Plato is the same as that in which Althusser and Fredric Jameson write about Marx, in which Maritain (and the young William Buckley) used to write about Thomas Aquinas, and in which many members of what Bloom (in his best chapter) calls "the Nietzscheianized left" now write about Foucault. There is no question of these authors having been fundamentally misguided; the only question is how to render what they wrote internally consistent.

From Bloom's point of view, however, it is misleading to suggest, as I have, that there is a free, open, forum into which the Straussians might come and argue Socratically with their opponents. For things are much worse than most people think. "We are," Bloom tells us, "like ignorant shepherds living on a site where great civilizations once flourished."[13] The idea (widely held in Europe and Asia) that America's universities are notably free and flourishing, that they are as splendid centers of learning and forums for Socratic discussion as the world has ever known, is wildly mistaken. On the contrary, the subtitle of Bloom's book tells us, "higher education has failed democracy and impoverished the souls of today's students." What passes for "liberal education", Bloom says, "has no content", so "a certain kind of fraud is being perpetrated."[14] Further, "the crisis of liberal education is a reflection of a crisis at the peaks of learning, an incoherence and incompatibility among the first principles with which we interpret the world, an intellectual crisis of the greatest magnitude, which constitutes the crisis of our civilization."[15] The American universities have, especially since the disastrous 1960s, "decomposed." In the humanities, in particular, "there is no semblance of order, no serious account of what should and should not belong, of what its disciplines are trying to accomplish and how."[16] In America, "the philosophic language is nothing but jargon."[17] Under these conditions, small wonder that the saving remnant of philosophers keeps to itself, and does not mingle with the jargoneering intellectuals—all those people clever enough to manipulate abstractions, but not patient or honest enough to see the incoherence of their own historicism. Small wonder either that, to these people, the Straussian remnant looks like just one more intolerant and self-obsessed sect.

Bloom's book raises three questions: First, is he right, over against common opinion, about the state of American higher education? Second, was Plato right, over against Dewey, in thinking that there is a permanent, a historical, truth about the nature of human beings and of the good? Third, can one argue the first question independently of arguing the second? Or do we have to figure out whether Plato was right before we can decide whether our universities are in bad shape?

Bloom thinks that we do—that we have to start from first principles. We Deweyan historicists think that "first principles" are abbreviations of, rather than justifications for, a set of beliefs about the desirability of certain concrete alternatives over others—that their source is not "reason" or "nature" but rather the prevalence of certain institutions or modes of life in the past. So we think that the method of political theory is what Rawls calls "the attempt at reflective equilibrium." Such attempts start with a realization that one's intuitive judgment that some recent development (e.g., a novel institution or mode of life) is desirable or undesirable cannot easily be reconciled with some old "first principle." One then qualifies either that first principle, or one's previous judgment about desirability, or both. One muddles through, without any clear antecedent criterion, in the hope of finding a way to balance competing claims.

The historicist claim that such criterionless muddling must take the place of the Platonic appeal to immutable standards presupposes that there are lots of institutions and modes of life which Plato (and, for that matter, Locke or Mill) knew nothing about. By contrast, it is essential to Bloom's position that Plato's and Aristotle's vocabulary is, for purposes of political philosophy, entirely adequate to everything that has happened since their day; there are no alternatives of which Plato was unaware. For if there were, then what counted as a rational, coherent, non-self-contradictory view for Plato would not necessarily count as one for us. We would have more material to make coherent than he did. If the historicists were right that history is always throwing up such new material, then Plato's test of coherence could not have produced a timeless standard in either morals or politics. Historicists would also be right in thinking that we shall never have anything firmer to fall back upon than our accumulated experience of the advantages and disadvantages of various concrete alternatives (judged by nothing more immutable than *our* common sense—the judgment of the latest, best-informed, and freest of the children of time).

Whether one is a Straussian "philosopher" or a historicist "intellectual" depends upon whether one finds this lack of a timeless and unvarying standard acceptable. Strauss thought it unacceptable. He thought that "if there is no standard higher than the ideal of our society, we are utterly unable to take a critical distance from that ideal."[18] Deweyans think this is a *non sequitur*. They think we can take a critical distance just by comparing the detailed advantages and disadvantages of our institutions and modes of life with other real (historical and anthropological) or imagined (literary) alternatives—without claiming that any of these alternatives are "higher" or "closer to nature." For Strauss and Bloom, this suggestion is incompatible with the Platonic picture of the philosopher as someone who seeks the good by nature, as opposed to simply sorting through alternative conventions. Deweyans accept the incompatibility, but rejoin "So much the worse for the nature-convention distinction." So much the worse, also, for what Bernard Williams has recently called "the rationalist theory of rationality"—the idea that if you cannot lay down a criterion for settling arguments in advance, then you are condemned to "irrationalism" and "relativism".

The contrast between Dewey's stance and Bloom's comes out nicely in a passage in which Bloom harks back to Plato's Myth of the Cave. He says:

A culture is a cave. He [Plato] did not suggest going around to other cultures as a

118

solution to the limitations of the cave. Nature should be the standard by which we judge our own lives and the lives of peoples. That is why philosophy, not history or anthropology, is the most important human science.[19]

Dewey *did* suggest going around to other cultures. He thought that the benefit of going around (via history and anthropology) to other cultures was the same as that offered by the arts—the enlargement of our moral imaginations. He thought that "imagination is the chief instrument of the good . . . art is more moral than moralities." He put his faith in the arts rather than in philosophy because he did not believe that there was such a thing as "nature" to serve as "the standard." For Dewey, as for Heidegger and Sartre, "human things" were human creations. The idea of "human nature" was a cowardly attempt to reduce a self-creating being to one which was already finished and unchangeable. The Greek idea of an historical super-science called "philosophy"—a physics of human things—was, for Dewey, an infantile "quest for certainty". Humanity gradually abandoned that quest as it matured—as it gradually gained the self-confidence which was urged by Bacon and Hobbes, and which bursts forth full-blown in Emerson and Nietzsche.

Dewey warned that, to people still immature enough to long for certainty:

To say frankly that philosophy can proffer nothing but hypotheses, and that these hypotheses are of value only as they render men's minds more sensitive to life about them, would seem like a negation of philosophy itself.[20]

That is, indeed, how it seems to Straussians. Strauss organized his history of political thought around a story of decay: the story of how we have lost touch with the notion of "philosophizing" as a distinct human activity—the activity which, he thought, affords "the only true happiness" and which, Bloom thinks, makes possible the only "real community of man." Dewey thought this change indicated maturity rather than degeneration. On his view, Plato's "spectator theory of knowledge", and his doctrine that only the "potential knowers" could form a genuine community, were early, primitive hypotheses—ones whose retention, even in diluted form, will make us insensitive to the possibilities of the democratic life around us.

Bloom sometimes accuses us historicists of no longer believing in truth. But, as Socrates would say, much depends on how you define "truth." The question "do the historicists still believe in truth and reason?" is like the question "do the Straussians still believe in democracy?" Both questions are pretty bad—and liable to be merely rhetorical—because words like "truth" and "reason" and "democracy" have, in the course of their careers, meant a lot of different things. We historicists think of "loving truth" not as "wanting to get in touch with something which exists out there, independent of the fluctuations of human opinions and passions" but as "wanting to hear all the arguments, dream up all the hypotheses, think in all the languages, before making up our minds." For Platonists like Bloom, the emphasis lies on being faithful to something timeless, something equally available to all (sufficiently gifted) human beings at all times and places. For us, the emphasis lies on the journey rather than the goal. That the journey will never end, that there will always (we hope) be novelties which will lead us to revise what we thought were immutable principles, is no tragedy. The important contrast is not reason vs. passion or knowledge vs. opinion but rather freedom vs.

constraint. What matters to us mere "intellectuals," as opposed to the Bloomian "philosopher," is the imaginativeness and openness of discourse, not proximity to something lying beyond discourse. Both Platonists and Deweyans take Socrates as their hero, but for Plato the life of Socrates did not make sense unless there was something like The Idea of the Good at the end of the dialectical road. For Dewey, that life made sense as a symbol of a life of openness and curiosity, an experimental life—the sort of life which is encouraged by, and in turn encourages, the American democratic experiment.

The Deweyan idea that society should worry only about the freedom of the universities and not about what is taught there is paralleled by the Rawlsian claim that social justice is a matter of procedure rather than of substance: that it swings free of alternative "conceptions of the good." Rawls's point is that we democrats—we who do not see democracy as a cynical prudential strategy, but as having made possible new and better forms of community than have been available to human beings in the past—have to bracket the question "what is the good for man?" when thinking about alternative social institutions. We have to substitute the Rawlsian question, "Is this institution fair to everybody, in the sense of not favoring one race, sex, IQ level, income level, or sense of the point of human existence, over another?"

Rawls's conception of justice as fairness is, for Bloom, a reductio ad absurdum of the lines of thought which have gradually, through Hobbes and Locke and Mill, led us away from the Greek question "What sort of person should a state try to produce?" and towards the question "How can we maximize freedom and equality?"—away from Strauss' claim that "the ultimate end of the city is the same as that of the individual" to Rawls's firm separation of "the right" from "the good." Bloom would like the question of whether this upshot is absurd to be determined by "first principles," and we Deweyans would like it to be determined by inspection of the merits of some concrete proposals for the reform of American institutions.

If one stops treating Dewey as just a "big baby" and sees him as the culmination of lines of thought which Strauss traced back to Marsilius of Padua and Hobbes—as the product of a conscious, careful, and reflective rejection of Platonism, rather than of ignorance or impatience or misreading—then one can see the limits of the test of "coherence." There is no way to show that either Plato or Dewey are incoherent; like all good philosophers, either can keep pace with his rival's detection of apparent contradictions by making distinctions which will eliminate those contradictions. Rather, one must, sooner or later, ask how well their respective vocabularies and doctrines chime with the rest of what we believe and desire.

This means that one has to come back around to the concrete, to questions like the first one I listed: is Bloom right about how things currently are with American higher education? But the trouble with this recourse to the concrete is, once again, that Bloom's account of what higher education should be like sounds plausible only if one already believes a lot of what Plato believed. A less inexact subtitle for Bloom's book would have been "how democracy has failed philosophy and made it difficult for students to take Plato seriously."

As Bloom's subtitle stands, it gives the impression that he is doing the same sort of thing as E. D. Hirsch tried to do in his *Cultural Literacy*. Because that book and Bloom's appeared around the same time, they have often been reviewed and discussed together—treated as if Bloom has done for the universities what Hirsch has done for the primary and secondary schools, or as if Bloom supplied the "philosophical basis" for Hirsch's criticism of current

122

educational practices. But the two books could hardly be more different. Hirsch is working within the framework of a Deweyan understanding of democracy, pointing out (quite rightly) that Dewey's ideas about "skills" as opposed to "content" have worked out very badly, and that very specific reforms are needed if we are to have an electorate able to understand the issues of the day. He is not interested in judging human character by reference to "nature", nor in diagnosing an "impoverishment of our students' souls." He just wants to make the students better citizens of a democracy. He wants them to recognize more allusions, and thereby be able to take part in more conversations, read more, have more sense of what those in power are up to, cast better-informed votes. Dewey would have cheered Hirsch on.

Bloom's advocacy of "the good old Great Books approach"[21] may seem like the same sort of effort, applied to colleges as opposed to high schools. But lots of people who would favor (as I would) both Hirschian reforms in pre-college education and a Great Books curriculum in the first two years of college will demur at what Bloom takes to be integral to a "Great Books approach." For Bloom is advocating not just that we make college students read "certain generally recognized classic texts," but that they be read in a particular, characteristically Straussian way, in other words:

> letting them [the texts] dictate what the questions are and the method of approaching them—not forcing them into categories we make up, not treating them as historical products, but trying to read them as their authors wished them to be read.[22]

This description of how to read may sound harmless enough, but think about it. Normally we read books with questions in mind, not questions dictated by the books but questions we have previously, if vaguely, formulated. It is not clear how we *could* avoid forcing books "into categories we make up," since it is not clear how we could make our mind a blank tablet. To be sure, we need to give authors a run for their money—suspending doubt or disbelief long enough to work ourselves into an author's way of talking and thinking, trying to put ourselves in her shoes, giving her every chance to convince us. But I doubt that that sort of initial sympathetic suspension is enough for Bloom. For it is characteristic of the Straussians to think that a student who throws himself into Plato and emerges with a clear preference for Mill, Dewey and Rawls has misread Plato—that his soul has already been so impoverished (by the insidious historicism which pervades contemporary intellectual life) that he is no longer capable of reading properly. The Straussian attitude toward reading Plato is the same as the fundamentalist attitude toward reading Scripture (if you don't believe it, you must have been pretty deep in sin to start with) or the Marxist attitude toward reading Marx (if you don't believe it, you must be in the grip of bourgeois ideology.) If the students who buy in on Platonism are relatively thin on the ground in the contemporary universities, then, so the Straussians reason, so much the worse for those universities.

When we professors start falling back on "an intellectual crisis of the greatest magnitude" or "repressive tolerance" or "the treason of the clerks" (i.e., of some other professors) to explain our failure to get more students to agree with us, what is to be done? From a Deweyan angle, the only thing to do is to check out the state of academic freedom. Are the students able to read and say whatever they like without getting (even covertly and mildly) punished for it? Are the teachers able to teach what they like and still get promoted? Do the faculties exert themselves to take in representatives of every conceivable movement—Deconstructionists, Marxists, Habermasians, Catholics, Straussians? Do the government, the trustees, and the university administration keep the money coming without asking what is done with it? Is the library open late at night, and is there enough scholarship money so that the students can be found there rather than taking orders at MacDonald's? Is truth being given every chance to win in a free and open encounter?

By reference to such questions, American universities are in better shape than any others known to history. But from a Bloomian-Platonic angle, these questions are not the only ones, nor the most important ones. Rather, we have to ask questions like "do the humanities departments share a 'serious account of what should and should not belong, or of what its disciplines are trying to accomplish and how'?" Or are they rather, to use Bloom's analogy, more like a flea market? Bloom thinks that we have to ask not just about institutional procedures but about the substance of what is being taught.

The trouble, of course, is that if the answers to Dewey's questions are "yes" then the answers to Bloom's questions are likely to be "no", and vice versa. About the last thing we Deweyans want is for the humanities departments to have a consensus about their function and mission. When Bloom speaks of "the problem of the humanities, and therefore of the unity of knowledge", we Deweyans cannot see why knowledge should be thought of as a unity (rather than, say, a bag of tools). The university as a flea market (though not, for reasons given by Hirsch, the primary or secondary school as flea market) is fine with us. Once the defects of our high schools have been made up for by a couple of years' worth of the Great Books, the students should be left free to shop around in as large and noisy a bazaar as possible.

If you start from Deweyan principles, both Rawlsian "merely" procedural justice and "merely" procedural academic freedom look pretty good. If you start from Platonic principles, both look pretty bad. If you put freedom and imagination first, as Dewey does, you will be willing to put up with less goodness and with a good deal of muddle. If you put goodness and order first, you will be willing to put up with less freedom and variety. So recourse to the concrete is not going to *settle* the Dewey-Plato issue, any more than will recourse to high a priori argument. Issues of that magnitude are never going to get "settled"—they just get continually redefined by going back and forth between the concrete and the abstract. Still, recourse to the concrete at least breaks the theoretical standoff. It makes us ask "what should we *do*?"

Bloom does not offer much in the way of practical proposals. It would be nice to know how he thinks we could restructure the universities so that they would cease "impoverishing the students' souls" while still hanging on to what we have come to think of as academic freedom. (For example, can he suggest a way of getting us historicists off what he calls "the peaks of learning" without giving somebody like the Secretary of Education the power to fill professorial chairs?) Maybe there is a way to do this, but it is not obvious. Or maybe we can afford to lose some of our academic freedom in order to serve other goals more efficiently—but this is not obvious either. Unless Bloom follows his book up with one which gets down from first principles to the nitty-gritty (in the way that Hirsch does), it is going to be hard to evaluate the apocalyptic claim with which he ends:

> This is the American moment in world history, the one for which we shall forever be judged. Just as in politics the

responsibility for the fate of freedom in the world has devolved upon our regime, so the fate of philosophy in the world has devolved upon our universities, and the two are related as they have never been before. The gravity of our given task is great, and it is very much in doubt how the future will judge our stewardship.[23]

This suggestion that there is a close relation between the fate of philosophy and that of freedom amounts to the claim that unless we can recapture belief in the Greek notions which, taken together, give credence to the claim that the philosophers are the only real human community—unless we can bring ourselves to go back to Plato—we have little chance of avoiding a relapse into tyranny. Only that old-time philosophy can save us now.

The claim that resistance to tyranny depends on agreeing with Plato goes back to Strauss' idea that we can blame Hitler on false theories about man and nature and truth—on "value-relativism" and historicism. Strauss shared with many other emigres—for example, Adorno, his opposite number on the left—the idea that reference to what had been happening in European intellectual life helped explain the coming of fascism. Bloom takes this idea for granted when he sardonically attributes to the American disciples of Freud and Weber the view that "the trouble with Weimar was simply that the bad guys won.[24]

On a Deweyan view, that *was* the only trouble with Weimar. The fact that, as Bloom says, "German thought had taken an anti-rational and anti-liberal turn with Nietzsche, and even more so with Heidegger" did not do much to tip the balance in favor of the bad guys, any more than the popularity of Deweyan pragmatism among American intellectuals of the 1930s does much to explain why fascism did not happen here. Disagreements among intellectuals as to whether truth is timeless, whether "reason" names an ahistorical tribunal or an Habermasian free consensus, or whether the "inalienable rights" of the Declaration are "grounded" in something non-historical or are rather (like education for women, and the transistor) admirable recent inventions, are just not that important in deciding how elections go, or how much resistance fascist takeovers encounter. The questions "did Socrates answer Thrasymachus? Did he (or Strauss) *prove* that justice was by nature rather than by convention?", like the question "can we answer Hitler?" get replaced, for Deweyans, with questions like "how can we arrange things so that people like Thrasymachus and Hitler do not come to power?" For Strauss and Bloom, this replacement is a confession of intellectual bankruptcy; for their opponents, it is a refusal to be encumbered by obsolete Academic requirements.

The public rhetoric of contemporary America is an inchoate mixture of religious, Platonic and Deweyan ideas. Words of praise and blame are constantly being used in diverse senses, senses which presuppose different understandings of background notions like "reason", "truth" and "freedom". This mixed rhetoric is just what one would expect of a pluralist society, but it makes it easy for opposing intellectual factions to find some tom-toms to beat, and to secure attention for warnings that their opponents are betraying the republic. You can always raise a scare by charging "relativism" or "irrationalism", but you can raise one equally well by charging "dogmatism" or "scholasticism." It would be easy, though cheap and dishonest, for us Deweyans to reply to Bloom by beating our own set and issuing our own warnings. We could easily go on about intellectual snobbery, failure to trust the Healthy Instincts of the People, and, of course, "elitism." We might (in revenge for all that Agnew-Buchanan stuff about pointy-headed liberals) view with alarm the ominous ubiquity of

Straussians in Reagan's Washington (sly *eminences grises*, slipping back and forth between right-wing think-tanks and the corridors of power, gently deceiving the rubes who are supposedly running the country).

But it would be better to mute the tom-toms, and for both sides to discuss, in a cool hour, whether our country's unease is a matter of the "deep spiritual malaise" of which we have been hearing so much lately. Perhaps this unease is just the result of running up against some unpleasant, stubborn, merely material, facts. For example: that this turned out not to be the American Century, that the "American moment in world history" may have passed, that democracy is unlikely to spread around the world, that we do not know how to mitigate the misery and hopelessness in which half of our fellow-humans (including a fifth of our fellow-citizens) live. Deweyans suspect that we Americans are not suffering from anything deeper or more spiritual than having bitten off a lot more than we turned out to be able to chew—that is, the task of saving the world from tyranny and want. We are now running scared, for we have increasing reason to think that the bad guys are going to win, and that no Larger Power (Inevitable Progress, the Working Class, the Human Spirit) is going to step in at the last moment. Perhaps our problem is not internal hollowness, but straightforward external failure—the shipwreck of the hopes on which we were raised. These hopes, like those with which Plato sailed to Syracuse, may seem naive in retrospect, but they were neither silly, nor disreputable.

If this hypothesis about the cause of our unease were right, there would be further reason to doubt that a return to that old time philosophy will be of any use—that if we turn away from Emersonian self-reliance and Deweyan experimentalism we shall feel, or do, better. For "nature"—that larger power with

129

which Plato hoped to supplant the Olympians—is no more reliable an ally for an embattled democracy than the God of the fundamentalist wowsers.

NARRATOR: Who would like to ask the first question?

QUESTION: Do you oppose historicists with Straussians as well as historicists with Platonists? It sounded like you were using Straussians and Platonists interchangeably. Is there a distinction there, and if so, what is it?

PROFESSOR RORTY: That's a good question, but you better ask a Straussian. It's just the kind of issue that gets difficult when Straussians and non-Straussians discuss it. I take the Straussian position to be not that Plato was right over against Aristotle, but that the kind of thing which Plato and Aristotle did is a distinctively human activity that has gotten lost in our day. It seems to me that if you'll hold that view you are committed to a lot of what Plato believed. For instance, nature or there being such a thing as the nature of the good. But Straussians often want to distinguish their "above the battle view" from an adherence to Platonism.

QUESTION: Do you think one can admire Plato, and do what Plato was doing and still be a good democratic citizen?

PROFESSOR RORTY: I think you can admire Plato but probably not do what he did. That is, I think you could admire him for getting us off to a good start but who simply didn't know very much.

QUESTION: Is what is happening to intellectuals that we find it hard to understand this concept of nature and pursue it and, at the same time be good democratic citizens?

PROFESSOR RORTY: Yes, exactly. I think that the theory of liberal democracy has to share Dewey's thinking about human beings making themselves up as they go along.

QUESTION: We'd like to suggest some alternative hypotheses about this conception you have spoken about. Is it possible, for example, that Bloom is simply appealing to one of these currents of rhetoric which is in a phase of ascendency? Do we necessarily have to believe that we are on the way to defeat to explain Bloom's popularity?

PROFESSOR RORTY: I guess what I find puzzling is why the rhetoric of immutable principles suddenly has come back in. We have lived with the Emerson-Dewey rhetoric for so long, that I'm looking around for some reason why we seem to be giving up on it and the best I can do is that we're suddenly terrified. But there are, of course, alternative hypotheses, namely that the public has noticed something wrong with the universities that people inside it don't notice. I just can't see what they think they've seen.

QUESTION: This concerns your suggestion that you subject students first to two years of the Great Books and then throw them into a bazaar. Are you saying that you can't have Deweyan juniors and seniors unless you have Bloomian freshmen and sophomores?

PROFESSOR RORTY: I guess I believe that they have no right to be Deweyans as juniors and seniors unless they have gone through the kind of training which Bloom thinks they ought to go through. The one thing he's right about is that if you're going to have any general views at all you'd better have read the books of the people who hold different theoretical views.

QUESTION: How much do you think the excesses of the 1960s contributed to causing a reaction to Deweyan philosophy?

PROFESSOR RORTY: I'm sure that has something to do with it, but within the American academic system there are two different memories of the 1960s. There are the people who remember the excesses. And then there are the people who play down the excesses and say well, at least it was a period in which our students went South in aid of the Civil Rights Movement. Some of them got killed. It was in that period that American universities led the anti-war movement. And some think that excuses a great deal. That's rather the way I look at it. But I don't know how to argue the point of what was the real essence of the 1960s.

QUESTION: Isn't it possible to argue that the system of structural binaries, where you have Dewey on one hand, and Plato or Strauss on the other is in itself a platonic argument? Wouldn't it be deconstructionist?

PROFESSOR RORTY: Well, you could always lay another grid of distinctions crossways over the Platonist-Deweyan one. I guess I don't believe that there's an activity called deconstruction as just an activity of proposing some other grids to replace the grid that is currently being used. And of course there are others, but I sort of wanted to pick up Bloom's and use it and just emphasize the merits of the other side, as he characterized the others.

COMMENT: The system of structural binaries is the theory we've attributed to the Platonic tradition.

Richard Rorty

PROFESSOR RORTY: I have no idea whether Darrydar really believes that you can somehow have some kind of argument in terms of binary oppositions. I've never seen what was wrong with binary opposition. It's sort of natural to say, "Well, there's the x's and there's the non-x's." And there you have a binary opposition. Whatever is wrong with Platonism, it can't be binary opposition.

QUESTION: Can you speculate for a moment on what the consequences for the future of American democracy might be if that democracy faced the shipwreck of hopes on which we were being raised?

PROFESSOR RORTY: I guess it would consist largely in talking practical politics again instead of talking ideology. It seems to me we now have a mindless administration, a mindless Left. Both simply chant slogans at each other, Rambo-like slogans on the one hand, and Foucault-like slogans on the other hand. And no one seems to ask questions like "If we don't help the Contras, what do we do in Central America?" and all these nitty-gritty things which people used to talk about but somehow no longer come up.

In the days when the American Academy was largely in the service of the left-wing of the Democratic party, that is, the 1950s and 1960s, you still got all kinds of intellectuals saying, "Why don't we do this, attempt foreign policy or legislative initiatives?" And the people on the Right would answer: "That's a lousy idea because . . . ." It seems to me that there was a lot more of that type of discussion than there is now, because somehow the Left has gotten sufficiently discouraged so that it's gone all philosophical, and the Right has no interesting intellectual figures as far as I can see.

QUESTION: What about the arguments that Strauss used to make, namely that, unless you make this return to Platonism, you will have a superficial reading of all the texts? Only through Straussianism do you actually discover the true intent of the reading. Secondly, that every great political figure wrote in the context of a certain period in history and with reference to certain regimes, that limited or gave him freedom to say whatever he or she wanted to say. These arguments certainly underscore what Bloom has said; is there any merit in either of them?

PROFESSOR RORTY: I think the Straussians, and Strauss in particular, have produced really fascinating readings of text that nobody else has produced. There is certainly a case to be made for them. What I'm dubious about is whether there's a reasonable case to be made for this sort of claim about whole sale Machiavellianism in the seventeenth and eighteenth centuries. I guess I can't really entertain the idea that, as it were, two centuries worth of political thinkers were in such fear of persecution that it takes Straussian readings to get at them. It seems peculiar to me that somehow everything changed so rapidly that we got people like Mill in the next century. This sort of move from reading everybody as Machiavellian to reading everybody as stupid seems to me too artificial.

QUESTION: I'd just like to say first of all, I would align myself with the position that the University is a community of ideas and not with the position that holds the university's job to be the pursuit of some kind of truth which lies beyond and exists by itself. However, I would also like to say, that the community of ideas implies that there is some kind of equal exposure to valid theories and philosophies. What worries me about our system of education right now is whether or not this is actually happening, or have intellectuals become so obsessed with ambiguity that their theory itself is ambiguous. Have they embraced a plurality of ideas to a point where we have no ideas to contemplate outside of ambiguity? I wonder if that is not as destructive to the idea of community of ideas as was Hume's theory of truth?

PROFESSOR RORTY: I think there's something to that. That's what I had in mind when I was criticizing the contemporary American intellectual Left for having gotten too philosophical. This has created a situation in which we go on and on about ambiguity but nobody ever gets around to saying, "Yes, but what are we supposed to do now," which one would think the Left ought to talk about occasionally.

QUESTION: It seems that for a community like this to exist, there has to be an idea and I'm not sure that ambiguity qualifies as an idea in and of itself that can lead us anywhere, and bring about a conclusion. I wonder if that is even a possibility?

PROFESSOR RORTY: If it isn't a possibility, we better give up on democracy; I mean, that was the idea. The whole system is based on Milton's idea of a free and open encounter. And if there's something wrong with the idea that truth emerges from that kind of clash, then I can't imagine what . . .

QUESTION: It seems to me you can't have a clash if everyone espouses the idea of ambiguity, as with the deconstructionists, for example.

PROFESSOR RORTY: Well, I can't quite imagine the situation you're describing of everybody espousing the idea of ambiguity. I guess deconstruction has been blown out of proportion. In the first place, it's a short-lived phenomenon in certain American academic departments. In my view it is a misinterpretation of the philosophy of Deridier while others seem to take it as the culmination of modern intellectuality. This strikes me as silly. It's just one more philosophical fad. We've had lots of philosophical fads.

QUESTION: What would be your answer to the people who say that if we wait for a standard to emerge through the Deweyan process, if we say there is nothing fixed, immutable, or firm, then in fact we're in worse shape than Machiavelli? Machiavelli at least embraces the notion of virtue.

PROFESSOR RORTY: I guess I think we have a perfectly good American sense of virtue. We call it self-reliance. I think that the Emersonian tradition is still alive and it has everything that Machiavelli had along that line. I don't see that there's any danger of a crisis of indecisiveness. I admit, I don't quite know what our problem is, but I don't think it's that. I tend to think of it as a crisis of realizing that, whatever we can work for, it isn't going to be what we thought America was put into the world for. It's going to have to be something much more limited. And this strikes me as mixing everybody up for a while. But I see no reason why it has to last forever.

NARRATOR: Many of you have heard, as I have, that in the halcyon days of the Harvard department of philosophy, William James and his colleagues regularly addressed themselves to the great issues of the day and critiqued them. Today we are failing to do that. But what we've heard today is a clear-cut refutation of that. We're all in debt to Richard Rorty because, in addition to his enormously valuable scholarly work on the most difficult philosophical problems, he has also been willing to address, as James, Dewey, and others were, these current, urgent, concrete issues which present themselves. For that reason and for many others we are delighted that Richard Rorty made the trip from Princeton to the University of Virginia. Thank you very much.

ENDNOTES

1. Allan Bloom, *The Closing of the American Mind*, (New York: Simon and Schuster, 1987), p. 382.

2. Ibid., p. 279.

3. Ibid., p. 288.

4. Ibid.,p. 289.

5. Ibid., p. 285.

6. Ibid.,p. 288.

7. Ibid., p. 29.

8. Ibid., p. 30.

9. Ibid., p. 43.

10. John Rawls, "Kantian Constructivism in Moral Theory," *Journal of Philosophy*, 1980, p. 519.

11. Leo Strauss, *Natural Right and History*, (Chicago: University of Chicago Press, 1953), p. 193.

12. Allan Bloom, "Justice: John Rawls vs. the Tradition of Political Philosophy," *American Political Science Review*, 1975, p. 662.

13. Ibid., p. 239.

14. Ibid., p. 341.

15. Ibid., p. 346.

16. Ibid., p. 371.

17. Ibid., p. 379.

18. Leo Strauss, *Natural Right and History*, p. 3.

19. Ibid., p. 38.

20. John Dewey, *Reconstruction in Philosophy*, (New York: H. Holt & Co., 1920), p. 22.

21. Ibid., p. 344.

22. Ibid., p. 344.

23. Ibid., p. 382.

24. Ibid., p. 149.

CHAPTER VI

Science and Policy Advising:
The Two Cultures

EDWARD TELLER

NARRATOR: Dr. Edward Teller is senior research fellow at the Hoover Institute of War, Revolution and Peace at Stanford University. He currently is director emeritus of the Lawrence Livermore Radiation Lab at the University of California after having been its director for many years. The history of much of nuclear science and science in general can be traced in the appointments that Dr. Teller has held and the service he has given at Los Alamos, at the Manhattan Project and at Argonne National Lab. His research covers topics as related, and yet varied, as molecular and nuclear physics, quantum mechanics, thermonuclear reactions, application of nuclear energy, astrophysics, spectroscopy of atomic molecules, and numerous other subjects.

Of immediate interest to us in this whole intellectual scientific journey he recounts in is his forthcoming book, *Better a Shield Than a Sword*, published in June of 1987.

Dr. Teller is the recipient of numerous scientific awards: the Joseph Priestly Memorial Award, the Albert Einstein Award, the General Donovan Memorial Award, the Research Institute of American Living History Award, several Gold Medal Awards, including one from the American Academy of Achievement, the Thomas White and Enrico Fermi Award, and many others.

It would be interesting to have Dr. Teller's thoughts about the role of the science adviser, his notion of what scientists can do in government, his analysis of the two cultures and his experiences in advising either this President or other presidents. I noticed that he served on the White House Science Council and also on the Science Advising Board of the Air Force. Did you find that in any of these cases your voice was heard and that you made a contribution?

DR. TELLER: Yes, to some extent my voice was heard. I would like to make one remark in some little detail which is not a direct answer to your questions. The problem is the extreme difficulty of the science adviser's job. I would say that the difficulties of giving advice to the armed forces are considerable but not overwhelming. The difficulties of giving advice to politicians are so great that I don't know what the value of the process is. I believe it has some value.

There is one country in which I have seen science and government work together in real harmony, and only one; I doubt that there is a second. I don't think that you will ever guess which country I am talking about.

COMMENT: I would guess that it is Israel.

DR. TELLER: No. In Israel I had a good friend who was an excellent scientist, and who also worked for the government but he is one of the few that you would find in this dual function. In general the connection between the government and the scientists in Israel is better than in most places. But my first choice, and entirely in a class of its own, is Taiwan.

This is something I did not expect. I was invited to give lectures and I went back several times so that altogether I might have been there five times. I don't agree with everything they are doing; there is no country where an individual, if he is honest, will agree with everything.

Taiwan has made incredible progress in the last four decades; it went from one of the most wretched places in the world to one that is practically industrialized. If you look at high officials in Taiwan (including the prime ministry, a number of cabinet secretaries, and politicians), approximately fifty percent of the most influential ones are educated in mathematics, physics, chemistry or engineering. Talking to these people who know what you are talking about, and having them ask pertinent questions that demand answers, is altogether a fine experience. I have not encountered anything like it, anywhere.

Let me dwell on this a little longer. In their process of industrialization the Taiwanese did not make the mistakes that almost every other backward country commits. They did not start with industry. They started with agriculture. This earned them the strong support of the peasants by helping not only with improved production but also with marketing. Today people in Hawaii are getting upset about Taiwanese pineapples because they are no longer the largest pineapple producers in the world. It was a natural thing to do, and it was the right thing to do.

I was more closely involved with (and was asked to come to give advice on) nuclear energy and nuclear reactors. They have started to provide for their own energy needs with the help of water power. These people did not have fuel, coal or oil; they would have had to import that. They tried to minimize imports by developing their water power, and they developed all of it, just like the Swiss. Moreover they did it in fifteen years. That was basic; they did it well. As

soon as they finished they went on to nuclear
reactors. They did not take any intermediate steps.
Their nuclear reactors were working, and they are
safe. I wish the people operating nuclear reactors in
this country would make them as reliable as they are
in Taiwan.

These are a couple of examples into which I
looked. The science advice is there. Now I would
like to point to some limitations. I remember a
dinner of maybe fifteen years ago where these people
started to discuss acupuncture in a very favorable
light. Maybe they were right, but I was doubtful. I
didn't say much; I wanted to be polite, but I did not
join in their enthusiasm. After dinner the science
adviser of Taiwan came to me and said we should pay
more attention to that, but I wanted to meet the
people who are doing the research. The next day five
of us—my wife and I, the two researchers and the
science adviser—had lunch together. The claims the
researchers were making were much more moderate
than the claims accepted by the people whom they
were serving. In fact they were saying that
acupuncture is not doing much more than deflecting
attention from the pain. The amusing thing was that
the whole project was paid for by the United States.
Our government had heard about acupuncture, but we
did not want to go ahead at that time to consult
China for it, so we went to Taiwan.

QUESTION: Why do you think Taiwan did this?
What was different about Taiwan that caused them to
do develop differently from other Third World
countries?

DR. TELLER: I don't know, but Chiang Kai-shek got
the best of education, and became a part of a reform
movement, a very important reform movement initiated
from above. Like many reform movements initiated
from above including the one in Iran, this one didn't

work. The communists beat him. It did not work for reasons that you know at least as well as I do, probably better. They were overwhelmed by the war, by the communists and by the perdition of corruption. The country was too big for them; they could not manage it. Then they came to Taiwan and here was a job that they could manage. Almost anything they did in Taiwan was an improvement, considering the horrible state the country was in. So where they did not succeed before, they started to succeed now. These people had received their education mostly in the United States, and finally put it to good use. Things were disorderly then, but they determined who the best people were. I have no other explanation than this trivial one.

I don't agree when people talk as if modern technology could solve all their problems. I'm convinced that most of the troubles are, in fact, administrative in nature. Furthermore, I tend to believe that most administrations, perhaps even the communists, have good intentions. They just don't know how to go about solving their problems. They don't know any better.

Let me get back to answering your question, by talking about Niels Bohr, perhaps the greatest of physicists. He was a very remarkable man in other ways as well. You probably never heard his definition of an expert: "An expert is a person who, through his own painful experience, has found out all the mistakes that one can commit in a very narrow field." Now Chiang Kai-shek was an expert in politics. He found out all the mistakes one can make, and the next time around he tried to do it better. Perhaps he persisted in some political mistakes; I cannot tell. But in starting to move a country forward, in starting to initiate industrialization, he was successful. Progress was in part possible because he rejected complete government control.

QUESTION: How many of those Taiwanese nuclear scientists were educated and trained in the U.S.?

DR. TELLER: I believe all of them.

QUESTION: What kind of educational capability do they have now to sustain their level of intellectual quality?

DR. TELLER: I don't know in detail but I lectured, and I worked with sponsors. I believe that their universities system functions well, though they have the reputation of oppression. The first evening I spent at the university, just after I arrived the first time, I walked into a big debate about right-wing oppression and felt completely at home. It was in the middle of the 1967-68 Berkeley upheaval and the students there were arguing about precisely the same things as students in Berkeley. They criticized their own government all over the place, though they were extremely polite, unlike many American students. In the objective statements they made, though, their criticism was just as sharp as those of American students.

I claim that their universities function, that they are working on interesting projects and that they have freedom of speech. How much money they have, and how much progress they make is another matter; it is a small country after all.

NARRATOR: Among the students we get, we have recently had a native Taiwanese who wrote a doctoral dissertation that I think is as good as virtually any that we've ever had.

DR. TELLER: You know the Taiwanese who came recently from China make up ten or fifteen percent of the population. (The rest of the people came 300 years ago.) All the officers used to be recruited from

144

this group but now only half the officers are. There is certainly some inequality in the representation of ethnic groups in government, but the transition is being made smoothly, and generally, I think it's a well governed country.

NARRATOR: The population program is also very successful, isn't it? They call it the "Military Dependency Program," and they were able through that to introduce a good deal of discipline into the program. (Madam Chiang Kai-shek took a role in it, I believe.)

DR. TELLER: Perhaps that is true. Now, though, I would like to talk about the picture in our community, and here I was not closely involved; I was too young. I was, however, involved in a very essential part of the development and production of the atomic bomb. At that early time, we scientists were new to the idea of intervention, but one of my friends, a man ten years older than I from Hungary, Leo Szilard, tried to bring the problem to the government's attention. There was nothing like science advising at that time. He went to Einstein, and Einstein wrote a letter to Roosevelt, a letter which in fact was composed by Szilard and which Einstein signed. Roosevelt, nonetheless, acted on it at once. I was involved in the transaction as Szilard's chauffeur; I drove him out to Einstein's summer residence. That was how my political career started. The decision on atomic energy was made not because of any organization, or any channel that existed. Szilard was ingenious enough to provide his own channel and Roosevelt had the right instincts. By the time the atomic bomb was practically ready, though, Hitler was defeated. Only Japan remained. What should have been done about it?

There are several sides to this story and good science advice at that time would have been valuable.

It was not available, not because there was no willingness to seek it, but because *the two worlds of the scientist and the politician were too far apart to allow communication to be effective.*

Scientists think that they know the truth and that they should make all the decisions. Politicians *know that decisions are rather difficult, that they themselves don't know what to do, but they are also firmly convinced that the scientists know even less. I believe that both are right, in a way.* To the *extent that they are contradicting each other, they are not quite right, and the cure will be a dialogue, particularly if the questions are difficult.* That dialogue did not exist then, does not exist now, and in the U.S. has never existed.

The job of the President's science adviser is a makeshift. Its present occupant, Bill Graham, is the best man ever to fill the job. He is knowledgeable and modest. He is doing about all one man can do in clarifying problems of science and technology. He is explaining science to politicians and politics to scientists. *It is very hard to try to interest the scientists in the political process, because they are interested only in their final decisions; they dislike listening to the problems.*

Let me come back to the situation as it existed in 1945. We had the atomic bomb, and Szilard made the proposal that it should be demonstrated to the Japanese and then used only if they would not surrender. I believe he was right. The proposal got nowhere partially because Robert Oppenheimer obstructed it. I would like to talk more about this if you are interested.

Actually, Oppenheimer chaired a panel to recommend what to do about the atomic bomb. (This is described in detail in Compton's book, *Atomic Quest.*) The panel had four members: Oppenheimer, Fermi, Compton and Lawrence. You cannot fault the government; for advice they had gone to the best.

Oppenheimer was determined that the bomb should be used; I think he was wrong. Fermi had come from Italy six years previously and had spent most of his time on the Manhattan Project, so he had no exposure to politics. The fact that he was doing secret wartime work served to isolate him further. I believe Fermi took a stance which one can easily understand given his political background. He was going to go along with the majority, no matter what the majority said, unless he had completely clear and logical proofs to the contrary. Compton and Lawrence wanted the atomic bomb demonstrated to the Japanese.

The compartmentalization within the Manhattan Project was such that Lawrence knew how to separate isotopes electromagnetically, and Compton knew how to build nuclear reactors, but neither knew anything about the construction of the bomb. Nor did they know what the bomb would do, or how it could be used. The only experts were Fermi—who knew a lot about everything—and Oppenheimer who was the director of Los Alamos, and hence literally understood all details. His knowledge was really remarkable and very comprehensive, but he had a firm political opinion which was not to be shaken by anything. He was very persuasive, and he managed to get a unanimous vote for dropping the bomb.

At the same time, Niels Bohr was visiting this country and England, and he was very anxious to bring the question of what to do with the atomic bomb to the attention of the highest offices. He sought interviews with Roosevelt and Churchill and managed to see them. You cannot ask for a better physicist than Bohr or much better leaders than Churchill and Roosevelt, but their interaction failed to produce understanding. There was no practical advice given or received. Roosevelt and Churchill were probably too preoccupied, with the decisions of the moment. Bohr, like Oppenheimer, had a firm opinion. It was not the same opinion as that of Oppenheimer, but it was a firm opinion, and he did not listen to what the problem was. What he should have done was to pose questions, but what he did was to give answers. The answers were unacceptable and, I think, objectively wrong, or at least not sufficiently conclusive. His answer was: atomic bombs will make war obsolete. We have to get an agreement now, and the first step is to tell the Soviets everything.

Neither Roosevelt nor Churchill were willing to go one step in that direction. Such an unlimited exchange could have meant a good deal under those conditions. Both Roosevelt and Churchill knew that something very important had happened, but they did not see how the obsolescence of war would fit into world politics. They didn't know to what extent atomic bombs could be used by others. Bohr looked at it as a problem that could be settled: this is good and this is bad. I believe he fell into the trap of assuming he knew the answer where the answer quite obviously was not simple. The result was that the question was never discussed at any significant level.

Let me now switch to science advice as it came about after Sputnik when the job of the president's science adviser was established. I believe no science adviser has ever been listened to and, furthermore, I'm not sure how often their advice was worth listening to. Kennedy was the one President who won the approval of academia; none of the others did. Republicans were respected even less than Democrats by our academic scientists but Johnson and Carter did not have scientific support either. Kennedy did have support but ironically the only important technical decision Kennedy made—to land a man on the moon—he made over the clear protest of Jerome Wiesner, his science adviser.

I believe that the advice is not there because scientists have not understood what the political questions really are and what the alternatives are. There is some receptivity on the other side; there had to be because after all science has had some successes. Since advice has not been effective for thirty years, the eagerness for advice is reduced.

President Reagan has been in complete agreement with his science adviser and the Advisory Committee of which I am a member. My advice to the President has been mostly given through George Keyworth. He is a good man but he always bypassed the great majority of the scientists who, as academics, are on the left-wing, and as left-wingers are uniformly opposed to SDI. In the whole debate, technical questions hardly ever played any role. The Physical Society has at last reviewed SDI in its recent report. The newspapers represented this report as opposed to SDI. The newspapers exaggerated. The Physical Society committee looked into all the directed energy weapons which are closely connected with their expertise in physics. Other aspects of SDI are connected with engineering, and that is outside their field. They don't say that directed energy weapons are infeasible; they only say that they are difficult. And they are correct. In my opinion they over-estimate the difficulties. The findings in this case are incomparably more positive than what you have heard here. I know Sidney Drell was here to talk about these issues.

An institution like the president's science advisory mechanism will not make an essential change as long as there is a wide split in the scientific community, and as long as the scientific community automatically negates everything that Reagan says. *To talk about the formalities of how the advisory process should work—who reports to whom—is a secondary question in my mind. The main question has been posed long ago in the well-known book Two Cultures. This is a situation with which we are stuck and it is quite obvious that a change for the better cannot come, except very slowly.*

QUESTION: I was on the Space Science Board for five years and, as you know, one of the burning issues there has been the investment in the space station and the difference between political and scientific perspectives. I was curious what your opinion was as to the course to be followed.

DR. TELLER: I'd be very glad to tell you. I happened to agree almost one hundred percent with Keyworth who was against it. In that respect, I disagree with the President. In this country we have systematically overemphasized manned space efforts. Practically everything we want to do in space can be done by robotics. We know that it is possible to put man in space, but it is a mistake to concentrate on putting more and more men in space. NASA is deeply involved with the complexities of the situation. I don't know for certain but I have a suspicion as to what happened. You know that these things are not publicly discussed but the administration appointed Bill Graham to become acting administrator, and he was by far the best man in the organization. He did not have things his way. The battle in NASA has been won, for the moment, by the people emphasizing man in space. A year and a half after the Challenger disaster, they still don't know what to do. We want heroes but we don't want risks and we don't want it to be too expensive either.

NARRATOR: There is one other issue which is only indirectly related to science advising. I wondered whether the media had been correct in reporting that you would go much further on exchange of scientific information than many others in government.

DR. TELLER: I would, so in that instance the media told the truth. Holding back information may make sense if it is for a limited period. We can hold back the information that we want to put people ashore on an island in the Caribbean, but trying to keep the multiplication tables secret is nonsense. Still that is essentially what we are doing. We know that the Russians know about nuclear explosives, yet we still keep them secret.

QUESTION: Dr. Teller, I would like to go back to the subject of a few minutes ago. *Do you think that a legislative science adviser with the Council would help to strengthen the relationship between the two cultures that you spoke about, or is this hopeless?*

DR. TELLER: *I do not expect that any legislation of that kind would make a great difference. I do think, however, that a well-established science adviser's office is an advantage, and I am for such legislation. But it is just one portion of a very big, difficult and old problem.*

QUESTION: What other functions are there? What other approaches are there?

DR. TELLER: In my mind, the main point is what you have just mentioned. It is a very remarkable situation. This administration has been effective in recognizing that where government interferes, it is apt to do damage. Reagan has recognized that in every field, except the field of national security. We do have realistic procedures of secrecy that have been practiced for two hundred years. Industry, for instance, won't keep secrets when they appear to be no longer effective. Government, on the other hand, keeps secrets whether they are effective or not. And in the case of SDI, administrative abuses of classification have been numerous.

It seems to me that the transmission of information from the technical community to the general public is incomplete because the information is complicated. It is hard to impart, as well as hard to absorb. If you add governmental secrecy the situation becomes absurd. Furthermore, secrets are not effective with regard to our enemies because they have a very good intelligence system. I believe that we should have more freedom of information, not in the sense that the newspapers can attend Advisory Committee meetings. (In any case the Advisory Committee won't discuss any sensitive problems in the presence of the press.)

Instead all technical information should be released after an appropriate period, one year at the very most. By that I don't mean intelligence information, such as the identities of our intelligence personnel; that is nobody's business. But trying to keep technological secrets that involve the cooperation of thousands of people for any length of time is not feasible. Incidentally, this was a point on which Niels Bohr was very strong and on that point I not only agree, but over the years have come to agree more and more.

COMMENT: I have a related question. One of the difficulties with an uneducated public, like ourselves, is that we hear opposite voices from qualified scientists on the same question, like SDI. How should we respond and what should we think?

DR. TELLER: What do you mean by qualified? If a person knows physics, he still does not necessarily know SDI, especially if he has not actually worked on it. If he has worked on SDI, then you may discard his opinion because he is an interested party. If we were allowed to openly argue the points now kept secret, the function of public judgment would be greatly facilitated. New information has not been allowed to be inserted into the public debate.

QUESTION: Are you saying that secrecy is what has prevented healthy public debate?

DR. TELLER: Yes, secrecy, and beyond that, the difficulty of the subject. *People are not persistent enough to try and understand the technical details of the problem at hand. Even without secrecy, we increasingly live in ignorance because problems have become too specialized. Moreover, the art of public information has gone into decline. In the days when Faraday discovered induction he demonstrated it in his Royal Society lectures, and explained it to the public and to children. There is nothing equivalent to that today. We have made a very remarkable discovery right now in which I am deeply interested. At the moment, I am neglecting SDI because I'm involved with superconductivity. The newspapers heard about it but one newspaper copies the other so that we hear little that is new about superconductivity. Secrecy brings many disadvantages with it but lifting secrecy will not necessarily solve all problems.*

COMMENT: Would you go beyond this in terms of education? *You mentioned earlier that there are scientists who don't know a thing about politics, and politicians who don't know a thing about science.*

DR. TELLER: *That's right. Furthermore each party is proud of their ignorance. A scientist may say, "I don't know anything about dirty politics," and you may hear politicians say in an election, "I know nothing about nuclear energy but . . ." and then he goes on and pronounces on nuclear energy.*

QUESTION: If you were me, how would you start?

DR. TELLER: I tell you how I started. In the 1960s just before the student revolt, I gave lectures at Berkeley.

COMMENT: I was there. I taught at Berkeley when you gave your lecture.

DR. TELLER: You know, I had a thousand students and it is a red letter day for me to meet somebody and then be told, "I attended your class." I think it is important to try to make sure that people know something, even outside their specialty. I discussed this once and said that admitting that I don't know what entropy is, is just as bad as *admitting I've never heard of Shakespeare. How many non-physicists know what entropy is though?* It is interesting; everybody can know about it; everybody should know about it. *Today most of the physicists don't know what superconductivity is. Although the theory was published more than thirty years ago, it went unnoticed and was not understood by most high energy physicists, which make up the majority of all physicists.*

NARRATOR: Well, thank you very much for your thoughts, Dr. Teller.

CHAPTER VII

Politicians and Physicists

IAN GRAIG

Some of the most contentious intellectual battles of the years since the Second World War have been fought over the relationship between the physical sciences and the humanities. While discussion of the relationship between what Sir Charles Snow termed the "Two Cultures" certainly predates the post-war era, debates on the subject have taken on a new vitality and passion during the years since Hiroshima and Nagasaki.

Snow fired the first salvo in the Two Cultures debate with his Rede Lectures, in which he warned of a growing gap in understanding between those trained in the physical sciences and their counterparts trained in the humanities. While even Snow himself admitted that portraying the sciences and the humanities as two sharply defined "cultures" is something of an oversimplification, his comments nonetheless hit a raw nerve in the intellectual community.[1] As Isaiah Berlin has written, "I have tried but altogether failed to grasp what is meant by describing these two great fields of human inquiry as cultures; but they do seem to have been concerned with somewhat different issues, and those who have worked and are working in them have pursued different aims and methods."[2]

Intellectual discussion of these differences reached a fever pitch in the early 1960s, when the notion of the Two Cultures was used to examine the relationship between science and government. As Don K. Price has noted, virtually every scientific meeting during that decade involved discussion of the relationship between science and government. President Dwight Eisenhower's warning that the nation's public policies might soon "become captive of a scientific-technological elite" prompted scientists and politicians alike to examine the interactions between their two "cultures." Sir Charles Snow's Godkin Lectures at Harvard University in 1960 warned, in Don K. Price's words, that "democracy was in danger from the great gulf in understanding between the Two Cultures of science and the humanities, and from any possible monopoly on scientific advice to high political authority."[3]

The primary cause of the increased passion in debates concerning the relationship between scientists and government is relatively self-evident: Scientific advice has become increasingly important to policy-makers during the post-war era, and scientists have consequently interacted more frequently with policy-makers during those years than during any previous era in history. As well, these interactions have occurred on an ever-growing number of topics ranging far outside the traditional areas in which scientists attempted to influence public policy. As a result, discussion of the relationship between the "cultures" of the physical sciences and the humanities—while it remains primarily an intellectual exercise—has grown in practical relevance and importance.

The growing importance of scientific advice to policy-makers is primarily a consequence of the increasing importance of scientific advances as elements of a nation's economic, military and political power. And the emergence of science as a key element in national policy—and of scientists as key advisers in the formulation of such policy—can primarily bc traced to the effort to develop the atomic bomb during the Second World War.

The $2 billion spent by the Manhattan Project to develop the atomic bomb was more than the U.S. government had spent on science and technology in the previous history of the country.[4] The weapon successfully developed by this project fully transformed the destructive power of the military and opened the door to a new era of military strategy.

The development of this weapon through a government program also transformed the role of science in determining a nation's position on the global stage. As Don K. Price wrote in 1954,

> The United States has come to see that it is in a new kind of rivalry with the Soviet Union—a rivalry that may well turn, not on territorial or diplomatic gains, or even (in the narrow sense of the word) on military advantage. The crucial advantage in the issue of power is likely to be with the nation whose scientific program can produce the next revolutionary advance in military tactics, following those already made by radar, jet propulsion, and nuclear fission.[5]

While science has certainly not trivialized the importance of diplomatic, territorial or military (not to mention economic) advantages, scientific leadership has nonetheless become an essential element of any powerful nation's arsenal.

This has changed the relationship between science and government. The increased importance of science as an element of national power—combined with the upwardly spiraling costs of scientific research—has led to the involvement of the government in a large proportion of the scientific research being conducted in the United States and around the globe.

As Hans Morgenthau has noted, governments before World War II "were typically the beneficiaries of scientific and technological innovations achieved accidentally by private enterprise." Governments did not initiate programs to pursue such innovations, but rather appropriated useful innovations which were developed in the private sector's free marketplace of scientific and technological ideas.[6]

This relationship between scientific innovation and government changed with the development of the atomic bomb at the instigation, under the auspices, and with the funding, of allied governments during World War II. Governments could no longer rely on the private sector alone to develop needed new technologies. As a result, much scientific research was brought under the government's wing. As Morgenthau wrote in the early 1960s,

> The commitment of unmatchable resources for certain scientific and technological projects chosen by the government exerts a well-nigh irresistible attraction upon scientific and industrial research. Thus the direction of scientific exploration and technological innovation is no longer left to the free interplay of intellectual curiosity and technical ingenuity but is pre-determined by the interests and the power of the government.[7]

This increase in government funding and direction of scientific research has led to a reversal of traditional patterns, as government-funded defense research in the U.S. has fed innovations in commerce and industry during the post-war era. Indeed, the federal government now supports the majority of scientific research conducted in the U.S. And this support has grown in recent years through what once seemed to be an endless supply of funds available for research on the Strategic Defense Initiative.

This trend has been furthered by a change in the relationship between basic scientific research and the advance of military technology. Before World War II, advances in military technology were generally developed independently of advances in basic science. University scientists did advise governments on military matters before World War II, but their advice, even during periods of wartime, was "sporadic and marginal," in William H. McNeill's words. As McNeill also notes, however, "World War II was different."

> The accelerated pace of weapons improvement that set in from the late 1930s, and the proliferating variety of new possibilities that deliberate invention spawned, meant that all the belligerents realized by the time fighting began that some new secret weapon might tip the balance decisively. Accordingly, scientists, technologists, design engineers, and efficiency experts were summoned to the task of improving existing weapons and inventing new ones on a scale far greater than ever before.[8]

Because of the important role scientists played during World War II in applying advances in the basic sciences—particularly in physics—to the development of weapons, basic scientific research became intertwined in the postwar period with improvements in weaponry and other military technologies. This naturally increased the involvement of the government in scientific research. Indeed, by the late 1950s—slightly more than a decade after Hiroshima—25 percent of the scientists in the U.S. were employed by the federal government, either directly or on contract, and about 65 percent of the scientific research in universities and 57 percent in private industry was government-funded.[9]

The increased role of government in funding scientific research, and the increased importance of scientific innovation in advancing a nation's military power, has given scientists an unprecedented role in shaping certain government policies. Naturally this role has been largest in areas of government science policy, but scientists have also had important roles in other areas, including foreign and defense policy.

This trend toward greater involvement of scientists in the policy process—especially in the area of defense policy—has been furthered by the increasingly esoteric nature of advances in basic science, advances which often have immediate implications for military technology. Traditionally, advances in military technology were readily understood by even technically-illiterate politicians, for, as noted above, these advances arose from advances in industry and engineering and not in the more theoretical sciences. But in today's world, where rapid advances in basic science can quickly lead to advances in military technology—and indeed are often given practical application only through the military—knowledge of relatively esoteric scientific topics has become essential to the shaping of foreign and defense policy. As a result, scientific advice at the highest levels of government has become increasingly important. As Hans Morgenthau has written,

> The ascendancy of the scientific elites in the modern state derives not only from the importance of the subject matter with which they deal but also from the monopolistic and esoteric character of their knowledge. By virtue of their training, the scientists have a monopoly of the relevant knowledge, and that knowledge is inaccessible to the layman.[10]

Finally, the power of scientific advisers has further been enhanced by the ever-increasing speed with which scientific advances are put to practical use. As University of Sussex science policy analyst John Irvine noted recently, "The time between the creation of new knowledge and its incorporation into new products and processes is shortening very rapidly. To a certain extent, science is becoming technology."[11] Policy-makers consequently must have virtually constant access to scientific advice.

An organized system through which scientists could offer advice to the highest levels of the American government was first established during the Second World War through the National Defense Research Council (NDRC), the Office of Scientific Research and Development (OSRD) and the Manhattan Project. The lines between these various administrative bodies were often blurred in the management of atomic weapons research, but scientists occupied many of the key administrative posts in each agency and thus determined many of the policies chosen during development of the bomb. This was only natural, for the bomb project was primarily a large scientific and technical undertaking, focusing on taking a revolutionary advance in basic physics and applying it to the development of a weapon. Thus this was an undertaking in which scientists and technicians inevitably were going to play leading roles.

But during the course of this undertaking, Manhattan Project scientists and administrators began to step outside the bounds of technical decisions and undertook efforts to influence broad political decisions on how (or if) the weapon they were developing should be used against the enemy, and what efforts the Allies should undertake to control that weapon in the post-war world.

Beyond this, many Manhattan Project scientists attempted to influence the very political philosophy of American and British leaders, arguing that the atomic bomb was of such importance that traditional political ideas would not be sufficient to direct policy in the post-war atomic world. These scientists argued that their understanding of the potential power of the atomic bomb—an understanding based on their knowledge of the tremendous advances in basic science which were leading to the development of the bomb—gave them a special insight into what policies needed to be followed by the superpowers if the world was to survive in the atomic age. These scientists thus undertook, using their power base developed through the administration of the Manhattan Project, to influence one of the most important areas of U.S. (and British) foreign policy during these years: the policy the Western Allies would follow with respect to control of the atomic bomb.

The development of the bomb probably ensured that scientists would play a role in addressing many of the key political and military questions facing the U.S. government throughout the post-war era. Their efforts to do so during the mid-1940s consequently formed the foundation for later interactions between scientists and politicians on broad policy issues and provided the earliest illustrations of the public policy implications of the differences between the Two Cultures and the relationship between science and government.

The Atomic Scientists and International Control

The most politically active of the Manhattan Project scientists were those who supported the international control of atomic weapons, and their first efforts to influence broad issues of U.S. foreign and military policy were taken to advance the cause of international control. But these scientists were advocates of one approach to international control, an approach which rested on a belief in free scientific interchange. The unique elements of this approach made it appealing to the atomic scientists, for this approach rested on their understanding of the implications of nuclear fission and on the traditional sense of international unity which characterized the scientific community in the years before World War II. And yet, these same unique aspects made acceptance of this approach by much of the political community highly unlikely.

This unique approach to international control was first formulated by Denmark's Niels Bohr in 1943. Bohr believed that "a disastrous competition" in atomic weapons between the Soviet Union and the Western powers would develop during the post-war years unless radical steps were taken. He was convinced that only a break with traditional power politics could forestall such a competition. He felt statesmen must understand that the development of atomic weapons would bring about, to use Hans Morgenthau's words, "quantitative changes of such magnitude as to amount to a qualitative transformation of the political environment."[12]

This new approach to international politics would have to be based on an understanding of mankind's common interest in meeting the threat posed by atomic weapons. "It would appear," Bohr wrote, "that the possibility of producing devastating weapons, against which no defense may be feasible, should be regarded not merely as a new danger added to a perilous world, but rather as a forceful reminder of how closely the fate of all mankind is coupled together."[13] Bohr hoped this common danger would help statesmen of all nations understand their common interest in controlling this weapon.

Bohr realized, however, that the mere existence of a sense of common interest would not prevent an arms race; this interest had to be codified if the world was to survive in the atomic age. Bohr turned to international control of atomic weapons as the vehicle through which the international system could be transformed.

Bohr envisioned a system of international control being implemented in three steps. He called on the U.S. and Britain to take the first step by telling the Soviets of the existence of the Manhattan Project before either that project reached fruition or the war ended. Bohr did not call for the transfer of technical information to the Soviets at this early stage, simply for a statement informing them that the U.S. and Britain were undertaking research into the feasibility of atomic weapons. They could be informed of the Project's existence without revealing military secrets because, as Bohr noted many times, the basic concepts of nuclear fission were well known to Soviet physicists. Once the Soviets knew of the Manhattan Project, their willingness to participate in the establishment of a system of international control could be determined.

Bohr believed such a early initiative was essential to establish the trust between East and West needed for successful control of atomic weapons. Any approach made to the Soviets after either the war ended or an atomic weapon was used might appear to be "an attempt at coercion in which no great nation can be expected to acquiesce." Thus the time to act was before the bomb became a reality, for a further delay would exacerbate Soviet mistrust of the West and push the Soviets toward development of their own atomic weapons.

The second step in Bohr's scheme was the establishment of a system of international controls through an organization similar to the League of Nations or the then-nascent United Nations. Bohr never really went into great detail on the structure he foresaw for this system. He was quite clear, however, in arguing that such a play must rely for compliance on a system of international inspectors with open access to nuclear facilities in all nation-states.

Once such a system was established, it would be possible to implement the third and most radical step of Bohr's proposal: the complete exchange of all technical information on military and industrial atomic research and development. Bohr believed that all nations should openly share information on the theoretical and practical elements of their atomic energy and weapons programs, and that all such programs should be subject to international control and inspection.

Bohr advanced this proposal believing that efforts to base a nation's security on "atomic secrets" were doomed to failure. Bohr believed that any advantage in atomic technology could only be temporary because the basic laws of atomic fission were so well known that any industrialized nation would soon be able to construct atomic weapons. Indeed, efforts at maintaining an "atomic secret" would doom the world to a dangerous arms race, for no nation could accept even the possibility that an adversary might be gaining a secret advantage in weapons of such destructive force. As Robert Oppenheimer described Bohr's plan, "In principle, everything that might be a threat to the security of the world would have to be open to the world."[14]

If there was an open flow of information guaranteed by a system of international inspections, however, the motivation for an atomic arms race would be defused. Bohr felt his radical plan was justified by the potential for security in an open world, a security which could never be found in a world marked by secret atomic programs.

Bohr thus foresaw the establishment of a system of international control of atomic weapons through which the whole system of international politics would be transformed, with nations coming to rely on international cooperation and the free flow of information to maintain peace and security.

This approach had two main premises. First, the approach incorporated the belief that peace could best be ensured through international organization. This belief, the heart of both Wilsonian philosophy and the internationalist peace movement which thrived in the 1920s and the 1930s, was obviously a basic premise of any plan for the international control of atomic weapons.

What made Bohr's approach unique was its second basic premise: a belief that open international scientific interchange was an essential element in the advance of civilization and the maintenance of peace, and thus must be an integral part of any international control plan. This belief clearly derived from the traditional belief among scientists that scientific freedom and the free exchange of scientific ideas was essential to the advance of human knowledge and the improvement of human relations. This second premise virtually ensured, however, that Bohr's scheme would find little acceptance among key policy-makers in the U.S. and Britain.

Bohr attempted, through a series of face-to-face meetings and lengthy memorandums, to persuade both Franklin Roosevelt and Winston Churchill of the validity of his approach to international control. But Roosevelt and Churchill rejected Bohr's approach—and all other plans for international control—preferring to rely for Western security in the post-war world on traditional balance-of-power politics and continued development of atomic weapons by the West. Both Roosevelt and Churchill believed that a transformation of world politics simply through the establishment of a system of international control was a pipe dream.

Both also distrusted the Soviets and doubted that they would abide by the terms of an international control accord.

Bohr's approach did gain support from a host of key figures within the Manhattan Project hierarchy, however. Vannevar Bush and James Conant—the two top scientists in administrative positions within the government—developed a similar approach on their own. Secretary of War Henry Stimson became the leading advocate of international control among top policy-makers drawn from the ranks of the military or government service. And several top Manhattan Project scientists eventually became advocates of Bohr's plans as well. Indeed, the basic elements of Bohr's approach can be found in such key wartime statements by the atomic scientists as the Franck Report.

This approach came closest to acceptance by top policy-makers with the drafting of the Acheson-Lilienthal report in 1946. This report was requested by Secretary of State James Byrnes, who called on Undersecretary of State Dean Acheson to establish a committee to draft a framework for negotiations on international control. This framework was to assist the U.S. representative to the U.N. Atomic Energy Commission (UNAEC) in impending U.N. negotiations on the subject.

Acheson asked Bush, Conant, Manhattan Project chief Gen. Leslie Groves and John J. McCloy of the War Department to serve on the committee. The actual report was originally drafted by a board of consultants to this committee, however. The board was headed by David E. Lilienthal of the Tennessee Valley Authority, and included J. Robert Oppenheimer and several leading scientists drawn from the ranks of industry.

The heart of the Acheson-Lilienthal plan was its call for the creation of an Atomic Development Authority (ADA). The idea of an ADA in particular, and the tone of the Acheson-Lilienthal Report in general, captured the spirit and incorporated the essential points of the approach to international control first advocated by Niels Bohr.

First, the creation of the ADA would have placed atomic energy in the hands of an international body. This body was to own or lease mines and processing plants, conduct or fund extensive research into peaceful uses of atomic energy, and distribute quantities of uranium to be used in such research. The authority would have monitored uses of raw materials through regular surveys, and would have had the power to inspect atomic energy facilities around the globe. As well, the ADA would have guaranteed the free movement of scientists and the free exchange of scientific information. Thus the creation of such an authority would have placed the control of atomic energy primarily in the hands of an international body, by definition the most important tenet of any approach to international control.

Second, the ADA would have sought, as its name indicates, to promote the development of peaceful uses of atomic energy. As noted above, the authority would have conducted research and funded outside research in the field. This would have met an important concern of such scientists as Bohr, who had long worried that efforts to deter the use of atomic energy for destructive purposes could hinder its development for peaceful uses. Bohr and most other Manhattan Project scientists believed that atomic energy could benefit mankind in such areas as transportation and medicine. The ADA's commitment to the development of that energy source thus addressed an important part of the scientists' approach to international control.

Indeed, the general tone of the Acheson-Lilienthal report, as captured in the idea for an international development authority, was positive and full of hope for international cooperation. This tone was also seen in the Acheson-Lilienthal committee's refusal to rely on sanctions to prevent nations from developing atomic weapons. The Acheson-Lilienthal report did not contain a listing of sanctions—military or otherwise—to be imposed by an international body on a state violating the ban on using atomic energy to create weapons.

Instead, the report expresses the belief that compliance could best be ensured through reliance on inspections of atomic facilities and a raw materials survey. The ADA would have the power to inspect atomic facilities in any state to determine if those facilities were being used for the construction of weapons. As well, the ADA would regularly conduct a systematic inspection of raw material deposits to monitor those deposits and ensure that they were not being used to create weapons. In relying on such an "open world"—i.e., one in which the ADA would have free access to facilities and mines in all nation-states—the Acheson-Lilienthal plan clearly captured another of Bohr's hopes.

Finally, the Acheson-Lilienthal plan called for reliance on free scientific interchange both as a trust-building step and as an additional method for determining states' compliance with an international control accord. The authors of the report argued that the free movement of scientists, and the free exchange of scientific information, would serve as one more method to determine the goals of scientific research being conducted around the globe, while also promoting cooperation among scientists from many nations. This was clearly an idea with which Niels Bohr would be in complete agreement.

Thus the Acheson-Lilienthal plan in many ways embodied the key elements of the approach to international control first advanced by Niels Bohr in 1943. But the Acheson-Lilienthal plan was not chosen to be the U.S. proposal to the UNAEC. Instead, a plan advanced by Bernard Baruch, the U.S. representative to the U.N. commission, was chosen. The reasons for this choice help reveal some of the key philosophical differences between the atomic scientists and top policy-makers in the Truman administration, differences which virtually ensured rejection of the international control approach favored by many of the scientists.

Three factors were most important in the choice of the Baruch plan instead of the scheme outlined in the Acheson-Lilienthal report. The first had little to do with philosophical questions but everything to do with political power. Bernard Baruch was a very influential man in Washington, and the Truman administration needed his influence to gain public and congressional support for both the McMahon bill—the administration's proposal to establish a system to regulate and promote the domestic development of atomic energy—and the U.S. proposal on international control. President Truman was therefore quick to support Baruch in crucial decisions, as was demonstrated several times during the drafting of the final American proposal to the U.N.

The second factor in the choice of the Baruch plan went straight to the heart of the differences between the atomic scientists and top policy-makers: opponents of the Acheson-Lilienthal plan argued that it would require the U.S. to give away secret scientific information. This impression was created by Acheson-Lilienthal's call for the U.S. to share basic scientific information as part of the effort to establish the ADA. Acheson-Lilienthal argued that such a sharing of basic scientific information was essential in the process of establishing the ADA, and could also serve as a trust-building step. The report emphasized that it did not envision the sharing of applied engineering information, but merely of basic scientific knowledge which could never be kept secret. The Baruch plan, on the other hand, stated flatly that no information would be exchanged before a system of sanctions and safeguards was in place.

Accusations that they favored giving away the "atomic secret" had long plagued the advocates of the approach to international control embodied in the Acheson-Lilienthal plan. Advocates of that approach had argued since early 1944 that an essential first trust-building step toward international control was for the U.S. to inform the U.S.S.R. of Anglo-American atomic research and to seek Soviet support for negotiations on international control. If such Soviet support was forthcoming, the U.S. would offer to exchange with the Soviet Union basic scientific knowledge about atomic fission. Originally, such advocates as Niels Bohr and Vannevar Bush wanted this approach to be made before the U.S. successfully tested the atomic bomb or, if not that early, then before the war ended or the U.S. used the bomb against an enemy target. But even after Hiroshima, Nagasaki and the surrender of Japan, the supporters of this approach to international control argued that the U.S. at least needed to take steps toward basic scientific interchange.

Their support of this position was based on the argument that one could clearly distinguish between basic scientific knowledge and applied scientific and engineering information. The former, they argued, could not be considered secret, for the basic knowledge about atomic energy was known by scientists around the globe even in the years before World War II. The latter, on the other hand, did involve secrets concerning the industrial, engineering and technological skills used by the United States to build a bomb. This information, they argued, should not be turned over to the U.S.S.R. or any other nation until an international control plan had been agreed to and safeguards put in place. The Acheson-Lilienthal approach was clearly of this school of thought.

Opponents of this approach to international control, on the other hand, felt that such a distinction could not be made. They argued that the United States should zealously guard any and all scientific information until such time as a system of safeguards and sanctions was in place. They saw no need for a trust-building step such as the exchange of basic scientific information, and indeed argued that any such step would involve a grievous violation of U.S. security.

The supporters of the Acheson-Lilienthal plan failed to bring about an understanding or acceptance of their position on this issue. This failure can in large measure be traced to one key factor: the leading proponents of the approach to international control embodied in the Acheson-Lilienthal plan were scientists, and they were making an argument based on their unique training and experience and their knowledge of other scientists around the globe. Their training taught them that a distinction could be made between basic scientific knowledge and applied industrial and engineering information. Their familiarity with their counterparts in other nations taught them that the basic concepts of nuclear fission were well-known even in the Soviet Union, and that only the applied technological information used to build the atomic bomb could be kept secret.

The failure of the scientists to convince leading policy-makers of the validity of their position was of vital importance, for the idea of an early trust-building step and the free exchange of basic scientific information were keystones to their approach to international control in general and to the Acheson-Lilienthal plan in particular. This failure contributed to the impression that the plan advanced by Bernard Baruch would better ensure that the U.S. did not give away the "atomic secret," and this impression contributed to the Truman administration's selection of the Baruch plan as the U.S. proposal to the U.N. Atomic Energy Commission.

The third reason for the choice of the Baruch plan is clearly related to the preceding point: The plan was perceived as being more realistic, particularly in its call for an explicit statement of sanctions to be imposed by the international control body. This was seen as particularly important because of distrust of the U.S.S.R. and a consequent belief that some form of coercion was essential to ensure Soviet compliance.

But was the Baruch plan more "realistic"? One could argue that Acheson-Lilienthal offered the more realistic vision of how successful an international organization could be in gaining compliance through the threat of sanctions. The history of international organizations in the inter-war period certainly offered no encouragement to the idea that the threat of international sanctions could be effective. And it was certainly unlikely that a major power intent on violating an international agreement would be deterred from doing so by clauses and provisions on sanctions.

In light of these arguments, the authors of the Acheson-Lilienthal report had chosen a different approach to preventing violations. A system of international inspections and raw material surveys would provide warnings of treaty violations. These warnings would give other states the opportunity to take steps on their own or together to punish the violator. Thus the threat of sanctions (through self-help) was present in Acheson-Lilienthal, but was not explicitly stated. The authors of the report argued that their approach was preferable, for a statement of sanctions would merely set a tone of punishment and control while not in fact increasing the impetus for states to comply.

Advocates of the Baruch plan nonetheless effectively characterized the Acheson-Lilienthal approach as unrealistic because it failed to threaten explicitly the imposition of sanctions. They argued that a system of open scientific interchange would not remove the impetus for nations to cheat by undertaking efforts to build atomic weapons, and could not provide adequate warning to ensure that such efforts never reached fruition. Supporters of the Baruch plan thus dismissed as "naive" the most important element of the international control plan first advocated by Niels Bohr—its reliance on free scientific interchange as a guarantor of security.

The idea of explicitly-stated sanctions was particularly appealing in the tense world of international politics in the early years of the Cold War, and the notion of free scientific interchange was thus easily dismissed. The Baruch plan contained a call for a clear statement of sanctions, and this call was the final factor in its being chosen by the U.S.

The choice of the Baruch plan marked the Truman administration's final rejection of the approach to international control advocated by Niels Bohr and many other atomic scientists. But the scientists remained hopeful that agreement on some system of international control could be reached at the United Nations. These hopes were destroyed when the Soviet Union rejected Bernard Baruch's proposals. An international control agreement consequently was never signed.

In the environment which had come to dominate U.S.-Soviet relations by late 1946, the failure to reach such an agreement can hardly be considered surprising, however. East-West relations were deteriorating rapidly during this period. Soviet actions in Eastern Europe, the Mediterranean and the Middle East overshadowed, and in turn shaped, the discussion of international control. The atomic bomb was coming up to be viewed in the West—even as early as 1946—as the "winning weapon," an essential element in countering Soviet military power. The maintenance of the U.S. atomic monopoly was seen by many as a counterweight to Soviet conventional military strength. As the Cold War heated up through 1946, the chances for negotiating an international control agreement grew progressively dimmer.

This supports the argument made by Niels Bohr as early as 1943 that the first steps toward international control—in particular, a direct approach to the Soviet Union by the U.S. and Britain—had to be taken either before the war ended or atomic weapons were used against enemy targets. An Anglo-American approach made after the power of the bomb was demonstrated would, according to Bohr's argument, be interpreted as atomic blackmail. Only an early approach could demonstrate a genuine interest in international control.

But these early steps were not taken. The U.S. made only a token approach to the U.S.S.R. at Potsdam. East-West relations began to deteriorate even before the war ended. The U.S. delayed formulating an international control proposal, for the Truman administration was preoccupied with the question of domestic control of atomic energy and passage of the McMahon bill through mid-1946. By the time the U.S. did formulate an international control proposal, East-West relations were extremely tense. Soviet actions in Eastern Europe and the Mediterranean heightened these tensions. In this environment, it is hardly surprising that the U.S. would have formulated a proposal such as the Baruch plan or that the Soviets would have rejected that, or perhaps any, proposal.

The Two Cultures and the International Control Debate

The Manhattan Project brought scientists into the policy process in more prominent roles than at any previous time in American history. The prominence of scientists in the Manhattan Project hierarchy was natural, for the effort to develop and produce an atomic weapon was essentially a scientific and technological undertaking. Efforts by scientists to influence the administration of such government-sponsored scientific projects, and of federal science policy in general, had clear precedents. Indeed, scientists had long held positions within the government administrating federal science policy.

Decisions concerning the use of the bomb, the sharing of information about the bomb, and the American approach to international control of the bomb, were not fundamentally technical or scientific decisions, however, but rather fundamentally decisions about politics, diplomacy and military strategy. As Albert Wohlstetter wrote in 1963,

> The decision at the start of World War II to develop a fission bomb, or the decision to use it against Japan, or the decision to develop an H-bomb, or to bomb German cities during World War II, called for much more than natural science or engineering. Such decisions have narrowly technological components, but they involve just as essentially a great many other elements: military operations and counter-operations by an enemy, the economies of industrial production, the social and political effects of bombing on populations, and many others . . . [These] are political and military, strategic decisions. Technology is an important part, but very far from the whole of strategy.[15]

Yet many Manhattan Project scientists undertook to influence such decisions even though they fell beyond the mere technical administration of the bomb project. In doing so, these scientists stepped outside the realm of federal science policy in which American scientists had traditionally been active.

The Manhattan Project scientists argued that their advice was essential to finding correct answers to questions concerning the control of atomic weapons, despite the fundamentally political nature of such questions. These scientists argued that only they could understand the scientific and technological bases of atomic weapons—and, therefore, the destructive potential of such weapons—and thus only they could truly comprehend the potential impact of the atomic bomb on international politics.

Beyond this, many Manhattan Project scientists argued that their political views were not shaped by the parochial concerns of a particular nation (or government or party), but rather by a desire to do what was best for mankind. They argued that this clearly distinguished them from most politicians, and that this "objectivity" made scientific advice essential in addressing even fundamentally political questions.

This argument arose from the tradition in which scientists were seen as members of a community which transcended national boundaries, a tradition which influenced Niels Bohr's faith in the ability of free scientific interchange to form the basis of a broader system of international political cooperation. As Eugene Rabinowitch has written, "International cooperation in science is as old as modern science itself . . . By its very nature, science is an international effort; it can be only temporarily made to serve the separate interests of part of mankind."[16]

This belief in the political objectivity of scientists was most evident during the Second World War among those Manhattan Project scientists, such as Leo Szilard, who distrusted the Washington bureaucracy. As Barton J. Bernstein has written, Szilard "believed in the superiority of scientists [and] extolled them for their capacity for objectivity." As Bernstein also notes, Szilard believed that "scientists, unlike politicians, seek the truth, and thus a critic need not ask why scientists take certain positions but only whether or not the positions are correct."[17]

Leo Szilard admittedly was an unusual character among the atomic scientists. But his beliefs reflected those of many Manhattan Project scientists, who accepted his view that key differences did exist between the scientists and policy-makers.

This view was not unique to the scientists, however, for many policy-makers within the U.S. government also believed similar differences existed. They argued that scientists lacked the political acumen and administrative skills to make valuable contributions to the political dialogue on anything but the most narrowly-defined technical issues. Just as many Manhattan Project scientists argued that the politicians and bureaucrats in Washington did not understand the basic problems encountered in (and caused by) building the bomb, many members of the Washington community argued that the scientists did not understand the basic problems encountered in developing an effective strategy for using or controlling that weapon.

These perceptions were based in part on real differences between the scientific and political "cultures." These differences are based in large measure on different educational backgrounds and work experiences, which result in different methods of framing and addressing problems. These method-ological differences are often apparent regardless of the topic being considered. In other words, the scientist will often apply scientific methodology even when addressing political, economic or social problems, for the scientist's way of approaching problems is naturally shaped by his or her training and life as a scientist.

The scientist is trained to work in a world governed by verifiable fact. The scientist's work is concerned with testing a theory or addressing a problem through careful and logical research. While Heisenberg may have demonstrated that some uncertainty must be accepted even in the physical sciences, the scientific world nonetheless is governed much more by certainty and logic than is the world of politics.

As a result, the scientist often tends to approach even non-scientific undertakings with the belief that one approach is the correct approach, the approach which is certain to lead to the desired result. This often results in the scientist framing political issues in an "either/or"manner—for example, either the world institutes this system of international control or the world is sure to be destroyed in a nuclear holocaust. As Sir Charles Snow wrote in 1961, "Scientists *know* certain things in a fashion more immediate and more certain than those who don't comprehend what science is . . ."[18]

And yet, one can rarely say in the world of politics and government that one approach is certain to lead to a desired result. One can rarely prove that one policy is the correct policy. One rarely faces "either/or" situations. For politics—despite the aspirations of political scientists—is not a science. The world of politics, government and public-policy is one in which policies are rarely undertaken with any guaranteed result. Compromise is often the key; the careful balancing of differing opinions may be the only way to attain any solution to a problem. One can never prove that any solution is the correct solution, the right solution, or certainly the perfect solution. For there are no absolute answers in politics—as there often are in science—and one cannot prove the absolute validity (or fallacy) of a particular policy.

These philosophical differences illustrate a key difference between the scientist and the politician. The scientist strives for—and can often attain—absolute solutions to soluble questions. The politician, in

179

contrast, strives for the best possible solution to often insoluble problems.

McGeorge Bundy illustrated this difference by citing a speech given by Sir Charles Snow in the early 1960s. In this speech, Snow presented a classic "either/or" argument: *either* the atomic powers accept "a restriction on nuclear armaments" *or* the arms race between the U.S. and the U.S.S.R. would accelerate, several other states would develop atomic weapons and "within, at the most, ten years, some of these bombs are going off." Snow stated that "the *or* is not a risk but a certainty."

"It's not as simple as Snow made it," Bundy stated in response,

> Moreover, he made it simple with the authority of a scientist, and in that, I suggest, there is a great danger . . . The prediction, which he made as a scientist, dealt with political as well as with scientific phenomena; it dealt with very complex questions of choice and allocation of resources as well as with what was conceivably possible, and it assumed certainties from possibilities.[19]

The differences highlighted by Bundy complicated the interactions between scientists and politicians during the period in which the U.S. was formulating an approach to the international control of atomic weapons. The scientists often claimed to *know* the answers to political problems, displaying an arrogance which obviously did not serve them well in their efforts to influence policy. The politicians, in contrast, frequently downplayed the potential contributions that could be made by scientists to the political debate, demonstrating an arrogance themselves which caused them to dismiss the scientists' ideas as "naive."

Such generalizations obviously oversimplify the situation. Niels Bohr, for example, displayed a clear deference to the political skills of the statesman, writing to Roosevelt at one point that "the responsible statesmen alone can have the insight in the actual political possibilities" of international control. And Secretary of War Henry Stimson clearly was open to policy suggestions by the atomic scientists and generally took their opinions quite seriously.

And yet these generalizations about scientists and politicians also often held true, probably to the detriment of U.S. policy. The suggestions of scientists needed to be considered by policy-makers in the formulation of U.S. positions on the use and control of atomic weapons, for both scientists and politicians had something to contribute to the policy debate.

For example, the scientists' knowledge of the technical potential of the bomb certainly needed to be considered when atomic policy was being formulated. No politician truly understood the potential of those weapons, particularly during the debates which occurred *before* Alamogordo, Hiroshima and Nagasaki (for example, the discussions between Bohr and Roosevelt and Churchill). Only the scientists had a real grasp of what power could be unleashed by the splitting of the atom.

And yet, this fundamentally technical knowledge certainly did not mean that the Manhattan Project scientists also were the sole possessors of the expertise needed to make decisions on fundamentally political questions. As Emmanuel G. Mesthene wrote in the early 1960s, "The belief is prevalent that the policy problems raised by the rapid advance of science and technology are best dealt with when professional scientists are appointed to policy-making positions in government . . . [But] policy-making, even when it concerns science, has its own problems and techniques, to the understanding of which scientists, I think, can lay no special claim."[20]

As Mesthene indicates, formulating government policy requires certain skills, training and experience. Yet Manhattan Project scientists, with a few exceptions, lacked any such skills, training or experience. They were not familiar with the workings of either political or diplomatic processes. For this reason, one must question what Mesthene has termed "the myth" that policy issues which involve scientific questions are "best handled by scientists *because* they are scientists."[21]

Beyond this, one must question the assumption that scientists—again simply because they are scientists—will be objective policy-makers, free from the political biases of more traditional actors in the political process. Like anyone interested in political issues, scientists approach those issues with preconceptions and biases. As Hans Morgenthau has written, "The scientist, in common with the rest of us, looks at the political world from the vantage point of his personal perspective and preferences, and what he sees and anticipates is determined by both."[22] Or, in McGeorge Bundy's words, "Scientists are people, a fact which is frequently forgotten, but verifiable experimentally."[23] As people, scientists have political biases, beliefs, aspirations and opinions, and these can obviously shape their recommendations on political issues.

The mere admission that scientists have political opinions obviously should not exclude them from participating in policy decisions which are in part affected by scientific and technological advances, including decisions in the areas of foreign and defense policy. Quite to the contrary, scientists can play an important role in broadening the political debate on certain issues. This was illustrated by the international control debate outlined above, in which the atomic scientists applied their technical expertise to raise important questions concerning the direction of U.S. policy toward the control of the atomic bomb. Many of the atomic scientists demonstrated great prescience on certain aspects of this debate (by accurately predicting, for example, that the U.S.S.R. would develop atomic weapons quickly and that the West's atomic monopoly would consequently be short-lived). Unfortunately, their views were often dismissed by policy-makers.

Yet scientists must be careful to offer advice which falls outside their narrow technical expertise with an air of certainty, as if their opinion had the imprimatur of fact. As Hans Morgenthau has written, both scientists and statesmen, "try to anticipate the future by guessing and, as history has shown, it cannot be presumed that the guesses of one are necessarily superior to those of the other."[24]

Both scientists and politicians have skills, training and experience which can be brought to bear on virtually any policy issue which is affected in some way by science or technology—in other words, on almost any issue in our technological age. Scientists thus need to be consulted on, and play an important role in the formulation of, a wide-variety of issues facing policy-makers, including many issues which fall outside the realm of federal science policy. Only when scientists and politicians work together can a policy emerge which incorporates both realistic approaches to international or domestic politics and an understanding of the implications of scientific and technological advances.

ENDNOTES

1. See C.P. Snow, *The Two Cultures: And a Second Look* (New York: Mentor, 1964) and Sanford A. Lakoff, "The Third Culture: Science in Social Thought" in Sanford A. Lakoff, ed., *Knowledge and Power: Essays on Science and Government* (New York: The Free Press, 1966), 1-64.

2. Isaiah Berlin, "The Divorce Between the Sciences and the Humanities" in Henry Hardy, ed., *Against the Current: Essays in the History of Ideas* (New York: Viking, 1980), 80.

3. Don K. Price, *The Scientific Estate* (London: Oxford University, 1965), 11-12. Snow's lectures were published as *Science and Government* (Cambridge: Harvard University, 1961).

4. William R. Nelson, preface to William R. Nelson, ed., *The Politics of Science* (New York: Oxford University, 1968), v-vi.

5. Don K. Price, "The Republican Revolution" in Nelson, ed., *The Politics of Science*, 5.

6. Hans J. Morgenthau, *Science: Servant or Master?* (New York: Meridian, 1972), 82-83.

7. Morgenthau, *Science: Servant or Master?*, 84.

8. William H. McNeill, *The Pursuit of Power* (Chicago: University of Chicago, 1982), 357; Warner R. Schilling, "Scientists, Foreign Policy, and Politics" in Nelson, ed., *The Politics of Science*, 360.

9. Schilling, "Scientists, Foreign Policy, and Politics," 361.

10. Hans J. Morgenthau, "Modern Science and Political Power" in Hans J. Morgenthau, *Truth and Power: Essays of a Decade, 1960-70* (New York: Praeger, 1970), 228.

11. Quoted in William J. Broad, "Science and Technology: The Gap is Shrinking Fast," *The New York Times*, April 5, 1988.

12. Hans J. Morgenthau, "Decisionmaking in the Nuclear Age," *Bulletin of the Atomic Scientists* XVIII (December 1962), 7. The discussion of Bohr's ideas is drawn primarily from his letters, memorandums and articles on international control, most of which can be found in the papers of J. Robert Oppenheimer, Manuscripts Division, Library of Congress, Washington, D.C. Other important sources include Ruth Moore, *Niels Bohr: The Man, His Science, and the World They Changed* (New York: Knopf, 1966); S. Rozental, ed., *Niels Bohr: His Life and Work as Seen by His Friends and Colleagues* (New York: John Wiley, 1967); A.P. French and P.J. Kennedy, *Niels Bohr: A Centenary Volume* (Cambridge: Harvard University, 1985); and Martin J. Sherwin, *A World Destroyed: The Atomic Bomb and the Grand Alliance* (New York: Vintage, 1977).

13. Niels Bohr, "A Challenge to Civilization," *Science* 102 (October 12, 1945), 363-64.

14. J. Robert Oppenheimer, "Niels Bohr and Atomic Weapons," *New York Review of Books* 3 (December 17, 1964), 6.

15. Albert Wohlstetter, "Scientists, Seers and Strategy," in Nelson, ed., *The Politics of Science*, 272-73.

16. Eugene Rabinowitch, "Scientific Revolution: The Beginning of World Community," *Bulletin of Atomic Scientists*, December 1963, 14-15.

17. Barton J. Bernstein, "Leo Szilard: Giving Peace a Chance in the Nuclear Age," *Physics Today*, September 1987, 40-43.

18. Quoted in McGeorge Bundy, "The Scientist and National Policy" in Lakoff, ed., *Knowledge and Power: Essays on Science and Government*, 426.

19. Bundy, "The Scientist and National Policy," 427-28.

20. Emmanuel G. Mesthene, "Can Only Scientists Make Government Science Policy?" in Nelson, *The Politics of Science*, 457.

21. Mesthene, "Can Only Scientists Make Government Science Policy?", 458.

22. Hans J. Morgenthau, *Science: Servant or Master?*, 110.

23. Bundy, "The Scientist and National Policy," 429.

24. Morgenthau, *Science: Servant or Master?*, 114.

PART THREE

THE TWO CULTURES AND POLITICS

CHAPTER VIII

Presidents and Religion

MARTIN MARTY

NARRATOR: Martin Marty has written about the relation between religions in present day America and political movements. He won the National Book Award for his book, *The Righteous Empire*, on the pros and cons of American religious movements and American religions. He is a professor at the University of Chicago, an associate editor of the *Christian Century*, has lectured widely throughout the country, and written at least twenty books in his career.

MR. MARTY: Recently, I read the presidential addresses and the correspondence of three presidents—Harding, Coolidge, and Hoover—with regard to their outlook on religion. To those who know the history of this subject, this is a little bit like the famous illustration about thorough German scholarship. There is supposed to have been a typically thorough work of German scholarship on *The Flora and Fauna of Iceland*. The table of contents included "Chapter 8: 'Snakes in Iceland.'" The chapter was one line long: "There are no snakes in Iceland." In the parallel case, one does not normally turn to these presidents for any assessment of the trends of presidents and religion.

PRESIDENTS AND RELIGION

I've read these Presidents' papers for a work on a four-volume work called *Modern American Religion.* I have just finished the first book, on the period between 1893 and 1919, which will be published soon. One of the sectors is on the public religion of American life. President McKinley was all but deified in the iconography of the era, for a lot of reasons. Theodore Roosevelt was quite possibly one of our few agnostic presidents. He convinced everyone he was religious, however, because of his "Muscular Christianity," a busy-bee, do-good attitude. Everyone, therefore, assumed there must be something religious going on. Woodrow Wilson was one of the most patently and deeply religious of the Presidents, for better and for worse. Many of the ambiguities of his career derived from his faith. Much of the legitimation for both the war and the peace he hoped would follow was done in general American religious terms, the way most presidents do, and also in specifically Wilsonian Christian terms. His southern Presbyterian convictions were very deep. Wilson was the last President for a long time to be that explicit. Then came the three, Harding, Coolidge and Hoover. I'll mention them in a different context later.

The modern understanding of the role of public religion was born with Franklin D. Roosevelt who was a life-long, undramatic, faithful member of the Episcopal Church. Harry Truman was a lively, rambunctious Baptist with some Presbyterian Sunday School background who could draw on it and often did. The Jewish Theological Seminary gave him an honorary degree for his contribution as a non-Jew to the birth of Israel. Truman is said to have surprised people there by saying, "I am Cyprus." He was referring to the passage in Isaiah 45 where King Cyprus, a non-Israelite, was commissioned to be God's servant. Truman was well grounded in these things, but he didn't come across as a contributor to the public religion role. Eisenhower had an explicit interest in articulating a generalized national religion to meet the mood of the post-World War II insecurities. Sometimes Eisenhower used the language of the "crusade against atheistic communism," but more often his was a genial religion of good will. William Lee Miller later wrote a book called *Piety Along the Potomac*, which was a summary of Eisenhower religion.

Kennedy was the first Catholic President, so his religion was very visible, but he very seldom resorted to Catholic imagery. He dealt with the much more generalized religions. It was his Inaugural Address that inspired the famous essay (1967) by Robert Bellah on "Civil Religion in America." Lyndon Johnson was a more ambiguous figure but the use of religious imagery came with ease to him. Richard Nixon was a little restrained in his rhetoric at first. Then he instituted religious services in the White House, and developed an image to the point where one theologian could find enough material to write a book called *The Nixon Theology*. The thesis was that Nixon transferred to the nation the attributes that are normally applied to God. Gerald Ford was personally pious. However, he was President too briefly to make much of an impact. Jimmy Carter's religion was so visible and was such a controversial element in his election that he had to restrain himself in the White House. His inaugural address has fewer religious references than are found in almost any other of the last seven or eight presidents. I think Carter knew everyone was watching. With President Reagan, of course, the role of religion is very up front. He chooses to be seen as the most explicitly Christian President since Wilson, although he more often resorts to the general rhetoric of religion. These are brief examples of the fact that religion is around in the twentieth century White House.

In 1749, Benjamin Franklin, while proposing the Academy of Philadelphia, listed elements that would be needed for that admittedly private school. He thought that there should be what he called a "publick" religion which would have some elements of Christian morality fused with morality in general. Franklin's is a kind of root text of American experience. The civil religion that Robert Bellah described in his earlier work was inspired more by the visions of Rousseau and Durkheim. They believed that every complex society has to have a single integrating set of symbols. Otherwise there can be no common basis of morality, no common base for debate. In the Rousseauean model, the State generates these symbols.

George Wills' book, *Statecraft as Soulcraft*, made many of his fellow conservatives very nervous by arguing, *contra* James Madison, that one can't rely simply on the factions in American life to provide this coherence. The state or the government or the elected officials or somebody has to generate elements for this common base of values. Then citizens are free to dissent against the consensus. But it has to be there, at least so we can know what he or she is dissenting against. Such an argument is—though George Will may not like to think of it this way—more the Rousseauean or Durkheimian model.

The other model is that of Franklin. That founder, in effect, was saying, "Obviously, you need a common basis. If there is to be civic virtue or public virtue there has to be some minimal consensus at least." But Franklin then looked around and said, "Now what are we going to do with all these nice churches and philosophies and interest groups?" He generated the notion that they all would naturally need their particularity for their own purposes. They all did something to hold themselves together, but they also made some contributions to the general morality. I think this model is at the root of the uneasy synthesis in American life between the two main spiritual traditions, the biblical tradition and the

Enlightenment tradition of the Founding Fathers. They live in an uneasy conjunction.

The generating of the general morality has often fallen upon presidents who evoke transcendent symbols. This is clear from their rhetoric. Abraham Lincoln is a good illustration of this because he was a rhetorician who could invoke a biblical tradition more explicitly than any other president. And he is, interestingly enough, the only President who never was a member of a church. At the juncture of the greatest conflict in American life, Lincoln called on religious symbols just as Wilson did at his juncture.

Why do some presidents contribute to public religion and why don't others? Why have the Harding/Coolidge/Hoover people not been seen in the succession of people who added to this common pool? Aristotle felt that effective rhetoric depended on the character of the speakers. They must embody or, as Machiavelli would say, they must at least *project*, the image of their being in harmony with the aspirations of the nation and still somehow be able to transcend them. In this sense McKinley is interesting because the halo was there, yet the rest of his career does not quite shine.

Roosevelt, Eisenhower, Kennedy and Reagan were perceived very broadly by the public as having the convincing kind of character. If citizens want to dissent against them, they are seen as dissenting against something of the majority's view of the present concept of national aspirations. The ethos or character of the speaker has to be patent. People have to believe it. Liberals have kept saying that President Reagan's imagery was a contrivance with the media because they have a hard time imagining that the public really did like and agreed with him. On the one hand, Reagan was speaking from a majority view, but on the other hand, he also inspired very strong reactions because his was a particularized view of one of the camps of Protestants. But Reagan was quite effective in relating to what Aristotle called the *pathos*, the public situation in which people were saying that they were henceforth going to have to do things somehow differently. Presidents Carter and Ford and Nixon were not as effective in relating to this pathos.

Paul Nagel's book, *This Sacred Trust*, talks about a half-century in the development of American nationalism in which small town speakers, Fourth of July orators, clergy, and lecturers like Edward Everett were the people who promoted the biblical image of a sacred trust. Literature has also helped. The Ralph Waldo Emersons played their part in the mainline poetic and essayist traditions. Occasionally also a hero could contribute, or a hostage could speak out in a language to which the public related at least for a few days. But in our kind of society the presidency is the principal moral spokesman. This is interesting because as candidates they did not explicitly run for that responsibility.

Some years ago I wrote an essay which always gets mislocated by the computer or in bibliographies because it is called "Two Kinds of Two Kinds of Civil Religion." Everybody assumes there is a typographical error there in the two "two kinds" but I *meant* "two kinds of two kinds" of civil religion. I believe that religion in most cultures has two roles; one is integrative, one is disruptive, unsettling. On the one hand, religion is to take people out of their isolation, their chaos, and give them meaning and transcendent hope. On the other hand, that same transcendent power is judging the people. The Biblical scholars find that religion serves two needs. One is priestly and one is prophetic. The president is almost always cast in the priestly role. Lincoln's Second Inaugural was a rare instance of a President playing the prophetic role. That is why Lincoln was so beloved by the theologians. He said of the warring sides in the Civil War that both sides pray to the same God.

194

Both claim God is on their side. Both want to prevail. But the Almighty has his own purposes. That was the prophetic approach.

There is also a "left" and a "right" priestly approach. If today the impulse toward the common symbols comes chiefly from the New Christian Right, in other times it may come from the left. Thus John Dewey, J. Paul Williams, and A. Powell Davies promoted the need for a nontheistic common faith of democratic process. Dewey's own book in 1934 was called *A Common Faith.* The heirs of the people who thought it was fine to have Roosevelt invoking these symbols on the moderate left in the 1930s and 1940s now think it is bad to have Reagan doing so on the moderate right—and *vice versa.*

There is another design for analyzing the rhetoric. Historian Conrad Cherry described four themes in the American public faith: sacrifice, exodus, destiny under God, and international example. In the public evocations of rhetoric, especially in inaugural addresses, he found the theme of *exodus* to be rare. Jefferson employed it once. Americans have been liberated, they have been moved out of slavery into freedom. One of the four Roosevelt inaugurals included a very casual reference to it. In some respects exodus remains a strong theme. It is the strongest single motif in black civil religion in America. Every black leader, for example Martin Luther King, used the language of the "Promised Land." They say, in effect, "I've seen a vision, I may not get there, but we are on exodus in American history." But the theme of exodus is very rare in the highest levels of rhetoric.

The theme of *sacrifice* appears now and then. President Kennedy used the rhetoric of sacrifice. He said that Americans would pay any price. They must ask what they could do for their country. The theme of sacrifice, however, is very rare on the highest levels.

The *destiny under God* is the overwhelming theme in presidential rhetoric. We are "one nation," we are "set aside," we are a "special people under God." International examples show that fairly frequently America is "a light to the world." Most students find that the presidents do their invoking "under God." Then when they describe God's attributes, they are assigned to the nation. Thus, Charles Henderson's book on Nixon kept saying that Nixon sounded like Billy Graham, because he would use the words "promise" and "hope." But when one read the end of his sentences, it would always be shown that Graham was promising hope in God, while Nixon would be promising hope in our children. Faith was not in God, or even in the nation, so much as faith in "ourselves."

The prophetic voices within religious groups, like that of Will Herberg, are always nervous about presidential leadership in public religion. Most recognize that it has to be there, and that it has a positive function, yet they are nervous about how it can be misused. The public does not worry much about it. Gibbons has a line in *The Decline and Fall of the Roman Empire* about the late Roman empire in which he notes that there were many religions. They were perceived, he said, by the philosophers to be equally false, by the people to be equally true, and by the magistrate to be equally useful. For all my historical suspicions and lack of sympathies with this kind of power, I suggest that if one compares the private letters of most of the presidents with their public expressions, it will become clear that they really do believe these things. There are momentary exceptions. Jefferson in 1774 in effect suggested that the people were very lethargic. We've had to get them whipped up. So, as one scholar noted, they rummaged around for some old prayerful ceremonies that they could use for the moment. Most politicians are going to do some things that are needed along the way. Yet, over his long career, Jefferson held an extremely consistent if complex view of religion. And so did many others. I have very little sympathy for the Reagan approach, but note that it was generated out of an outlook on life that has been very consistent from the late 1940s until now. In general, the public tends to look for this kind of thing in political leaders. If they can not summon it, there is a kind of breach.

QUESTION; What do you think of Lou Cannon's thesis that until the middle of the first term, Reagan kept his politics fairly separate from an explicit religious view?

MR. MARTY: I think that there are explanations. Certainly in the second election, Reagan did not have to follow the direction of the religious right to get reelected. They had no place to go. They do vote generally for all kinds of self-interest and local interest. On certain issues like anti-abortion they will be united, but on social policy there is more diversity. But the religious right had no place else to go. Reagan had them in the bag. They needed him a good deal more than he needed them. Apart from getting elected, Reagan did need them for some things, like defense policy. For the most part, they are for high military expenditures. The turning point came very early in his Orlando speech on the Soviet "evil empire." It did not alienate people; it congealed them. While he lost many Jewish votes the morning after his nomination when he spoke to evanglicals in terms of the Christian America, he didn't lose all Jews. Reagan was not above calculating how he could keep these constituencies happy, but he did not make up a religion in order to satisfy them. He drew on resources that were there, and found sympathy there.

QUESTION: I always thought of Mr. Hoover as being an absolutely dedicated Christian because of his work in food relief.

MR. MARTY: The problem is who is going to define what a Christian is. Hoover certainly was a humanitarian with a complete humanitarian ethic and probably was as consistent as any president in this century. This is one of the things that revisionists of the Hoover legacy keep coming back to. On the other hand, there are a lot of people who say that theologically he was fairly near being an agnostic. Hoover was extremely wary of using the name God. He somehow avoided references to God but stood in a high humanitarian tradition that projected religiousness all through his career. His leadership in World War I relief efforts illustrated this humanitarian tradition. But now let me keep my promise to talk about the presidents of his era.

Religion was a kind of media creation for Harding. Mrs. Harding made him go to church. He learned it was popular. He fit an image. He looked like a President so he should be a church goer. He was a kind of a well-meaning small-town boy, with a service-clubby view of life. He had an ability to apply these symbols. I think Harding really believed them, but there was nothing deep about his approach.

Coolidge is interesting because he was a Puritan of the Puritans and he knew that tradition. He invoked it "non-religiously" with considerable regularity. The work ethic was a very strong part of this. He would constantly call people back to what they had been about. But before he joined the congregational church in Washington—his wife brought him, too—Coolidge almost never made a reference to the nation under God or the God of the Puritans. He probably was the nearest of the three to a mainstream theological tradition in America but he arrived at it late in life.

198

Hoover consistently expressed values that people associate with religion and Christianity. Harding, both personally and publicly, expressed a religious role. At the time of Harding's death, there were florid writings about how God was waiting for him because he had been the one President without a flaw. A year or two later a different kind of book came to be written as Harding's corruptions came to light.

I studied Harding, Coolidge and Hoover out of sense of duty. After McKinley, Roosevelt, Wilson and the most recent five or six Presidents, the interesting thing to note is the presence of two Americas. Just before the 1920s, World War I pulled people together. There were few decades in American history when more people seemed more angry with each other in the name of religion than in the 1920s and 1930s. The Klu Klux Klan and "wets" and "drys" and the fundamentalists and modernists, for example, were mad at each other. Yet many seemed to be looking to the White House for a kind of assurance that everything was all right.

News people remember that when he was in New Hampshire in 1976, somebody said, "Mr. Carter, is it true you've had a personal experience with Jesus Christ?" And Carter said, "Yes, I'm born again." "Born again" was a new thing in some parts of the country. Kennedy's Catholicism, Carter's born-againism and Reagan's explicit use of evangelical symbolism existed in a culture where power was invoked everywhere in the world in the name of people who had a strongly religious sense of togetherness.

QUESTION: Could you say something about the concept of civil religion versus public philosophy? The public philosophy symbol is what Bellah seems to prefer in his latest book, *Habits of the Heart*. Couldn't it also embrace the civic republicanism or whatever you want to call the Jefferson enlightenment?

MR. MARTY: First of all, one would answer, yes. Across the board more people than before seem to be saying that there cannot be a common morality if it isn't explicitly grounded in a specifically agreed upon theology. This idea is very popular these days. What we see today is not the disappearance of the secular order but signs of disarray in it. We don't have many good articulators of it. There is now no Lippmann writing on the "public philosophy," nor a John Dewey writing on the "common faith." Most of the gifted columnists and publicists today come up out of separate camps. They don't often transcend the camps.

Habits of the Heart has been characterized by some neoconservatives as a socialist vision of the American economy. It does call for community against individualism. However, Bellah does inspire respect even from many of those who disagree with him. They need somebody on his end of the spectrum because there haven't been many people over there recently. His book is dedicated to keeping the dialectic between the two alive.

A theologian colleague, David Tracy, and I repeatedly teach courses called "Public Religion and Public Theology." We finally have come to the 1920s and 1930s. We treat Walter Lippmann, H. L. Mencken, W. B. DuBois, FDR, Eleanor Roosevelt, Dorothy Day, etc. Only three or four of these could be explicitly identified with religion. In the 1920s there was a strong tradition of American education as a kind of coherent secular philosophy. Now it is widely felt that an ethic cannot be based on Plato or Aristotle or Kant or Mill or whatever. Rather, it has to be based on specific revelations. The battle between Cardinal O'Connor and Governor Cuomo in 1984 was between two Catholics who are on two sides of this issue.

Cuomo said philosophy must tie into some sort of rational or consensual pattern. O'Connor said some of that, but he also said that the truth ran in a specifically religious course.

Our impulse to force our candidates to be so religious these days may be born of the breakdown of the concept of the public philosophy. All the Democratic candidates in 1984, Reverend Jesse Jackson, Walter Mondale, George McGovern, for example, were minister's sons or ministers. All of them were carrying on the social gospel tradition. John Anderson, Gerald Ford, Ronald Reagan, and Jimmy Carter were born-again. It is part of the phenomenon of re-tribalization in which people get their strength by having their particularities projected. I think it is going to be a real problem.

I have always been somewhat nervous about the concept of civil religion. I liked Bellah's later phase much better than his earlier one. He has not lost his sense of religious or theological transcendence; it is very deep in him. If anything he is more explicitly religious than he was twenty years ago. But he still argues that the republic will need to move beyond its present discord wherein people can not understand each other because they do not share anything. William Sullivan has written a good book called *Reconstructing Public Philosophy.*

Sidney Mead wrote a classic called *The Lively Experiment.* This is a history of the development of "the religion of the republic." Mead took Jefferson, Madison, Franklin, and other such figures as founders of the normative religion in America. He said this religion of the republic was heretical and un-American. This was said with a little ironic twist but he meant it. What Mead wrote is relevant. His prime years were the Eisenhower, Kennedy, and early Johnson times when there were left and right consensuses and when there was a faith in progress. Today's philosophers don't often believe that reason is so unassailable. Progressivism is *passe*. Often Mead did still talk in a language like that of John Dewey, that one should give a kind of privilege to the "religion of the republic." Mead did it so subtly that he never became a target of the people who attack secular humanism. His wasn't a very secular view; it was a very religious view.

There are some basic shared elements. One is that churches and synagogues do a lot to generate a commonality. They do try to prepare people for life in the republic. They see it as everybody's burden to do that. Secondly, there are many ways in which religion can be taught in public schools. Although a faith can not be taught as the truth about life, the role that religion plays in society can be taught. The civil religion of presidents can be discussed. There is a public philosophy. I personally think we have to teach people again that people who do not agree on ultimates can find a whole range of reasons to meet and discuss.

As an illustration, I think of the county west of where I live. Page County, Illinois, is a moderately conservative, hi-tech county with 700,000 people. Most are Republican, many are Catholic, some are Protestant. But every weekend at least forty-five religious groups worship in this county. They are not countercultured. They are professional people. As another illustration, there are now probably about as many Muslims as Episcopalians in America. There are approximately two to five million. They are getting more articulate. While America at large grew by eleven percent, the Asian population here grew by some four hundred percent. On one level they are super Americans. One-fourth of their children now get straight A's in American schools. On another level many have a Buddhist mentality. They aren't going to fit in on those terms. They are increasingly respectable upper-middle class people. The neighbors like them. America has just gotten more complex.

We have to use these other three kinds of instrumentalities to achieve coherence.

COMMENT: The whole Reagan phenomenon has shaped the religio-political environment and given it a partisan ideological twist. You might compare the 1980s and the 1920s. I see a lot of comparison also between the '80s and '50s. There is also a new kind of religio-political configuration. It isn't continuous with the whole stream of presidential experience either. Now it is "God, Reagan and America" together over against the Supreme Court. This hasn't been the case before, this mingling of a rather sharply etched ideological and partisan politics that will affect us for a long time.

MR. MARTY: There is little doubt in my mind about that. In a global view, at mid-century, the popular image was that of a "family of man." The images that developed in the next decade were of "spaceship earth," the formation of the World Council of Churches, the United Nations, and United World Federalism. It was always portrayed that somehow, for all our differences, there would be a growing convergence. Thirty years later Harold Issacs wrote a book which describes our times. He says that around the world there is a massive, convulsive gathering of peoples into their separatenesses and over-acquisitivenesses, to protect their pride and power and place from the real or presumed threat of other people with their concerns over their pride and power and place. America has a mild version of that compared to Iran's, but I think the "Evil Empire" speech was typical of this phenomenon.

Reagan's theological advisers and some of his political people have a Manichean view of the world. It is God *versus* Satan, Christ *versus* anti-Christ, Christian *versus* secular humanist, the good people *versus* the Court, so there is exclusion. Eisenhower on the same day would meet Catholic Bishops and Billy Graham. Today only one camp ordinarily has access to the president. He is not talking to the National or World Councils of Churches. He has continued to hold an antagonistic view of wider Catholic leadership. With the Jewish leadership, there is an agreement on Israel but not on much of anything domestic. The blacks are frozen out. When Reagan says, "I've been talking to the theologians," he means Tim LaHaye and Hal Lindsey. Not even many conservative theological schools would call these men "theologians."

Roosevelt was the moderate left priest and Eisenhower was the moderate right priest, but they didn't freeze others out. Here there definitely is an exclusion principle. I call it "mild tribalism." Reagan does not himself project or embody the meanness of some of the people who are supporting him. That might be where we are lucking out. I often said in the 1950s, that if America really wanted to measure its being lucky it should notice that Billy Graham didn't have a mean bone in him. Today mean streaks characterize some celebrity evangelists.

COMMENT: You put everything in terms of exclusion and inclusion, both worldwide and within this country of groups. I feel it also with respect to public policy ideas. They seem to be grounded in either the civil religion or in Christianity. But the young people who are Reagan era products generally have lost the notion of Christianity as being for social justice. What the Christian religion means or what belief in God means add up to issues of family life, self-discipline, and things that fit with the new social agenda, including a kind of raw capitalism. There once was such a thing as Christianity which had social justice as its very central meaning. That seems to be gone.

Martin Marty

MR. MARTY: During the two most recent presidential campaigns I did not mind—in fact, I liked the fact in social policy—that the New Christian Right was saying that the Bible should play a big part. Fine, except I wanted them to have us read the whole Bible. If you read the pages of the prophets, the proportion is about fifty to one in favor of caring and justice, the needs of the widow, the orphan, and the stranger at the gate, compared with being against homosexuals or pornography. Pornography is an evil, but that is not the main emphasis of the Bible.

Columnists Evans and Novak, who are friendly witnesses, have written that one reason the merchant Republican party has to mute some of the social issues now is because it has attracted a lot of the young climbers who are semi-secular; their whole thing is "what's in it for me." The leadership has muted social issues a bit because these are people who for the most part are not going to follow the book. The Republican party, they have said, is on the verge of becoming a coalition of these two groups; it would then be "the party of greed and sex." They would like to prevent that development.

This is a dimension of our current culture. It was not just invented by President Reagan, but has been prominent for the last ten or fifteen years. I'm not tempted to see the 1960s as "the good old days" because I don't think that decade's version of social justice serves as much of a norm. The last fifteen or twenty years has been seen the emergence of this other style. It can lead to a society that is very good at generating private morale, but it pays very little attention to social or public morale. There is, consequently, a postponement of the question of the larger social order. In Robert Bellah's *Habits of the Heart*, there is a character who is asked, "What do you believe in, Sheila? What is your religion?" She answers something like, "Sheilaism, I'm Sheila and I'm for me." Here is a one-person religion.

205

I think the key struggle for this generation will be to find its public voice. That is going to be hard. The South African divestment issue has attracted some, but it can be quite frankly a fairly cheap one on campuses. Students need make no sacrifice themselves. The peace movement, by and large, has been regarded as a cause for senior people. For all the diversity of the generation—and I want to celebrate its diversity—it hasn't found that public voice yet. There are many things in Reagan's civil religion that the generation is not picking up. There is no high-level projection of an alternative set of symbols at this time, either. Much remains "up for grabs."

NARRATOR: We are indebted to Professor Marty for this thoughtful presentation.

CHAPTER XIX

Religion and Law: The First Amendment in Historical Perspective

HAROLD J. BERMAN

The interrelationship of church and state is not only a political-legal matter. It is also a religious matter. Analysis of it should begin, in my view, with a consideration of the interaction between our religious belief, in the broad sense of our concern for the ultimate meaning and purpose of life and faith and commitment to transcendent values, on the one hand, and the legal process, on the other, in the broad sense of the process of allocating rights and duties and thereby resolving conflicts and creating channels of cooperation.[1] It is in the context of the interaction of religion and law, the interaction of our sense of the holy and our sense of the just that the more *specific* question arises of the proper relation between religious and political *institutions*.

Just as the topic "Church and State" is a part of the larger topic "Religion and Law," so the topic "First Amendment" is a part of the larger topic "Church and State." Indeed, the religion clauses of the First Amendment had only a small impact on church-state relations prior to 1940 since prior to that time (as is universally acknowledged) those clauses only applied to the federal government. "*Congress*," the Amendment said, "shall pass no law respecting an establishment of religion or prohibiting the free exercise thereof." The several states remained free to continue to support religion and to restrict its exercise. It was only in the 1940s that the Supreme Court of the United States held for the first time that the religion clauses of the First Amendment, by implicit incorporation into the Fourteenth, are applicable also to the states.[2]

To speak, then, of the history of the First Amendment, and of the intent of the Framers—as courts and writers continually insist that we must do if we are to understand what the Constitution requires in the sphere of "Church and State"—is to run up against the plain facts that the First Amendment left the protection of religious liberty at the state level to the states themselves and that the Framers expressed no intent concerning how the states should exercise their responsibilities in the matter. As Justice Story wrote in 1833, in commenting on the First Amendment, "[T]he whole power over the subject of religion is left exclusively to the State governments, to be acted upon according to their own sense of justice and the State Constitutions."[3]

To take a religious, and not only a legal, view of the relation between religion and law, and to ask how not only the Founding Fathers but also the authors of the state constitutions understood the relation between church and state, is to raise—but not necessarily to answer—sharp questions concerning the understanding of the First Amendment which has come to prevail in America in the twentieth century.

Prior to World War I the United States thought of itself as a Christian country, and more particularly as a Protestant Christian country; since then it has ceased to do so.[4] James Madison's conception of the religion clauses of the First Amendment, of which he was the principal draftsman, was based in part on his belief in a divine covenant between God and man;[5] in the twentieth century the interpretation of those clauses has been based on a political, and not on a religious, concept. Some now argue that we should return to the religious and legal values and beliefs of the eighteenth and nineteenth centuries. Yet to repudiate the past two generations of our history in an effort to return to the generations that preceded them cannot be justified in the name of history. Indeed, the strength of a historical argument, in the American legal tradition, depends on the concept of history as an ongoing process rather than as something that stopped at some particular date in the past.

By the sake token, however, we cannot understand our ongoing history without reference to where we have come from. In the American legal tradition the question "whither" cannot be divorced from the question "whence." Some argue that the record of the past is simply used—and distorted—by partisans of one side or the other. Yet it is important that that record be examined dispassionately if only to see whether it might not lead in a direction different from that espoused by either side.

Not only partisans of a "wall-of-separation" theory of the First Amendment but also partisans of a theory of "accommodation" between church and state[6] should be somewhat discomfited by the fact that in the early part of the nineteenth century many states enacted laws that had the effect of making Christianity the official religion of the state. One may find state constitutional and statutory provisions declaring it to be "the duty of all men to worship the Supreme Being, the great Creator and Preserver of the Universe;"[7] regulating membership in Christian denominations; imposing fines for failure to attend worship services on the Lord's day; requiring elected officials to swear that they "believe the Christian religion, and have a firm persuasion of its truth;[8] and establishing public education for the purpose of promoting "religion, morality, and knowledge."[9]

In 1811 in New York the highest state court upheld an indictment for blasphemous utterances against Christ. Speaking for the court, Chief Justice Kent stated that "we are a christian people, and the morality of the country is deeply ingrafted upon christianity. . . ."[10] The New York State Convention of 1821 endorsed the decision in that case, declaring that the court was right in holding that the Christian religion is the law of the land and to be preferred over all other religions.[11] These statements were confirmed in an 1861 New York case in which the court said: "Religious tolerance is entirely consistent with a recognized religion. Christianity may be conceded to be the established religion, to the qualified extent mentioned, while perfect civil and political equality, with freedom of conscience and religious preference, is secured to individuals of every other creed and profession."[12]

Similarly, in Pennsylvania in 1822 a man was convicted of blasphemy for saying that "the Holy Scriptures were a mere fable" and that "they contained a great many lies."[13] The Supreme Court of Pennsylvania in affirming the conviction, stated: "Christianity, general Christianity, is and always has been a part of the common law of Pennsylvania. . . . not Christianity founded in any particular religious tenets; not Christianity with an established church, and tithes and spiritual courts; but Christianity with liberty of conscience to all men."[14]

On the same grounds, laws restricting commercial activities on Sundays were upheld by courts of many states. In one such case Scott, J., speaking for the Supreme Court of Missouri, stated:

> Those who question the constitutionality of our Sunday laws seem to imagine that the [Missouri] constitution is to be regarded as

210

an instrument framed for a state composed of strangers collected from all quarters of the globe, each with a religion of his own, bound by no previous social ties, nor sympathizing in any common reminiscences of the past;; . . . [S]uch is not the mode by which our organic law is to be interpreted. We must regard the people for whom it was ordained. It appears to have been made by Christian men. The constitution, on its face, shows that the Christian religion was the religion of its framers.[15]

Similar judicial statements may be found in other states in similar cases, involving blasphemy, violations of Sunday laws, and other religious offenses—notwithstanding the fact that the constitutions of virtually all the states contained provisions proclaiming religious liberty.

In addition, states did not hesitate to require the teaching of the Christian religion in prisons, reformatories, orphanages, homes for soldiers, and asylums. State colleges and universities as well as elementary and secondary schools required the reading of the Bible and singing of hymns and saying of prayers.

In 1890 the Supreme Court of Illinois considered the case of a student at the University of Illinois who had been expelled because of his refusal to attend daily chapel exercises. He contended that the chapel requirement violated a provision of the Illinois Constitution stating that "[n]o person shall be required to attend or support any ministry or place of worship against his consent."[16] The Court held that so long as the rules of chapel attendance were reasonable, permitting excuse on grounds of religious or other conscientious objections, the University had a right to impose the requirement, and the student could not escape it on the mere ground that he considered it unlawful. There is nothing in the Illinois Constitution, the court said, that prevents state colleges and other institutions of learning from adopting "all reasonable regulations for the inculcation of moral and religious principles in those attending them."[17]

With regard to religious exercises and religious education in elementary and secondary schools, the courts of many states went so far as to uphold regulations requiring attendance, on pain of expulsion, regardless of religious objections. The Supreme Court of Maine stated:

> . . . The right of one sect to interdict or expurgate would place all schools in subordination to the sect interdicting or expurgating.
>
> If the claim is that the sect of which the child is a member has a right of interdiction [in fact she was a Roman Catholic who objected to the reading of the Protestant version of the Bible as part of a general course of instruction], and that any book is to be banished because under the ban of her church, then the preference is practically given to such church, and the very mischief complained of, is inflicted on others."[18]

Thus far I have recounted instances of government support of religion and government restrictions upon the free exercise of religion at the state level, under state constitutions, during the period prior to World War I. If we turn to our national experience at the federal level, we find a similar situation: it was generally assumed that America is a Christian country, and more particularly, a Protestant Christian country, and that the First Amendment was intended to reinforce Christianity by giving all denominations equality before the law and by permitting no government interference with the religious beliefs of any person. The notion of a "wall of separation" which would prevent any government aid to religion was wholly alien to the realities of American constitutional law in the late eighteenth and nineteenth centuries.[19] As Joseph Story wrote of the First Amendment in 1833:

> Probably at the time of the adoption of the Constitution, and of the [First Amendment], the general if not the universal sentiment in America was, that Christianity ought to receive encouragement from the State so far as was not incompatible with the private rights of conscience and the freedom of religious worship. An attempt to level all religions, and to make it a matter of state policy to hold all in utter indifference, would have created universal disapprobation, if not universal indignation. . . .
>
> The real object of the [First] [A]mendment was not to countenance, much less advance, Mahometanism, or Judaism, or infidelity, by prostrating Christianity; but to exclude all rivalry among Christian sects, and to prevent any national ecclesiastical establishment which should give to a hierarchy the exclusive patronage of the national government. It thus cut off the means of religious persecution (the vice and pest of former ages), and of the subversion of the rights of conscience in matters of religion, which had been trampled upon almost from the days of the Apostles to the present age. . . . (Footnotes omitted.)[20]

From the Constitutional Convention itself, in which Benjamin Franklin proposed that the delegates should resort to common prayer to break an impasse in its deliberations;[21] from the explicitly religious Presidential Proclamations of Washington, Adams, and Madison;[22] from the designation of chaplains for the army and navy and for the U.S. Congress itself; from the Northwest Ordinance of 1787 with its provisions for religious education;[23] from federal support of Christian education of Indians, including Jefferson's own treaty with the Kaskasia Indians providing for a salary to be paid by the United States government for a Catholic priest and for United States funding of the erection of a Catholic church (the Kaskasia Indians having been converted to Roman Catholicism);[24] from exemption of religious activities from federal taxation; and from a host of other similar circumstances—it must be concluded that the Establishment clause of the First Amendment, drafted not by the Deist Jefferson, but by the Protestant Christian James Madison, was not intended to prevent any government aid to religion but was intended rather to prevent the establishment of a national religion.[25]

But Jefferson, too, though against *organized* religion, believed firmly in "nature's God," "the Creator," the "Supreme Judge of the world"—all terms to be found in the Declaration of Independence. In a Thanksgiving Proclamation issued in 1797 when he was governor of Virginia, Jefferson appointed "a day of public and solemn thanksgiving and prayer to Almighty God, earnestly recommending to all the good people of this commonwealth, to set apart the said day for those purposes, and that the several ministers of religion to meet their respective societies thereon . . . and generally to perform the sacred duties of their function, proper for the occasion."[26] Jefferson also believed that all religions share a common morality which is essential to the welfare of any society, and that, more specifically, America needed religion to give it the necessary inner strength to survive. The First Amendment, Jefferson said, was an "experiment," designed to test whether religion could flourish in America without government support. He was confident that it could, and that its ability to do so was essential to the maintenance of peace and order.[27]

In contrast to Jefferson, Madison derived the principle of religious liberty not primarily from its political utility in a pluralist society but also, and more immediately, from God's own will. In attacking legislation proposed in the 1780s in the state of Virginia, which would have levied taxes to contribute (among other things) to the salaries of ministers, Madison stated that it is God who forbids the establishment of religion; that God wants men to worship Him freely, and not by coercion; and that this divine requirement transcends all political considerations. The covenant between God and man, Madison said, requires free exercise of religion, and that covenant takes precedence—"both in order of time and degree of obligation"—over the social contract.[28] This statement of Madison makes implicit references to the Lutheran doctrine of Two Kingdoms—the heavenly kingdom of grace and the earthly kingdom of law—as well as to the Calvinist doctrine of two covenants, one between God and man, the other between government and people.[29] For Madison, the non-believer was in effect a third-party beneficiary of the divine covenant.

To stress the importance of Christian concepts and values in the final achievement of religious freedom in America is not to minimize the importance of Enlightenment concepts of rationalism and individualism. It was the combination of the two—Christian faith, strongly influenced by Calvinist theology, and Deist skepticism, with its strong anticlerical tendency—that eventually prevailed. The religion clauses of the First Amendment owe at least as much to Jonathan Edwards as to Thomas Jefferson.[30] Also the struggle of the various sects—especially the Baptists, the Quakers, and the

Congregationalists—against repression by one denomination or another was a decisive factor in bringing about what may be called a Christian pluralism. Madison supplemented his theological argument with an ecclesiastical one: that the "multiplicity of sects, which pervades America, . . . is the best and only security for religious belief in any society."[31] This position was not grounded solely in pragmatism; it was grounded also, and primarily, in principle: the principle that religion itself—religious belief—depends for its validity on the freedom to disbelieve.

In uncovering the religious roots of our constitutional guarantees of religious freedom, we also uncover the religious basis of American public discourse in general prior to the 1930s. In 1835, De Tocqueville wrote: "[T]here is no country in the world where the Christian religion retains a greater influence over the souls of men than in America. . . ."[32] "Religion," he wrote, "is the first of their political principles."[33] In 1888, James Bryce wrote that "the influence of Christianity seems to be, if we look not merely to the numbers but also the intelligence of the persons influenced, greater and more widespread in the United States than in any part of western Continental Europe, and probably as great as in England."[34]

Prior to World War I, and into the 1920s, America professed itself to be a Christian country. Even two generations ago, if one had asked Americans where our Constitution—or, indeed, our whole concept of law—came from, on what it was ultimately based, the overwhelming majority would have said, "the Ten Commandments," or "the Bible," or perhaps "the law of God." John Adams' conception that our law is rooted in a common religious tradition[35] was shared not only by the Protestant descendants of the English settlers on this continent, and their black slaves, but also by tens of millions of immigrants from western

216

and southern and eastern Europe, a large proportion of whom were Roman Catholics and Jews. Indeed, throughout the entire nineteenth and into the early twentieth century, America studied its law chiefly from Blackstone, who wrote that "[the] law of nature . . . dictated by God himself . . . is binding . . . in all countries and at all times; no human laws are of any validity if contrary to this; and such of them as are valid derive all their force, and all their authority, mediately or immediately, from this original."[36]

Within the past two generations the public philosophy of America has shifted radically from a religious to a secular theory of law, from a moral to a political or instrumental theory, and from a communitarian to an individualistic theory. Law is now generally considered—at least in public discourse—to be essentially a pragmatic device for accomplishing specific political, economic, and social objectives. Its tasks are thought to be finite, material, impersonal—to get things done, to make people act in certain ways. Rarely, if ever, does one hear it said that law is a reflection of an objective justice or of the ultimate meaning or purpose of life. Usually it is thought to reflect, at best, the community's sense of what is expedient.

Likewise, it is only in the last two generations that the concept of religion as something wholly private and wholly psychological, as contrasted with the earlier concept of religion as something public, something partly psychological but also partly social and historical, indeed, partly legal, has come to dominate our discourse.

These contemporary views of law and religion find support in the Enlightenment philosophy of the late eighteenth century, with its emphasis on rationalism and individualism, and its attempt to divorce law and morality from religious faith—the sense of the just from the sense of the holy. It is no accident that in recent decades our courts and writers have so often cited Thomas Jefferson, America's leading apostle of the Enlightenment, when they interpret the religion clauses of the First Amendment in such a way as to separate entirely the sphere of government from the sphere of belief.

Justice Rehnquist, relying on recent scholarly research, has presented an account of the origins of the religion clauses of the First Amendment which is similar, in some. respects, to the one that I have presented here.[37] He has attached to the historical record a very different significance, however, from that which I would endorse. He would turn the clock back to the founding period. He contends, in effect, that since the religion clauses were not originally intended to be applied to the states, therefore they should be restricted—as they were until the 1940s—to *federal* legislative, executive, and judicial action involving religion. Justice Rehnquist contends, further, that *if* the religion clauses are to be applied to *state* legislative, executive, and judicial action, then they should be interpreted to mean what they were understood to mean in 1791: more especially, "establishment" should be understood to mean not state "aid" to religion but rather state endorsement of a religious creed.

There are at least two strong objections to that solution. First, it would be a sign not of respect but of disrespect to constitutional history to overrule the precedents of the past forty-five years in favor of precedents of a more distant past. Our constitutional history is an ongoing history. It is a living tradition, not a mere historicism. Jaroslav Pelikan has defined tradition as the living faith of the dead, traditional*ism* as the dead faith of the living. It is an example of traditional*ism*, not tradition—of historic*ism*, not a belief in history—to try to restore the original understanding of the First Amendment.

Second, the religious context of the First Amendment as originally understood—and as understood at least until World War I—no longer exists, and the public philosophy generated in that context no longer exists. Today we are groping for a new public philosophy—one that will build on the past but will not be bound by the past. Such a public philosophy must be grounded in something more than the practical need to maintain peace among warring factions. It must look beyond our pluralism to the common convictions that underlie our pluralism. It must come to grips with the fact that freedom of belief—which includes freedom of disbelief—rests, in the last analysis, on the foundation of belief, not on the foundation of skepticism. That is what John Adams meant when he said that the Constitution, with its guarantee of freedom to believe or disbelieve, "was made only for a moral and religious people. It will be wholly inadequate to any other."[38] It is not to be regarded as an instrument framed (in Judge Scott's words) for a society "composed of strangers . . . each with a religion of his own, bound by no previous social ties, nor sympathizing in any common reminiscences of the past."[39]

At the same time—and here I speak in the spirit more of the last two generations than of the first two-and-a-half centuries of our history as a people—our public philosophy must also come to grips with the deep conflict in our society between orthodox religious belief-systems and widespread indifference or opposition to such belief-systems. We have in the past sought to resolve this conflict largely by trying to sweep it under the rug. We have pretended that all belief, both religious and non-religious, is the private affair of each individual. Public figures and others who participate in shaping public opinion have for the most part been unwilling to express publicly—that is, outside their own like-minded groups—their deepest convictions concerning religious questions. When they have done so, they have been attacked as overstepping the bounds of public discourse. This has inhibited the articulation of a public philosophy grounded in our fundamental beliefs concerning human nature, human destiny, and the sources and limits of human knowledge.[40]

Especially with regard to debate concerning the religion clauses of the First Amendment, there should be open discussion of the significance of its historical roots in the combination of Christian and Deist beliefs. Such a discussion might lead to a new understanding of those clauses. More particularly, a reconsideration of Madison's conception that religious freedom can only be secure if it is undergirded by religious faith could lead to a reinterpretation of the relationship between the establishment clause and the free-exercise clause—a reinterpretation which would permit government support of any or all belief-systems, whether religious or irreligious, so long as such support does not discriminate among belief-systems (and therefore does not constitute an establishment) and so long as it is non-coercive (and therefore does not restrict free exercise).[41]

Harold J. Berman

ENDNOTES

1. See Harold J. Berman, *The Interaction of Law and Religion* (1974), pp. 24-25.

2. In *Cantwell v. Connecticut*, 310 U.S. 296 (1940), the Court held for the first time that the "free exercise" clause of the First Amendment is made applicable to the States by the Fourteenth Amendment. In *Everson v. Board of Education*, 330 U.S. 1 (1947), the Court held for the first time that the "establishment" clause of the First Amendment is made applicable to the States by the Fourteenth Amendment.

3. Joseph Story, *Commentaries on the Constitution of the United States* (2d. ed., 1851), vol. 2, 1879, p. 597.

4. Cf. Winthrop S. Hudson, *American Protestantism* (1961), pp. 128-130.

5. See infra note 28.

6. On the "wall-of-separation" theory see note 19 infra. Recent presentations of the "accommodation" theory—whose proponents argue that the First Amendment permits, and at times requires, the government to accommodate the institutions and programs of any religious group—include Thomas Derr, *The First Amendment As a Guide to Church-State Relations: Theological Illusions, Cultural Fantasies, and Legal Practicalities in Church, State and Politics* (J. Hensel ed., 1981), p. 75; Canavan, "The Pluralist Game," *Law & Contemporary Problems*, vol. 44 (2) (1981), p. 23;

221

Louis J. Sirico, "The Secular Contribution of Religion to the Political Process: The First Amendment and School Aid," *Missouri Law Review*, vol. 50 (1985), p. 325.

7. Connecticut Constitution of 1818, art. VII, 1.

8. Massachusetts Constitution of 1780, ch. VI, art. I.

9. Northwest Ordinance of 1787, art. III, 1 Stat. 50, at p. 52 n. (a).

10. *People vs. Ruggles*, 8 Johns. 290 (N.Y. 1811), at p. 195.

11. New York State Convention of 1821, pp. 462-574.

12. *Lindemuller v. The People*, 33 Barb. 548 (N.Y. 1961), at p. 562.

13. Updegraph v. The Commonwealth, 11 Serg. & Rawl. 393 (Pa. 1822), at p. 394.

14. Id. at p. 399.

15. *State v. Ambs*, 20 Mo. 214 (1954), at pp. 216-17.

16. Illinois Constitution of 1870, art. 2, 3.

17. *North v. Board of Trustees*, 137 Ill. 296 (1891), at p. 305.

18. *Donahoe v. Richards*, 38 Me. 379 (1854), at p. 407.

19. In a letter written in 1802 to a committee of the Danbury Baptist Association, Jefferson stated: "Believing with you that religion is a matter which lies solely between man and his God, that he owes account to none other for his faith or

222

his worship, that the legislative powers of government reach actions only, and not opinions, I contemplate with sovereign reverence that act of the whole American people which declared that their legislature should 'make no law respecting an establishment of religion, or prohibiting the free exercise thereof,' thus creating a wall of separation between church and state." The *Writings of Thomas Jefferson* (1904), vol. 16, pp. 281-2. Jefferson's phrase "wall of separation between church and state" was first used by the U.S. Supreme Court in *Reynolds v. U.S.*, 98 U.S. 145 (1879), which held that the "free exercise" clause of the First Amendment was not violated by the federal prohibition of polygamy in a U.S. Territory inhabited largely by Mormons. The concept of a "wall of separation" goes back to Roger Williams's metaphor of "a hedge or wall of separation between the garden of the church and the wilderness of the world." Williams stated that when people "have opened a gap" in that wall, "God hath ever broke down the wall itself . . . and made His garden a wilderness." For the full quotation, see Mark DeWolfe Howe, *The Garden and the Wilderness: Religion and Government in American Constitutional History* (1965), pp. 5-6. Howe stresses the difference between Williams's "principle of theology" and Jefferson's "principle of politics" based on "enlightened rationalism." Id., pp. 6-9. In neither Williams's nor Jefferson's conception, however, did the phrase "wall" have the meaning attributed to it by Justice Black in *Everson v. Board of Education*, supra note 2, at pp. 15-16: "The 'establishment of religion' clause of the First Amendment means at least this: Neither a state nor the Federal Government can set up a church. Neither can pass laws which aid one religion, aid all religions, or prefer one religion over another. . . . Neither a state nor the Federal Government can, openly or secretly, participate in the affairs of any religious organizations or groups and vice versa. In the words of Jefferson, the clause against establishment of religion by law was intended to erect 'a wall of separation between church and state.'"

20. *Story*, note 3 supra, 1877, p. 594.

21. *Benjamin Franklin's Works* (1844), vol. 5, p. 153.

22. See James D. Richardson, *A Compilation of the Messages and Papers of the Presidents*, 1789-1897 (1901), vol. 1, p. 56, 66, 123, 141, 219, 229, 274, all of which are reprinted in Robert L. Cord, *Separation of Church and State: Historical Fact and Current Fiction* (1982), pp. 251-260. Cord notes that Madison later stated that he believed it to be unconstitutional for the President to issue proclamations establishing a day of national thanksgiving. Id., pp. 29-36.

23. See note 8 supra.

24. *Treaty Between the United States of America and the Kaskasia Tribe of Indians*, art. III, 7 Stat. 79 (Aug. 13, 1803), reproduced in Cord, note 22 supra, p. 261 ff.

25. Madison's original draft stated: "The civil rights of none shall be abridged on account of religious belief or worship, nor shall any national religion be established, nor shall the full and equal rights of conscience be in any manner, or any pretext, infringed." *1 Annals of Congress* (1789), p. 434.

26. *The Papers of Thomas Jefferson*, vol. 3 (1951), p. 178. Jefferson's gubernatorial proclamation started by quoting the recommendation of the President that each state appoint "a day of public and solemn thanksgiving to Almighty God . . . that he would grant to his church, the plentiful effusions of divine grace, and pour out his holy spirit on all Ministers of the Gospel; that he would bless and prosper the means of education, and spread the light of christian knowledge through the remotest corners of the earth. . . ."

27. "Our sister States of Pennsylvania and New York . . . have long subsisted without any establishment at all. The experiment was new and doubtful when they made it. It has answered beyond conception. They flourish infinitely. Religion is well-supported; of various kinds, indeed, but all good enough; all sufficient to preserve peace and order; . . . Let us too give this experiment fair play. . . ." Thomas Jefferson, *Notes on the State of Virginia* (1782) in *The Writings of Thomas Jefferson* (1904), vol. 2, p. 224. Cf. Sidney E. Mead, *The Living Experiment* (1963), pp. 40, 59, 63.

28. In the Memorial and Remonstrance against the bill, which Madison drafted, he stated in his first objection that the right to free exercise of religion "is in its nature an unalienable right. . . . It is unalienable . . . because what is here a right towards men, is a duty towards the Creator. It is the duty of every man to render to the Creator such homage, and such only, as he believes to be acceptable to him. This duty is precedent both in order of time and degree of obligation, to the claims of Civil Society. Before any man can be considered as a member of Civil Society, he must be considered as a subject of the Governor of the

Universe: And if a member of Civil Society, who enters into any subordinate Association, must always do it with a reservation of his duty to the General Authority; much more must every man who becomes a member of any particular Civil Society, do it with a saving of his allegiance to the Universal Sovereign. We maintain therefore that in matters of Religion, no man's right is abridged by the institution of Civil Society, and that Religion is wholly exempt from its cognizance." "Memorial and Remonstrance Against Religious Assessments, 1785." *Writings of James Madison*, vol. 2 (1901), pp. 184-185. Cf. William Lee Miller, *The First Liberty: Religion and the American Republic* (1956), pp. 96-106. The Lutheran and Calvinist implications of Madison's reference to the relation between man as "a member of Civil Society: and man as "a subject of the Governor of the Universe" seem to have gone unnoticed in the literature on religious freedom.

29. Madison's theology, strongly influenced by his mentor at Princeton, the Presbyterian theologian Joseph Witherspoon, should not be wholly identified with Roger Williams's Baptist conception of an impregnable wall between the "garden" of faith and the "wilderness" of the world. (See supra note 19.) Madison had a much more positive view of the role of the church, including the clergy, in reforming the world, including the world of politics.

30. See Sanford H. Cobb, *The Rise of Religious Liberty in America* (1902), pp. 484-89. Cf. Howe, supra note 19, p. 9: "The fact that there is a theological theory of disestablishment traceable to Roger Williams, is recognized by all those historians who insist that the American principle became a political reality only because it was

sustained by the fervor of Jonathan Edwaids and the Great Awakening." This valuable insight neglects, however, the important differences between Williams's theology and that of Madison. Cf. supra note 29.

31. James Madison, "Speech Before the Virginia Convention" (1788), in Saul Padover, *The Complete Madison* (1953), p. 306.

32. Alexis de Tocqueville, *Democracy in America* (1956), vol. 1, p. 303.

33. Id., p. 305.

34. James Bryce, *The American Commonwealth* (1915), vol. 2, p. 778.

35. See *Works of John Adams* (1856), vol. 3, pp. 423, 424.

36. William Blackstone, 1 *Commentaries on the Laws of England* (1765), vol. 1, p. 41.

37. Wallace v. Jaffree, 105 S. Ct. 2479 (1985), pp. 2508-2520. Cf. Howe, supra note 19, p. 15: ". . . the Court, in its role as historian, has erred in disregarding the theological roots of the American principle of separation." Justice Rehnquist has now gone far to correct this error, though he has drawn legal conclusions quite different from those which Professor Howe drew.

38. *Works of John Adams* (1856), vol. 9, p. 229.

39. See text at note 15 supra. Judge Scott's phrase "each with a religion of his own" is parallel to the conception of "private religion" which has been said to characterize much of American

religious life today. See Robert N. Bellah, Richard Madsen, William M. Sullivan, Ann Swidler, and Steven M. Tipton, *Habits of the Heart: Individualism and Commitment in American Life* (1985), pp. 220ff.

40. The need for a religiously-grounded public philosophy has been forcefully argued by Richard John Neuhaus, *The Naked Public Square: Religion and Democracy in America* (1984). The interaction of the profane and the sacred in American history is the subject of an important study by George Armstrong Kelly, *Politics and Religious Consciousness in America* (1984). The latter work discusses critically the concept of an American "civil religion" advanced by Robert N. Bellah and others. Cf. Bellah, *The Broken Covenant: American Civil Religion in Time of Trial* (1975). The existence of such a "civil religion," which would include the belief in the Constitution as a sacred instrument, receives some support from Judge James L. Oakes's remark that the Bill of Rights is "not only a charter of our rights, but an inspiration for our daily lives . . ., a document that embodies as close as we may come to a national religion." Oakes, "The Proper Role of the Federal Courts in Enforcing the Bill of Rights," *N.Y.U. Law Review*, vol. 54 (1979), p. 922. It should be stressed, however, that such "civil religion" generally avoids metaphysical and theological questions and appeals chiefly to political justifications.

41. Writing in 1965 from a historical perspective similar in important respects to that taken in this essay, Mark Howe reached a different conclusion with respect to bringing agnostic and atheist belief-systems within the religion clauses of the First Amendment. "Of course," he wrote, "the

atheist's safeguards *can* be found in the free exercise clause. I would suggest, however, that structurally and grammatically the First Amendment's assurance of free speech provides a more natural safeguard for irreligious utterances than does its assurance that religion may be freely exercised. ... I stress this analysis ... because of my belief that its acceptance confirms ... that the religious [*sic*] clauses of the First Amendment expressed an evangelical, and not merely a Jeffersonian, theory of separation. ..." Howe, supra note 19, p. 154. While this may still be a satisfactory resolution of problems arising under the free-exercise clause, it does not meet the objection that under the establishment clause theistic and deistic belief systems have been denied government support equal to that granted to agnostic and atheist belief-systems. This is due in part to the fact that "structurally and grammatically" the First Amendment addressed itself to a situation in which, as Joseph Story put it (supra p. 12), "the general if not the universal sentiment in America was, that Christianity ought to receive encouragement from the State so far as was not incompatible with the private rights of conscience and the freedom of religious worship." In the radically different situation that has come to prevail in the twentieth century, for the courts to continue to give a narrow definition of "religion" as used in the First Amendment, while at the same time giving an increasingly broad definition of "establishment" is to discriminate in favor of non-theistic belief-systems.

CHAPTER X

Religion and Politics: Four Possible Connections

ROBERT BENNE

NARRATOR: Although its meaning is often confusing, it is striking that in three or four areas the relationship between ethics and politics, or values and politics has come to the fore. The Gary Hart case is a recent example of something that we thought for the moment had been brushed aside as an issue, but it came to the fore. Someone once said that if Adlai Stevenson, the divorced man, had run for the presidency in 1962 rather than in 1952 he would have been elected. Because of these types of comments one might assume that these issues are in flux, moving one way and then taking a totally different direction in another instance.

Therefore, in a hard-boiled, tough-minded public affairs center it is important to include some discussions of ethics, religion, and politics, and we've done that. In the first lecture that he gave at a major university, we had president-elect Edward Malloy of the University of Notre Dame speak on religion, ethics, society, and politics. We've also had a former colleague of Professor Benne, Martin Marty, speak on ethics and presidents. In other words, the Miller Center has worked on this subject, and nothing could be more appropriate, because of his proximity to Charlottesville and in terms of the standing of our colleague at Roanoke College, that Robert Benne would continue that discussion today.

Robert Benne received his doctorate from the University of Chicago. He taught at the Lutheran Seminary in Rock Island, Illinois for a time and returned to Chicago to teach at the Lutheran School of Theology, where he was fully recognized and widely respected in his field. In 1982 he moved to Roanoke College.

I did a little review at Roanoke College during the Fowler Lecture Program several months ago. What impressed me most was when I asked faculty members and administrators who was the one faculty member who was most trusted (because there was some controversy about the Fowler Lecture Program), without exception everybody said Bob Benne. Two of his writings are of interest to today's discussion. One is his book *The Ethic of Democratic Capitalism: A Moral Reassessment*, which was published in 1981, and a more recent paper that has provoked a great deal of discussion is a piece titled "Neoconservatism and Neoliberalism: Is There a Difference?" He continues to write and teach, gaining even further respect of friends in the field. We look forward to a discussion this morning on the connections between religion and ethics and politics. No one can look at these connections better than Bob Benne. I understand that in his mind there are four ways of looking at this problem, and with that we are absolutely delighted that he is with us.

PROFESSOR BENNE: Thank you. Well, anybody from the University of Chicago would see four ways of looking at things. It is a great honor to be here and I'm looking forward to a fruitful discussion of this very timely subject.

I want to reflect on the possible connections between religion and politics. It is a particularly appropriate time to discuss that relationship. Many

commentators on this issue, particularly Richard
Neuhaus in his book *The Naked Public Square*, claim
that we are in a first-principal investigation of the
relation of religion and politics. A book by James
Reichley called *Religion in American Public Life* has
created a great deal of discussion, and there has been
a whole spate of books connected with the First
Amendment: *The First Liberty* by William Lee Miller
of this university, *The First Freedom* by Thomas
Currie, and *The Establishment Clause* by Leonard
Levy. Many of those books have been stimulated by
the Bicentennial of the Constitution, but these studies
are all made vastly more interesting by the fact that
we have a lively, practical dynamic between religion
and public life in this country and, indeed, around the
world. That comes as somewhat of a surprise to
those who thought that the influence of religion
would wane as modern industrial civilization advanced.
That doesn't seem to be the case.

We have many examples abroad, of course, and
perhaps foremost among them are the Islamic
revolutions. Others also come to mind: the Roman
Catholic effect on both Philippine and Polish politics;
the Christian Church's involvement in the present
turbulence in Korea; the Catholic preferential option
for the poor in Latin America; the Church's resistance
to the Sandanistas in Nicaragua; the World Council of
Church's involvement with the African National
Congress and SWAPO, in Southern Africa; and church
involvement in peace activism in many of the
European countries. All of these examples are from
the world scene, but the domestic scene has, perhaps,
an even more focused and lively dynamic between
religion and public life. The debate on the abortion
issue, the Catholic bishops' letters on the American
economy and nuclear policy, and the great struggles
on education issues (evolution versus creationism; how
shall our young be morally formed in the public
schools; the role of the Ten Commandments) are all

examples of the domestic debate on religion and
politics. The debate over the portrayal of the
religious factor in American life and American history
is even more sophisticated and subtle. Have the
schools neglected that or given children a slanted
view? That is a very interesting discussion. The role
of prayer in the public schools is another heated
educational issue. Further, we have the religiously-
sponsored think tanks and political action committees
in Washington. Many of the churches also now have
advocacy offices both in Washington and in the state
legislatures around the country.

A very interesting case is our own Lutheran
Church in America, where hunger funds are used for
advocacy in this country, not only in Washington but
in the state legislatures as well. One of my students
who is supported by hunger funds works as an
advocate in the state legislature in Wisconsin, and the
main issue he has been working on is the issue of
comparable worth. People wondered, well, is that
where hunger funds should be going? At any rate, it
is illustrative of this lively interaction between
religion and politics. Now that we have identified
numerous examples, we can investigate what we make
of this lively issue.

The question is not whether religion does or
should have an involvement in public political life.
Judeo-Christian religion has a public dimension; it
cannot be relegated completely to the private sphere
without diminishing its significance or, more seriously,
truncating its very message. Certainly from the
societal side, the Constitution ensures the public
expression of religion. So the question is not
whether religion should be related to public life or
politics, but how it actually is and should be
connected to politics. In other words, in what ways
can and should these two poles interact?

My next step is to analyze the connections
between institutionalized religion and public political

life. I'm not going to focus on constitutional issues. There are people here that are far better at that than I am. I am going to focus on institutional religion (the church) simply because if you talk about religion as personal preference or orientation, it's very difficult to trace because it's so amorphous. In talking about institutional religion, one means the church's concern for political life. In examining its political role, I will include both a descriptive and analytical side of that life as well as the normative side. Finally, when I use the word 'political' I mean it in a broad sense of public discussion, debate, and decision-making.

What I will do now is to develop a typology of how the church affects the political order and make comments about how it ought or ought not to proceed. I believe that if the church relates in inappropriate ways there is a great danger to its own integrity and to its ability to serve the world positively. Also great damage can be done to society: "religionized" politics can be a very dangerous thing.

My typology includes four categories moving from the noncontroversial, low-profile to the very controversial, high profile kinds of relations. The first category is *indirect* and *unintentional influence.* By indirect I mean that the church as an institution does not get involved in public, political decision-making; it does not become a public actor as an institution. Unintentional is just what it indicates: the church has no particular conscious intent to affect a policy or a practice. There is no specific blueprint toward which it wants to move the society. As far as its influence is concerned, it aims primarily at persuading its own members; there is less concern about persuading the society. In fact, it doesn't have any real intent to influence the society as such. It is also important to note that the church is using persuasion, not power, and it is necessary to distinguish between persuasion and power. Persuasion is exactly what it says, persuasion by argument. Power, in contrast, is, according to Reinhold Niebuhr's definition, getting people to do what you want them to do whether or not they want to do it. Power moves from subtle kinds of pressure to outright coercion.

This first approach could be called the ethics of being or character. When using this approach, the church, a narrative-formed community, shapes people, their outlook, their character, and their moral values. When the church is really the church its preaching, teaching, worship, and discipline form and transform persons so that their innermost beings, both their outlook and moral values, are powerfully shaped.

To affect people so deeply in this way is arguably the most important, fundamental, and potentially most effective way the church influences the public order: its politics, its economics, and the society. There have been many historical studies that have traced this influence, the most celebrated being Weber's study of *The Protestant Ethic and the Spirit of Capitalism*. Weber argued that without a certain kind of reformed piety, which he called innerworldly asceticism, capitalism would not have developed in the West. Now the Calvinists were not intentionally shaping Capitalism. They didn't do this directly as an institution. But certainly because of the way that they influenced people they also enabled capitalism to develop. This is a good example of indirect, unintentional influence.

Another example is Ernst Troeltsch's thesis about the two great syntheses of civilization in the West. He believed that Catholicism brought forth a medieval synthesis and that Calvinism brought forth a reformed synthesis of culture which had its fullest emergence in America. Like Weber, Troeltsch also traced this indirect, unintentional influence on the public order.

Another fine study is Lord Lindsay's book, *The Essentials of Democracy*, in which he argues that the

Reformation doctrine of equality of all sinners before God's judgment and grace worked through nonconformist sects in England and gradually surfaced to affect political ideas of equality and democracy. Lindsay also asserts that in Reformed churches the practice of democracy influenced the public political order.

The point of all these examples is that religious communities can create a powerful ethos among people. These people then shape the world around them. This mode of church influence is still effective and prevalent in many places today. I teach courses in business ethics, and when you scrape below the surface of those people sitting in class (most of them are adults coming from the community), you can see that they have been shaped powerfully by basic Protestant religious values in the Roanoke Valley. They really want to do good according to their religious backgrounds, and this overflows into their business lives.

Although this type of influence is still very obvious in the United States, it is less powerful in European countries. The church does not seem to have the powerful effect on people that it once did. In fact, one of my theses about the eruption of working-class violence and disorder in England is that this eruption corresponds directly with the collapse of the dissenting churches of England. Although the Church of England has been declining, the Reformed, the Methodist, and the Welsh chapels are declining even more rapidly, and those were the groups that had once evangelized and formed working class people.

The churches of America strongly illustrate this indirect connection. For instance, when I search for religious communities that operate in this way, I think of, in the Lutheran family, the Missouri Synod. The Missouri Synod rarely talks about public issues in its churches nor has it often preached on them. It doesn't intend to affect the society in any direct way, and the church generally doesn't take stands on political issues. Yet, they have had a powerful ethos, and have influenced their members greatly. Therefore, you find a person like Senator Paul Simon, a member of the Missouri Synod, who is running for the presidency, and when you hear Paul Simon talk, those religious notions are clearly evident. They influence the way Paul Simon looks at politics and the way he acts politically.

On the other hand, you find Edwin Meese, who was also raised in the Missouri Synod and formed powerfully in that tradition. But, he seems to be on the other side of the political spectrum. These two individuals are politically divergent, but nevertheless both persons would find the religious formations very important in their vocation as political people.

The distressing signal, I think, is that this molding capacity probably is declining among the older, mainline denominations in the United States. This is not the case among the expanding religious groups: Southern Baptists, Evangelicals, Fundamentalists. They seem to be performing this task of forming their youth and laity quite well and with great vigor. In the mainline denominations one can see the declining number of young people. The mainline denominations have not been able to retain the membership of their young people or inform them in a way that really sticks.

Many people both in the churches and in society would like to stop with this mode of influencing the public order—indirect, unintentional influence. Many laity at least, and probably many secular people, as well think that if the churches would really do their job well, that's all they would have to do. In other words, if the church vigorously preached, taught, and nurtured, it could then let the laity live out their lives in the world based on a firm religious foundation. However, most of us are not satisfied with this mode of influence as the only way in which organized religion can affect the public sphere. It is too long-term and too indirect. Can we address something more specifically in the short-term? It is great to plant oak trees, but now and then we like to harvest a few pumpkins which not only grow more quickly but which yield the fruits of one's efforts in a more direct and tangible way.

So, I will expand the typology by introducing a second type of influence called *indirect* and *intentional influence.* Again, it is indirect because the church, as an institution, is not a public actor. It primarily influences its own people. But in this case, it is intentional; that is, the church directs its vision to specific public policy issues. It focuses on specific public issues self-consciously in the light of its own teaching and vision. The church begins with its biblical roots, works through the theological modulations of its tradition draws upon secular knowledge, and tries to relate all of that to specific issues in a self-conscious, reflective way *within* the institution. But the church doesn't make public statements to the society purporting to represent the members of that community.

It aims at inculcating its social teachings in its people, forming a common conscience, and bringing that into interaction with specific public or political issues that are before the society. It tries to arrive at a common vision (common principals, goals, aims), but it encourages a wide discussion among the laity of the means by which these goals and ends are achieved. The church assumes a wide variety of political and economic persuasions within the church and provides the context for this kind of discussion to go on. It tries to distinguish between what is permissible and what falls beyond the pale of Christian practice. But by and large, the church provides a wide latitude for discussion of the ways in which the church's ends and purposes can be achieved

239

in society. Then after this heightened awareness, the laity can make up their own minds.

I want to elaborate a couple of concrete examples of this mode because it may not be so familiar. During my years in Illinois, I was a participant in what was called Illinois Impact. This was a division of the Council of Churches in Illinois which watched the issues coming through the state legislature. It would pick six issues per year that were not the frontline issues with which other great lobbying groups would be involved. These would be important issues but ones that weren't receiving a lot public attention. Then Illinois Impact would publish study documents on these six issues, laying out what the legislation meant and elaborating its pros and cons. There was a persistent effort to give a critical and balanced analysis of each piece of legislation.

Many local churches would use them in their social ministry committees, and it gave people the opportunity to become much more educated about issues before the state legislature. In this way the individual would be encouraged to relate to Christian social teachings to those issues. However, Impact did not take a position either way on the issues, and the local church was not expected to take a stance either. When the issue came before the legislature for consideration, people were given the signal to contact their representatives. This contact was left up to the individual, and although there was heightened awareness among people within the churches, there was no dictated position behind which they were supposed to stand. All that persons had were reasons pro and con for the particular legislation. This is an example of what I mean by indirect but intentional influence.

Perhaps a better example, drawn from the German experience, is provided by the evangelical academies in Germany. These centers were set up after World War II by the churches. These centers never take positions on social issues no matter how clear things seem to be. What they do is bring competing sides on an issue together at their beautiful academies. These various groups meet intensively for a few days and ask the question: what does it mean to be responsibly engaged in this issue?

These centers have had a forty year history of encouraging dialogue between the management and unions of Mercedes Benz. They bring management and labor together, focus on an issue, and work it through without taking a position. One week when I was visiting Bad Boll, teachers and school administrators were brought together. The question before them was: "What does it mean to be Christianly responsible in this school system?" Thus, the academy provided a graceful context in which competing views and interests could come together, where people could admit their partialness and narrowness of vision, refuse to demonize the other side, and work through issues in a way that was thoroughly dialogic. The church was playing a mediating role.

Now this approach is emerging more strongly in the United States in various lay movements. The lay ministry groups that are emerging in a lot of the mainstream churches are composed of laity who have grown a little tired of all the official pronouncements in the church. They bring together competing perspectives on, for example, the farm issue in the Midwest. A lay group I have worked with brought together small farmers, large farmers, farmers who were involved in bankruptcy, and farmers who were prospering. These people came together to work through various aspects of the issue, but they generally refrained from taking any position at the end of the conference.

My hope is that this kind of intentional but indirect influence—the church as a mediating institution—is getting under way in the United States.

I believe it should be a more dominant way that the church affects the political order. Many more laity in the church would want to stop with this mode; they think this would be pretty good if it's pulled off well. I'm more and more sympathetic with this sentiment as I read the frequent public statements that the church is making on too many issues with not enough careful thought or balanced moral discourse.

I would finally not, however, be satisfied with stopping here either. The church is called to speak God's word as both law and gospel to the world. There is a prophetic dimension in the church's message in the public world though I believe that the church has often done that so poorly in recent years that it has lost a great deal of credibility with its own laity, as well as with the world.

The next category—escalating to a little higher profile—is *direct* and *intentional influence*. By direct, I mean that the church becomes a public actor as an institution, not indirectly through its laity. Again, it is intentional because it tries to shape and affect social policy or public policy. And it is working influentially, first of all with its own members but also with members of society in general.

Now we don't have to look hard for good examples of this mode of influencing society. The Catholic bishops are a vivid case in point with their last two pastoral letters, the letter on the American economy and their statement on nuclear issues. However, all the mainline churches have their battery of statements on the economy and on issues of peace and war. Whenever these statements come out, particularly from people as significant and influential as the Catholic bishops, it creates a great deal of public discussion and debate. First it is asked whether it is proper for the church to do this. I say, yes, it is proper: the church does have a calling to speak God's law to the society and to the public power. From the society's point of view, our society encourages, or at least does not prohibit, the public expression of conviction on public, political issues. So, it is proper for the church to do this.

There is a second question which always arises in this debate: does the church do it as well as it should? And to that I say, no, it generally doesn't. However, I think it has been getting better, and particularly the Catholic church has improved in the way it has exercised this direct and intentional influence.

I do want to list several guidelines regarding how I think this direct, intentional influence should be exercised by the church. These guidelines will judge the way that many Protestant churches go about making their statements and affirm in many ways, how the Catholic bishops have been going about it.

First of all, I think these statements ought to be infrequent. They shouldn't be made about every issue that comes up. A litmus test would be: does this particular religious community have something to offer from its own religious perspective that is unique to the discussion? If it doesn't, the church should be reluctant to speak because it will tend simply to reflect the current political biases of the church bureaucracies. Church statements should be made only when the respective religious vision has something unique to contribute, and this implies that these statements should be infrequent.

Secondly, churches ought to do their homework on the issues they are addressing. On the positive side, I believe that the Catholic bishops really have done their homework. They spend years working out their pastoral letters, and they try to take all perspectives into account. Perhaps the most inter-esting thing is that they revise their document publicly after a year's worth of feedback. If you trace the way that the Catholic bishops' statement on the economy changed, you can detect how seriously the bishops did take the feedback.

243

The third guideline, suggests that every statement by a church on public, political issues should distinguish between levels of authority. The central symbols of redemption that the church holds as its reason for being may be nonnegotiable and relatively unchanging through the ages. Therefore, these symbols are not very debatable. The key ethical principles that flow from those central symbols are not very debatable either. However, as you modulate those ethical principles into middle principles and draw upon philosophical sources and theories of justice to move toward political policy applications, you get into more ambiguity, more room for debate, and more disagreement. And finally, as you get to judgments on specific policy issues, you find a great deal of room for debate and disagreement.

The bishops, again, have been very instructive and helpful on this. They have recognized and analyzed the three levels of authority and invited people to disagree vigorously at the policy level, less vigorously at the middle level, but the bishops have also said that if you are a good Catholic, you will never disagree with these top level judgments.

These distinctions are contrasted with what one could call "straight line" thinking, where even judgments on particular policies are elevated to the same level as the central religious symbols. In this case a straight line is drawn in which even policy pronouncements are elevated to the level of the central symbols. In this situation people are willing to throw other people out of the Christian community if they disagree on a particular policy position.

The Christian Right is well known for this type of activity. For instance, the Christian Round Table has a list of what the "Christian" position is on all these hotly debated items. They rate members of Congress according to their list and have been known to give people like Paul Simon a zero rating while giving far less reputable members much higher ratings.

244

I think this straight line thinking does a great disservice to the mission of the church and diminishes the integrity of Christianity.

The Christian Left also uses straight line thinking when it gets too confident about certain policy applications. I find that the Left tends to do this more on foreign policy issues than it does on domestic issues. If you take the wrong stand on Nicaragua, you can find yourself very quickly beyond the pale of true Christian identity, according to the Left. But both the Right and the Left have often failed to distinguish these levels of authority and to allow disagreement on practical, specific issues of public policy.

Finally, when the church does make statements directly as an institution it should remember the means-ends distinction. Most of us agree on the ends that we should be pursuing. For example, no one wants high unemployment, so the church can affirm that most people within churches agree on such goals. The big discussion is on the means to get to those goals, and it is here that much more latitude has to be allowed. It would be very good for the church to encourage fair, moral discourse at this level of means. That sounds relatively easy and trite, but I find it very rare in the churches. If you go into the bureaucratic side of the church's life, you will find one orientation, generally left-liberal, but if you go to the local parishes, you will find a relatively conservative orientation. The bureaucracies don't like to invite anybody who might introduce a different viewpoint into the fray, and local parishes don't like to be disturbed by inviting people in for moral discourse on different means for reaching the same end.

It would be most helpful when the church makes a statement to the society that it state its goals and principles clearly. It might then put forth two or three models for reaching those goals and engage in some critical reflection on each model, on both the good points and the bad points of each. And if it really is clear that the church should encourage a specific direction, then perhaps it should make a clear and reasoned policy recommendation. But, I think in most cases it would be very useful to present those models and the critical analysis of each to the laity for their own consideration and decision.

Before I leave this type, I want to mention what is perhaps the most effective mode of direct, and intentional influence on society. This mode is what H. Richard Niebuhr called "social pioneering." Niebuhr didn't criticize the churches for their public and social statements, but he said that it is a lot more persuasive if the church uses its own resources to respond to a social problem first within its own life. By using its own resources to create a response to that social problem, the church creates a model for the surrounding society. In a very famous little treatise on the church as social pioneer, he traces historically how the church did this with hospitals, orphanages, universities, and kindergartens. The church sensed a need in the society, created a model, and then the secular society picked it up later on down the line.

In the contemporary world, we have some examples of that modeling. Churches have shaped fine inner-city education programs, and the secular society says, "Wow, how did you do that? Let us come in and examine how you did that." Then the state tries to duplicate the churches' model in the secular society.

There are some examples of emergent modeling on the part of the churches. For example, churches are engaged in lively discussions about the ethical investment of their money. Ought churches invest blindly or ought they consciously and conscientiously decide where their money should be invested? This is a hot issue in the churches and we can see a movement toward a more self-conscious use of church money for ethical investment. I believe that this model is going to be picked up by groups within the broader society. These are examples of what Richard Niebuhr called social pioneering—a kind of direct and intentional influence on the rest of society.

The final type of church-political relations is very controversial and risky for both church and society. This is what I like to call *direct* and intentional action. It is direct because the church is an institutional actor in society. This action is intentional; that is, it intends to change policy or move society in certain directions. Further, the church finds that its actions are no longer meant just to influence, but these actions involve the use of power, even leading up to coercive methods. It is the commitment of the institution, with its funds, political weight, and human power, in an effort to achieve a certain policy objective. This is very high-profile, risky, and controversial. The church recognizes this intuitively. Generally, when it gets into these kinds of activities, the church will spin off a voluntary association. This association will be the visible actor because the church itself doesn't want to be directly involved.

For example, when I was in England last year, the churches were all leaning toward the Labor position on nuclear issues. In fact, the churches were not only leaning but were making explicit statements along Labor party lines. But the churches themselves didn't participate directly in the demonstrations that were being promoted. There was a large voluntary association called the Campaign for Nuclear Disarmament (CND), and that group did all of the power work involved in the campaign. So the church itself recognized the danger of this kind of involvement by the institution in power politics.

Many examples of this kind of involvement can be found on the domestic level. One that immediately comes to mind is the boycotts. Years ago, I interned in a church in Chicago. Operation Bread Basket was just emerging, and there was a sense among those people that the local dairy wasn't hiring black people. On my first Sunday there the pastor got up and announced that after the church service we were going to boycott Bowman's dairy to press them to hire more black people. Well, the church happened to be a Danish church that was just beginning to be integrated, and as you might guess, this announcement was really explosive. The church was very divided on whether Bowman's was being unjust or not. Beyond that there certainly was a division on the kinds of methods in which the church, as a local congregation, was going to involve itself (i.e., boycotts, picketing, etc.).

The community organization movement, particularly in the 1960s and early 1970s but still continuing today, illustrates another kind of direct action. The emerging community organizations insisted that churches as organizations join the community organizations. Membership was not open to individuals. The churches had to decide whether they should belong to these community organizations that used a lot of conflict-oriented tactics for reaching their goals. That touched off all kinds of debates, and it still does. In fact, we have a very painful example in the Lutheran Church in America right now. There is a community organization in Pittsburgh that had invited a number of Lutheran churches to join their group which used numerous conflict-oriented methods as the means to their goals. Those churches joined as churches and blew those congregations sky high. The result of this action was that pastors were defrocked and disbarred from their pastorates in the Lutheran Church.

These examples are some historical reminders of how the churches have engaged in direct action. Presently the question is raised in a milder form by

248

the advocacy offices that have sprung up, not only in Washington but around the country in the state legislatures. Here the church is committing large amounts of funds and claiming to represent a lot of people on specific public policy issues. Should the churches be involved that directly in exercising pressure on particular public policy issues? Advocacy is a mild example of this direct and intentional action, but nevertheless, it is an example.

I believe that, in general, this mode should be avoided. It makes the church too easily a partisan political society that tends to run roughshod over the political opinions of too many people in the church. It infuriates people who have a different perspective on these particular public policy issues. More seriously, there is the danger of using the sacred symbols of the faith for very secular purposes, resulting in a secularization and instrumentalization of those symbols. Also, the church loses its needed distance from all worldly conflicts; it loses its claim to transcendence. Consequently, it has a more difficult time proclaiming the gospel universally to all sinners, regardless of what side of the fence they are on. Therefore I believe that this mode is threatening to the church's integrity. It can be damaging to the society, too, if religious political energies are inserted into the political debate in a raw fashion.

By and large, if issues arise that need direct action, it is much better to encourage the involvement of voluntary associations that are distinct from the church. Then the church itself can maintain some needed distance. Nevertheless, I believe there are occasions when this mode becomes necessary, though it is fraught with danger. There may be compelling reasons for the church to get involved directly in the use of its power in society. For example, I would defend the direct political activities of the church in Poland because it is the only relatively free and representative institution in a Polish society threatened by totalitarian impulses. It is also possible to defend the church's role in Latin America where it organizes peasants and workers to demand individual rights from their governments. It also seems reasonable to affirm the Philippine church for tipping toward Aquino rather than Marcos.

So there are certain times and places that almost demand direct action as the responsible strategy for the church. But we should be very careful and judicious about when those kinds of interventions are made.

Those, then, are the four ways in which the church can affect the political order, running from the relatively uncontroversial to the most controversial and risky. I believe, though, that if the church is really the church, the first level is the most potent and powerful way that it affects the political order. In a relatively just and stable society, I would hope that only the first three modes of interaction would be used. Nevertheless, there are areas of injustice in this society and certainly around the world where the church ought to responsibly engage in direct and intentional action. But it should only do so with full awareness that what it is doing should be temporary and should be done with a great deal of care. Thank you.

COMMENT: You enumerated actions that you would defend in terms of intervention which are all uniquely Roman Catholic. You haven't mentioned any Protestant actions you would also defend.

PROFESSOR BENNE: Although I don't know that much about it, the Presbyterian Church in Korea has been very important in carrying the flame of democratic practice and spirit. I don't know whether what's going on currently would be in the category of direct, intentional action. I suspect it is much more on the third level, with the church making statements and its laity being involved indirectly in these matters. But if the church is committed to the fray more directly, that would be a Protestant example. Also, in the community organization movements around the country, Protestant churches are involved in this direct action mode.

QUESTION: What about the SCLC (Southern Christian Leadership Conference) in the 1960s and 1970s? Does that fall into the fourth category and was it something that was necessary?

PROFESSOR BENNE: Well, the SCLC would be a voluntary association, I believe, which was warmly supported by the church.

COMMENT: It was awfully close.

PROFESSOR BENNE: It was awfully close because it was led by clergy and very closely identified with black Baptist churches. Those churches were often involved in direct action. That is true.

In order for direct action to work, there either has to be a great deal of authority in the church to commit itself to these controversial issues or there has to be a great deal of consensus. I believe that among black churches, for example, you can generate a great deal of consensus on some of these issues, and the black church can engage in this direct action with a lot less of the explosiveness than Protestant mainline churches.

For example, the boycotts that I was talking about before were generated right out of the black Baptist churches without a great deal of fragmentation because at the time, there was so much consensus among the black people and black churches that this was an issue which had to be addressed. When you have neither a great deal of authority nor much consensus, that last mode can be very divisive.

251

QUESTION: There is one issue that you touched on implicitly from time to time, the question of who is the church. Who is entitled to speak for and as the church? Occasionally in your remarks, you seemed to differentiate between the church and its laity, and as if the church consisted of only the clergy. But, obviously, it is a tough issue, and I should think it would affect virtually all of these points that you are making. Obviously, there are internal, political problems in churches, and there is wide diversity inside particular churches. There may even be an ethical question as to whether any group within a diverse church is entitled to monopolize the name of the church when taking a particular position. Do you want to comment further on that subject?

PROFESSOR BENNE: That is a tough question because, on the one hand, we want to claim that when the laity acts out its calling in the world, that's the church influencing the world. But I wanted to get around that problem by saying that what I'm talking about here is primarily institutional religion and how it acts *vis-a-vis* the public, political sphere. The first and second categories are really—I call them indirect—the ways that the church affects the world, but it is very indirect and through its laity. I think that one would want to distinguish between the laity's actions outside the walls of the church and the kinds of positions and actions the church as an institution takes. I'm not sure that throws any light on things; it's just a tough problem. And the problem of representation—who is speaking for the church?—is one that has to be worked through very carefully.

I think the Protestant churches try to be democratic, but many analyses have been conducted about who finally shows up at church conventions and how they are quite different from the general laity within the church. For example, the American

Lutheran Church, upon merging with the Lutheran Church in America, has just completed a document reflecting on its social statements for the last twenty years, and reflecting particularly on what was good and bad about the process. The one thing that kept cropping up, at least in recent years, is that the church's statements always have been on the side of the Democratic opposition with regard to political issues; yet in the ALC around 70 percent of the people voted for Reagan. The next question is—how does that happen? It's not that the church should represent the political composition of its members, but certainly the church should have some way of involving these varying political and economic philosophies in the process of making a statement. I think that the Protestant churches have not done that well. That's why you have a great, even dangerous gap between where the church bureaucracies are going and where the laity are.

COMMENT: You were talking about lines of authority in relationship to statements made; that is, some statements relate general policy to people. Of course there is also a very important question of lines of authority within the church structure itself. I think in a Presbyterian church you have a congregation, a presbytery synod, and a general assembly. It seems to me that as you move upward in the hierarchy, you do have a greater tendency to have policy statements being made which tend to be more divergent from the grass roots people. Perhaps if a statement were made by a local congregation, you'd feel much more comfortable, in many cases, that the congregation had the feeling that the grass roots were being reflected more clearly than when statements were made by the highest hierarchial branch.

PROFESSOR BENNE: I agree because one of the characteristics of large religious organizations is that

they have staffs that generally do the primary work
on these statements. The Catholic bishops have had a
very well educated and large staff to do work on
their statements. One of the charges has been that
the staffs primarily do the work, and the staffs tend
to be of one ideological orientation. Because the
staff has the initiative in formulating the statement,
they also set the direction of the things in a rather
undemocratic way. It can be challenged and
modulated a bit from the grass roots, but the basic
direction is set by the staff. I think that generally
holds true.

I followed our Lutheran Church in America
statement on economic issues from its beginning to its
end. From the beginning it had a very sharp
liberationist argument with regard to international
issues; on domestic issues, it was very interventionist
on the side of the government. Although the LCA
went around the country listening to people, holding
conferences, and revising each version of the
statement slightly, in the end the major ideological
tone and direction was set by the staff.

We talk about inclusiveness in our churches so
much, yet we tend to ignore one very important
element of inclusiveness, and that is political and
economic ideology. I think it would be very helpful
and healthy for the churches to involve that kind of
inclusiveness from the very beginning, particularly at
the staff level where these things are generated. If
this were done, I think we would get more statements
along the lines that I suggested. There would be
agreement on certain purposes and ends, but there
still would be various ways that Christians could
involve themselves on a particular issue, leaving it a
bit more open.

A very good example is the South African issue.
The churches have very much wanted to make a stand
against apartheid, and I agree with that. Who doesn't
agree that apartheid should be dismantled? However,

I believe there are several permissible models of how people should go about that, and churches have tended to close that plurality off by saying divestment is the only way. I think that's a mistake because there are good arguments for selective investment and divestment. The churches have attempted to push that idea down. I believe that if there were diversity at the very highest staff levels, you wouldn't get this movement toward closure or narrowing things down so much.

QUESTION: On that question, why should there be this kind of ideological tendency at the staff level?

PROFESSOR BENNE: I think it is something of a generational thing. I believe that a lot of the key people in those staff positions were very much affected or formed by the experience of the 1960s. To make a long story short, I think in the experience of the 1960s the whole myth of American innocence was flipped on its head to become the myth of American guilt. Therefore, staff members tend to have a very deep sense that the United States is at fault for most of the world's problems, and they are ideologically shaped very much with that vision, particularly in foreign policy. It has been a long march through the institutions; it's beginning to pay off for the people of the 1960s.

I don't object to those opinions or that outlook being represented. I think it should be represented, but it has to be in a lively encounter with other positions at all levels. I think the church could do much better.

QUESTION: But isn't that the problem of the religious mentality? It is intolerant, isn't it? Doesn't it have a doctrine it wants to promote? Isn't that the heart of the Western position? I'm trying to avoid just picking on one of the churches.

PROFESSOR BENNE: It depends on what level you are addressing. Certainly the church claims that its vision of life is true. But I think at the heart of that kind of claim ought to be a deep sense of paradox that we, finite human beings, are claiming to know the truth when, in fact, the only truth is God's truth which we have no direct way of appropriating. So at one level you humbly confess that this is the truth as we have received it from other limited human beings—the truth about sin and salvation. But those central religious convictions are quite a distance from public policy questions. There is no warrant for claiming revealed truth on those issues of policy. Indeed we are sinners and see things through distorted spectacles; we have our own interests connected with what it is we propose, even when we try to be objective. As you get into these more ambiguous areas, there ought to be a deep sense of humility and impartialness coming out of religion itself.

QUESTION: I'm curious as to whether you would draw a distinction within your hierarchy in terms of the danger to the church as an institution (which is how I interpreted your hierarchy) versus the danger to the institution of government. As most of us in this room know, Mr. Jefferson chose to put on his tombstone the fact that he was the author of the Declaration of Religious Freedom in Virginia, and my vague recollection is that he was really concerned about the power of the church as it might influence the institution of government. It seems to me that an argument can be made that it is not so bad if the Council of Churches stands up and makes some pronouncement, as long as I know that it is the Council of Churches. If I am able to do this, I can discount my own view in light of that of the pronouncing body. This might be more difficult to do if, for example, you took a *Wall Street Journal* article about the influence of the United Jewish Appeal. It seems to me that it is a concern to the institution of government if the source of the political pressure of the church is unknown, and I'm curious as to whether you would say that this is valid or not. If it is valid, it seems to me that the concern in terms of your hierarchy might be from the perspective of the citizen down on a lower level who can't identify the church's role as readily as when the bishops are making the pronouncements.

PROFESSOR BENNE: What you are saying is that at the very first level, if the church really was forming people powerfully and uniformly and was growing in strength in this indirect way, it could finally be more . . .

COMMENT: More insidious.

PROFESSOR BENNE: I would think that wouldn't be the case if religious faith was held to the influence mode, the persuasion mode. This is fascinating because in one way—maybe this is nostalgia for Christendom—I would hope that our society could find more cohesion around moral values and less fragmentation. I have a hope that some day we could move toward more of a synthesis of culture than we presently have. Maybe I'm the insidious one about whom you are worried. But I would want this only in a persuasive mode, that more people were persuaded that this was the way of life to which they should adhere. It would be a percolating model, starting from the grass roots and moving up. I would not find this terribly threatening unless you are a philosophical relativist who says that there is something terribly dangerous about having more coherence in a culture. I would find that threatening if it is done oppressively. But I do think your point is well taken, that it is a human tendency that once there is adherence to one frame of reference, it is common to claim too much for it and use power to maintain it.

I've always wondered when considering my categories, how the Mormons operate. I don't have any special knowledge of it. Maybe this is an interesting case in point. I wonder whether within the operation of the Mormon Church they specifically address public policy issues or whether it is in that first mode that the powerful formation occurs. Mormons do tend to come out on the same side of things with regard to public policy issues, and this may be a good case of what you are suggesting. Maybe the formation is so powerful and so narrow that they could, were they to spread sufficiently enough, present the kind of problem about which you were talking. Their elders don't make public announcements, at least not very often, do they? They do it on some issues, but they don't try to make any specific appeal to centers of government.

QUESTION: I noticed you didn't make any comment about the church having ministers of the cloth run for office. I'm thinking specifically of Pat Robertson and Jesse Jackson running for the highest office in the United States. These are two examples of church involvement that you didn't touch. In contrast to the Catholic position under which a priest was forced to resign from Congress, do you see any trend on the part of certain Protestant denominations to have their leaders be candidates for not only public office but the highest office in the land?

PROFESSOR BENNE: Well, I don't see any trend in that direction. Of course, when you are talking about Jackson and Robertson you are not talking about ordained clergy who are under much hierarchical authority or direction. They are almost completely independent operators, aren't they? No one could tell them that they shouldn't be ordained, or rule that they should give up their ordination. They are independents. My own viewpoint, as a lay person, is that clergy probably should shed their clerical role if they become public, political figures. I wouldn't insist on that, but if they do become elected public figures they shouldn't make much of their ordination. They shouldn't make a public issue of their status. I would be against Lutheran pastors wearing their collars in the Congress or in the state legislature because I think that would call forth too much religious authority for their very partisan acts of political decision-making.

NARRATOR: Not everyone may know this but we used to, in political history questions, ask Dumas Malone to ask the final question. We don't always have Dr. Fletcher with us, and yet he wrote a book on situation ethics some years ago that sold one million copies. This work had a profound impact on the thinking of a lot of people. Therefore, if he wants to, we ought to let him ask the last question.

QUESTION: I listened to and appreciate the helpful breakdown you made in various modalities of politics and religion. Several questions have occurred to me. Let me just ask you to confirm the impression I have. I have the impression that, given the historic saying in the Christian tradition, the business of the churches is to both afflict the comfortable and comfort the afflicted (the prophetic and priestly principles). In the bureaucracy of the churches the prophetic principle is a very vital and active one. But contrary to that, in the rank and file of the church, in the church's membership, the preoccupation is with comforting the afflicted and not afflicting the comfortable. Is there any validity in that impression?

PROFESSOR BENNE: Oh, I think you are right, and there are probably reasons for that which have been well-rehearsed in other places. In a world of fragmentation, violence, mobility, and turbulence, when the laity come to church on Sunday, they want to be comforted and want to be addressed in a way that is comforting. If I understand the laity, they don't like to be afflicted by what they might consider to be partisan, political haranguing. But if we rest comfortably with that, I think we will have a very poor arrangement because, at least from a Lutheran perspective, the law must be preached in a dialectical relationship with the gospel. The law does afflict, and I believe that has to be done not only with regard to personal morality or personal life but also with public life. It must be done in ways that are very skilled and in ways that allow people to disagree and to engage in a discussion with the person who is preaching.

I was at a Unitarian Church in the Roanoke Valley recently, and one of the marvelous things they do (which I am told the Puritans also did) is that the guest speaker makes a twenty or thirty minute statement, and then there is fifteen minutes for debate and feedback. I think that kind of arrangement—maybe not within the worship service itself—would probably encourage pastors to afflict the comfortable a little bit more if they felt they weren't offending the laity, then the laity could really talk about it. But I think you are right, and your impression of the description is accurate.

QUESTION: Could it have the opposite effect of scaring the pastor into preaching a less prophetic kind of message?

PROFESSOR BENNE: Yes, it could encourage him to take more care with the topics he chooses.

NARRATOR: We are very pleased to have had this opportunity with Professor Benne, and we hope that some of you who are in touch with activities in Roanoke will also be in touch with him. I didn't read his titles but they are impressive. He is Jordan Trexler Professor of Religion and Philosophy and chairman of the Religion and Philosophy Department at Roanoke College. He is also director of a major center on church and society. Reinhold Niebuhr once said, when somebody criticized him rather sharply, "I didn't just stumble in from the street." Bob Benne hasn't stumbled in from the street when he talks about these subjects and neither has Joe Fletcher. We hope very much that we can stay in touch.

CHAPTER XI

Religion and Politics in the United States: An Overview

KENNETH W. THOMPSON

Theologians and political philosophers through much of the twentieth century have found that the separation of church and state provides a unique source of strength in the U.S. constitutional system. Yet friends abroad are puzzled by the American justification for a division between the secular and sacerdotal worlds. Muslim, Confucian, and other non-Western thinkers would unite and bring together what American religious and political thinkers keep separate. Even in Western countries such as England the existence of a state church draws church and state closely together. In a recent monograph, Don K. Price, of Harvard University, traces the inter-connection between a religious establishment in England and the existence of a political establishment.[1] He finds that because the political establishment derives from the religious establishment, its credibility is enhanced. In the United States, science and administration have been substitutes for the trustworthiness of religiously acknowledged leaders.

THE FOLLOWING

Whatever questions outsiders may raise, the intention of the Founding Fathers seems clear. They believed in religious and political freedom. The political edifice they sought to build was dualistic in conception, balancing religion and politics. Not only Thomas Jefferson but also his most respected political allies feared an established religion and religious tests for political office. Nor did the author of the Declaration of Religious Freedom stand alone among presidents. In 1815, John Adams wrote to Jefferson, "The question before the human race is whether the God of nature shall govern the world by his own laws, or whether priests and kings shall rule it by fictitious miracles." This most balanced system has not prevented fear of abuse arising from the convergence of religion and politics. Writing to Adams six years after his second term, Jefferson described "this loathsome combination of church and state." Earlier he had warned that history provides no example of a clergy-ridden people maintaining a free civil government. The lack of such a government, he felt, marks "the lowest grade of ignorance," of which political as well as religious leaders will always "avail themselves for their own purpose."

Fear of the abuse of religion by political leaders reflected deep-seated underlying doubts concerning human nature. To keep lesser mortal motives within bounds, religion and politics were to exist in an equilibrium ordered by an intricate network of checks and balances. Not Hamilton but Jefferson declared, "Free government is founded on jealousy and not confidence which prescribes limited Constitutions to bind down those whom we are obliged to trust with power: that our Constitution has accordingly fixed the limits to which and no further our confidence may go."[2]   Jefferson was more emphatic about human nature in the debates over the Kentucky Resolutions of 1798, saying, "In questions of power then let no more be heard of confidence in man, but bind him down from mischief by the chains of the Constitution."[3]

Thus the outlook of the founders on human nature was grim. With certain contemporary philosophers, they believed in the mutually reinforcing quality of the two independent forces, religion and politics.   Indeed, that reinforcement constituted for them the genius of American society.   With a few tragic exceptions, notably the Civil War, the United States has escaped the fierce and destructive conflicts that have torn other societies asunder.   In that war, a sitting president was forced to speak of warring factions who read from the same Bible, prayed to the same God, and invoked His blessings on their cause. They went to war for principles, not politics or possessions.   For the most part, however, Americans within territorial boundaries have been spared those conflicts that stem from crusades for righteousness. Ordinary citizens have not rallied to fight holy wars or wars of religion; those who have fallen have not been helpless victims of *jihads* conducted in the name of religion.

The different aims of religion and politics

The cornerstone on which the separation of church and state rests, then, is the belief that religion cannot be equated with politics or politics with a particular religion without threatening their mutual destruction.   Each has its own imperatives. Historically, every attempt to substitute the pursuit of one for the realization of the other has been doomed from the start.   The ends of religion are not the ends of politics.   The claim that religion and politics are interchangeable will not stand scrutiny, especially in the long run.

The end of religion is to discover a purpose beyond all human purposes, according to Nikolay Berdyayev.[4] Men and women yearn for a perspective that transcends all the fragmentary purposes of human existence. Politics and nationalism remain fragmentary endeavors; when a political regime crowds out a higher religion, a religion is made out of politics, nationalism, or science. Societies will not long tolerate a spiritual vacuum.

Yet religion is more than a political necessity. It is the ground of man's being, as Paul Tillich has maintained,[5] and religious faith stands above and beyond religious practices.[6] Faith is a matter of a person's ultimate commitments, while religion expresses itself largely in ceremonies, practices, and institutions. To place every person's faith in a single doctrinal straitjacket is to trivialize that faith. Religious faith is above politics and institutions. It is not exhausted in observances or procedures. Ideologies and political religions are, at best, approximations—at worst, corruptions—of religion. Religion's province is human life and the cosmos, good and evil, judgment and salvation. Even in its most noble expression, politics' ends are not the same as religion's.

To be more specific, the ends of politics are order and justice. Whether through social compacts or conquest, we seek to bring nature and the war of each against all under control. We strive for justice, which John Dewey described as giving each man his due. Hans J. Morgenthau wrote of "equality of freedom" as the distinguishing characteristic of American politics.[7]

Politics is not allegiance to a single moral principle but the ability to coordinate and adjust multiple principles such as order and freedom, justice and equality, or peace and national security. It was

Justice Oliver Wendell Holmes, with his eye on politics, who explained, "Some people admire the man of principle. I admire the man who can find his way through a maze of conflicting principles."[8] The art of politics is that persons who hold convergent and divergent purposes and interests work together. Toward certain of these goals and interests, legitimate resentment may be felt, a resentment that moral sentiment alone cannot sweep away. The constituents of a religion are the faithful, but the constituents of most politicians are not members of a single religious faith. For example, along with voters of many religions, some 100,000 Hindus helped elect Senator Daniel Patrick Moynihan of New York. It is deception, therefore, when the leader of a religiously diverse constituency presumes to speak for his or her acts in the name of one God.

Looking back, we remember leaders who displayed cosmic humility concerning the will of God. At the time of the Civil War, Abraham Lincoln was visited by a group of Presbyterian ministers bearing a petition calling for the emancipation of all the slaves. He replied saying that in every great contest each party claims to be following the will of God. Though God cannot favor two opposing causes, proponents of both believe they act in his name. Lincoln went on to ask why, if God had revealed His will to others, He would not have revealed it to him, the president, accountable to all the people. He said he was anxious to learn the will of God and to follow it, but this was not the day of miracles. In politics he had chosen as his guide "to study the plain physical facts, ascertain what is possible and learn what is wise and just." In practical affairs, he had to balance the desirable with the possible.

In defining the role of church and state, constitutionalism speaks from two historical traditions. One of them is the Judeo-Christian legacy, which is the source of the higher law and the moral and political standards on which the Bill of Rights in the Constitution is based. Love and its approximation in justice are the guideposts of higher religion. Such a religion drives the individual in the direction of what Reinhold Niebuhr called "the impossible possibility," which is the law of love.[9]

Within the most intimate communities, and especially the family, the law of love is at least a tenuous possibility. In politics and business, love is almost always beyond reach. Great collectives such as political parties and nation-states do not love one another. For them, not love but respect is a practical possibility. Yet political leaders and nations, whose moral possibilities are of a lower order than the Judeo-Christian ethic, tend to justify themselves in the highest moral terms. Within the American constitutional system, they translate the practical politics of limited policies and programs into the language of moral absolutes. They sanctify their pragmatic actions as though they were universal truths and, in the process, hamper those who search for political compromises and agreements. We know that moral principles resist compromise. It is interests that yield in the political process.

The second historical tradition undergirding the constitutional order is the Graeco-Roman inheritance. Its focus is on politics and law. As the University of Chicago poet-philosopher T.V. Smith was wont to say, politics brings relations among people down from the heavens. Politics means the harmonization of interests and differences. The seamy side of politics is bargaining and horse trading in smoke-filled rooms. A political agreement means settling for half a loaf. John F. Kennedy observed that Lincoln was a sad man because he learned that in politics one cannot get everything one wants. Hard-boiled politicians know, as did Boss Tweed, that "this God-business" may have little to do with politics.

However, both traditions in politics—the Judeo-Christian and the Graeco-Roman—when carried to their logical conclusion are imperiled by certain excesses. Put too simply, the one suffers from moralism, the other from cynicism. Religious men and women can be excessively moralistic in defending the righteousness of their cause but singularly ineffective in reaching positions of consensus in a sinful world. Perhaps this is why Harold Nicolson described religious people as the worst diplomats.[10] They cannot escape the illusion that morality is bound up in a single moral principle. Yet we know that our versions of good and evil are almost always colored by the taint of self-interest. Dean Acheson once complained, for instance, that for Nelson Rockefeller stealing was the only sin. Politics, on the other hand, struggles with an opposite vice: an excess of hubris in putting means before ends, procedures ahead of purpose, and success above virtue.

The signal accomplishment of the Founders was in achieving balance and proportion in the relationship between religion and politics, between church and state. Because they recognized that each must have its place, they sought for each a position of independence. Neither was to rule the other, both were to serve in accustomed and well-understood constitutional spheres. How the ordering of that relationship and the accepted definitions of the constituent roles has been challenged, if not upset, in the 1970s and 1980s is the theme of the section that follows.

THE CHALLENGE

The challenge to the separation of church and state has come in the last quarter of the twentieth century. The causes are both immediate and long-term. The more immediate causes are social and political.   The long-term reasons for the challenge stem from religious changes.

The Indonesian social philosopher Soedjatmoko, who is currently president of the United Nations University, directed attention to one of the deeper causes of change when he wrote of mankind's loss of an unquestioning faith in the afterlife. Soedjatmoko argued that this change has transformed people of faith into people in a hurry. The perspective from which they view social problems is radically altered. Their time frame has shifted and they pursue salvation here and now. Political goals have become infused with religious fervor. Utopianism has replaced survival. The motivating force of political movements on both the Right and the Left is social transformation in the reformer's image.

At one level, the struggle is being waged within religious bodies themselves. Denominations in which opposing trends have long coexisted find themselves locked in self-described holy wars. Fundamentalists and theological moderates face one another across a deep spiritual chasm, as in the Southern Baptist Convention. Religion writer Ed Briggs quotes Baptist moderates as saying that "fundamentalism is not so much a doctrinal position as it is a style of life that is negative, judgmental and suspicious of anyone who doesn't agree with the way they see things."[11]   A seminary president denounces "unholy forces . . . at work in our midst" and "campus subversives" recruited and indoctrinated by the fundamentalists. Conservative leaders call for a reversal of the drift into biblical liberalism and predict a takeover of all the church's institutions in less than 10 years.[12] Church factions are at war.

As viewed by the public, the more visible manifestation of the change in church-state relations is in the political arena. Religion and politics seem to be merging into what one church historian—George Marsden, of Calvin College—calls "shallow folk religion." Thirty years ago, the United States was witnessing the greatest surge of churchgoing in its history. A record-level 49 percent of the population attended weekly church services. That level has dropped to 40 percent. Liberal Protestantism and the National Council of Churches were in the ascendancy, symbolized by President Dwight D. Eisenhower's laying the cornerstone of the Council's building in New York City. Today fundamentalists and conservatives alone have access to the White House. *New York Times* columnist Kenneth A. Briggs describes the changing patterns of religion and politics as follows:

> Armed with moral agendas, some conservative Christians who once felt excluded from the centers of political power are seeking to regain public backing for values they believe were wrongly stripped away by legislative and court action.
>
> At the same time, liberal Protestants, many of whom enjoyed close ties with official Washington in the past, are pushing a set of such issues as disarmament and improved social services that they consider neglected.
>
> Roman Catholics, meanwhile, have found a new, independent voice through their bishops that is measuring United States nuclear arms strategy, domestic social programs and foreign policy in a more sharply critical manner.
>
> These developments stem from a common perception among Christian groups that the civil authorities no longer offer sufficient support for their beliefs and moral standards. Often their interests overlap as they separately seek to gain a stronger hearing in shaping public policy. The situation is

urgent, they believe, because America is morally floundering and its values are up for grabs.[13]

Religion's influence on the political process

On the extent of the renewal of the public's commitment to religion, the debate goes on. Most observers see it in terms of mixed signals at best. The religious reawakening has done little to narrow the gulf between religion and morality. "People can feel spiritual and still indulge their secular yearnings for wealth and power."[14]

On the reemergence of religion as a factor in politics, more consensus exists. Two decades ago, Harvard theologian Harvey Cox prophesied an irreversible tide of secularism in politics. Now, in his latest book, he discovers a religious revival. At the forefront of religious groups striving to seize a firmer foothold in public affairs are the fundamentalists, many of whom turn to the Reverend Jerry Falwell of the Moral Majority for guidance and direction. Briggs writes, "Fundamentalists and their somewhat more moderate evangelical brethren believe that moral degeneracy and court decisions, especially those against school prayer and Bible reading and in support of abortion, have undercut America's divinely sanctioned mission."[15]

To turn back moral degeneracy, the Reverend Falwell claims to have registered 8.5 million new voters since 1978. In 1984, the focus of the group's efforts was the reelection of President Ronald Reagan—called an "instrument of God"—and Senator Jesse Helms of North Carolina, whom Falwell once described as "a national treasure." In an interview following the election, he revealed that the Moral Majority employed a full-time coordinator for North Carolina for a year before the election. He added,

Kenneth W. Thompson

"We worked on a daily basis with 2,400 pastors and churches in that state."[16]   The Moral Majority also campaigned for senatorial and congressional candidates who opposed abortion and favored a strong national defense.   In preparing for the 1988 presidential election, it plans to register a million new voters each year.

If the Moral Majority represents a more or less direct form of religious intervention into the political process, the leader of conservatism within the Roman Catholic hierarchy in the United States, Archbishop John J. O'Connor of New York, recently named a cardinal by the Vatican, stands for a more ambiguous interventionism.   He spear-headed the church's more subtle initiative during the 1984 presidential election centering on a litmus test for candidates on the abortion issue.

O'Connor, who was the major dissenter to the bishops' pastoral letter "The Challenge to Peace," joined conservatives Archbishop Bernard Law of Boston and Cardinal John Krol of Philadelphia in seeking to make abortion the paramount issue of the campaign.   According to United Press International columnist David E. Anderson, "O'Connor publicly questioned whether Catholic officeholders such as Democratic vice presidential nominee Geraldine Ferraro and New York Governor Mario Cuomo could remain good Catholics without actively joining the bishops' anti-abortion campaign."[17]   By indirection, he questioned their acceptability as candidates.   Governor Cuomo, himself a Catholic, responded that "the church has never been this aggressively involved in politics," adding, "You have the Archbishop of New York saying that no Catholic can vote for Ed Koch, no Catholic can vote for Jay Goldin, for Carol Bellamy, nor for Pat Moynihan or Mario Cuomo."[18]   Representative Ferraro, who had earlier stirred controversy by expressing skepticism about the Christianity of President Reagan's social policies, answered the

273

archbishop through an aide, "I am amazed at how times have changed. Twenty years ago people were afraid that John Kennedy would impose his religious beliefs on his decisions in government. Now some people are afraid that I won't."[19] Archbishop O'Connor replied that Mr. Cuomo had misinterpreted his views, but approximately 55 Roman Catholic theologians, some belonging to Catholics for Free Choice, cautioned bishops against trying to penalize priests or politicians who disagreed with them. Besides, Catholics, whether in theory or practice, were not of one mind on abortion.

Whatever the judgment of historians may be on the intentions of bishops or politicians, it seems clear even in the minds of its own members that the Catholic Church in the 1984 elections was walking a fine line that threatened the separation of church and state. Daniel Callahan, head of the Hastings Institute of Society, Ethics, and Life Science and a former editor of the liberal Catholic journal *Commonweal* has commented,

> The tradition [of the church] has been to speak to broad themes and let individuals reach their own judgments about how to apply church teachings to specific elections. But as the church gets more and more specific about the policies it supports and [as] it asserts that Catholics should consider its moral guidance as they decide how to vote, the people can pretty much deduce whom they should be voting for.[20]

Some fear a backlash against the integrity of religion if partisanship continues. Others would have the church resist the temptation to remain silent, a criticism of some of the German clergy in the time of Nazism. Seeking to put the controversy to rest, Bishop James W. Malone of Youngstown, Ohio, president of the United States Catholic Conference, proclaimed in a clarifying statement for the Catholic bishops that clergy should speak out on public policy issues but not "take positions for or against political candidates." The bishop's statement of 9 August brought Catholic thinking back into line with the tradition of separation of church and state. It also brought the church back to positions it had taken in the 1960s.

A month later, on 5 September, the issue was raised again by a group of Protestant, Roman Catholic, and Jewish leaders. Here the issue was President Reagan, who, speaking to fundamentalists at a prayer breakfast in Dallas, declared there was no inseparable link between religion and morality. Those who disagreed, he explained, were "intolerant of religion."

In response to Reagan, the Reverend Dr. James M. Dunn, executive director of the Baptist Joint Committee on Public Affairs, warned, "We are seeing in this political campaign a deliberate attempt to collapse the distinction between mixing politics and religion."[21] The group called on the leaders of both parties to reject the "notion that only one brand of politics or religion meets with God's approval and the others are necessarily evil."[22] Rabbi Mordecai Waxman, head of an umbrella group for Reform, Conservative, and Orthodox movements in Judaism, declared that "the question of whether Americans are a religious people is not an issue; of course we are. But we are not one religion but many religions."[23] Howard I. Freedman, president of the American Jewish Committee, further warned that "the state has a duty not to intrude itself in religious terms."[24] The statement of the multireligious group added, "The state should not behave as if it were a church or a synagogue. The state should not do for citizens what, in their rightful free exercise of religion, they are perfectly capable of doing for themselves."[25] The

275

First Amendment of the Constitution, after all, protects the freedom of religious conscience.

Reagan's Challenge

In these latter-day criticisms, it is the state, not the Roman Catholic Church or the Moral Majority, that is viewed as the source of the challenge to historic church-state relations. The object of criticism has shifted to President Reagan's efforts to legislate various moral positions of particular religious groups, including tuition tax credits, school prayer, the outlawing of abortion, and the establishment of formal diplomatic relations between the United States and the Vatican. Columnist James R. Dickenson, in appraising the main themes of the 1984 Republican National Convention, wrote, "Religion was as powerful an issue in the Republican National Convention . . . as the traditional secular themes of tax cuts and a strong national defense." Dickenson explained, "The Republican platform all but made religion a Republican virtue. The Democrats, it says, 'tried to build their brave new world by assaulting our basic values. . . . They attacked the integrity of the family and parental rights. They ignored traditional morality. And they still do.'"[26]

Thus Ronald Reagan stands at the center of the debate about the challenge to church-state relations. The controversy over religion and politics swirls around the person and practice of President Reagan. It may be no exaggeration to say that other controversies might have disappeared if the President were less central to the debate. For one thing, his own religion came to occupy the attention of columnists and the media. What is the average newspaper reader to make of reports that President Reagan seldom goes to church? Is he a deeply religious president who is prevented from going to church by security considerations? Or does habit play a part, as the Reverend Billy Graham, a friend of presidents since Dwight D. Eisenhower, explained when he said, "He has been hindered by the security situation and the fact he didn't always attend church regularly."[27] The Reverend Graham has acknowledged that he probably gave the President bad advice in 1981 when he was recuperating from an assassin's attempt on his life. As Graham remembers it, he told Reagan that "worship of God is disrupted if it becomes a media event." It might have been better, Graham now says, to suggest that the President hold church services in the White House. He is forgiving of the President and says he is sure that he misses not going to church.

Less forgiving are those who accuse Reagan for failing to practice what he preaches. Reagan's long-time observer and friend Lou Cannon explains, "He extols religious and family values while rarely going to church or seeing his grandchildren."[28] Increasingly his piety seemed directed more at political ends than at radiating an inner faith. However, his former minister, Donn Moomaw, declares, "His faith is very pious and very personal."[29] When Graham called on Reagan in Sacramento, the then-governor asked Graham if he thought the Second Coming was imminent. How could anyone pose such a question, Graham asked, if he had any doubts about God or his own faith?

Nonetheless, it is difficult not to take notice of a shift in Reagan's public use of religion as a political weapon. Lou Cannon writes:

Most biographers, including this one [Cannon], have played down the importance of religion in Reagan's life. This may reflect our lack of understanding. But another reason is that Reagan, before yielding to temptations of the political season, treated religion as a private matter. His campaign vow that he would not "wear religion on my sleeve" reflected his basic attitude.[30]

To point the finger at the shift in the President's attitude, Cannon argues, does not deny that Reagan is religious. Reagan's intimates say that he prays before making decisions and that he offers spiritual consolation to those who have lost loved ones. He appears to be a compassionate and caring person, particularly in traditional areas. The Reverend Graham supports this version, recalling that "by your fruits shall you know them, not by their church attendance. In his life, we have seen that he bears these fruits."[31]

The change that is being questioned, however, involves not Reagan's church attendance but his mixing of religion and politics. Cannon found that Reagan, in campaigning for reelection, violated an unstated understanding he had with the electorate. Throughout most of his political career he had "conveyed the impression of being a religious man who understood the difference between government and religion. He seemed to recognize he was President of Jews, Roman Catholics, Protestants, secularists, and unbelievers. Now he presumed to speak as an adviser on faith and morals."[32] He joined with fundamentalists and the right wing of his party in pressing the cause of school prayer. He championed the views of Catholics on abortion and on granting diplomatic recognition to the Vatican. He spoke to a Jewish leader about the coming of Armageddon, linking it with the Soviet-American conflict. He intensified the use of religion in an election year. Such actions cause consternation among those who do not share his religious views while they trivialize religious truths for those who do. In short, Reagan's admixture of piety and politics disturbs any number of religious groups, and irreligious groups as well.

Looking back on the president's most recent use of religion in politics, Mr. Cannon concludes,

> When Reagan cites public opinion polls as a basis for a school prayer amendment and portrays his opponents as less religious than he, he gives the impression that he puts reelection ahead of his faith. What it suggests is not hypocrisy but opportunism. It is a question more bothersome and of greater consequence than any computation of his church attendance.[33]

Historically, most churches and politicians have exercised a measure of self-restraint in the moral and religious claims they make for their policies. The need to build electoral coalitions among peoples and groups who do not share a leader's religious beliefs contributes to that restraint. When Senator Paul Laxalt sent his "Dear Christian Leader" letter to 45,000 fundamentalist ministers in 16 states, challenging them "to organize a voter registration drive in your church," his critics say he abandoned self-restraint.[34] As a rule, the churches have not endorsed a particular party or candidate, even when rallying public support for such issues as abolition of slavery, civil rights, or ending the war in Vietnam. The black churches are an exception because the church has been the one social institution available to blacks for promoting political concerns.

The challenge by President Reagan and his political associates in 1984 led Walter Mondale to accuse the President of "moral McCarthyism." In saying that "most Americans would be surprised to learn that God is a Republican," Mondale himself did a certain amount of mixing of religion and politics. In an address on 6 September to B'nai B'rith, he spoke, albeit uneasily, as the son of a Methodist minister, confessing, "What I am doing here today is something that, in 25 years of public life, I never thought I would do. I have never before had to defend my faith in a political campaign." But he did defend his faith and his stands on racism and anti-Semitism and concluded, "A determined band is raising doubts about people's faith. They are reaching for government power to impose their own beliefs on other people. And the Reagan administration has opened its arms to them."[35]

A POSSIBLE RESOLUTION

Invoking religion in 1984 was good politics, and it is unlikely that politicians will forget the lesson of that success. It would be heartening if the result were a profound and socially relevant religious reawakening, but the data do not support so profound an event. Therefore, we must seek the more long-term lessons elsewhere. One lesson may be the truth that religion often serves selfish as well as exalted purposes. What Jefferson and Lincoln said about religion has echoed through the ages. Lincoln spoke often of religion and social problems, but one of his most memorable passages dealt with religion and slavery:

> Certainly there is no contending against the Will of God; but still there is some difficulty in ascertaining and applying it, to particular cases. For instance we will suppose the Rev. Dr. Ross has a slave named Sambo, and the question is "Is it the Will of God that Sambo shall remain a slave, or be set free?" The Almighty gives no audible answer to the question, and his revelation—the Bible—gives none—or, at most, none but such as admits of

a squabble, as to its meaning. No one thinks
of asking Sambo's opinion on it. So, at last,
it comes to this, that Dr. Ross is to decide
the question. And while he consider[s] it, he
sits in the shade, with gloves on his hands,
and subsists on the bread that Sambo is
earning in the burning sun. If he decides
that God wills Sambo to continue a slave, he
thereby retains his own comfortable position;
but if he decides that God wills Sambo to be
free, he thereby has to walk out of the
shade, throw off his gloves, and delve for his
own bread. Will Dr. Ross be activated by
that perfect impartiality, which has ever been
considered most favorable to correct
decisions? But slavery is good for some
people!!! As a good thing, slavery is strik-
ingly peculiar in this, that it is the only good
thing which no man ever seeks the good of,
for *himself.*

Nonsense! wolves [devour] lambs not because
it is good for their own greedy maws, but
because it [is] good for the lambs!!![36]

Whatever Lincoln's skepticism that men were able
to know the will of God, he could not believe that
God willed either slavery or the destruction of the
Union. American slavery, he felt, was "one of those
offenses which in the providence of God . . . He now
wills to remove." Yet Lincoln also believed that
God's will as to the time and place of the ending of
slavery was unknown and unknowable. God's purpose
might be different from the purposes of either party.
If God willed that the war continue "until every drop
of blood drawn with the lash, shall be paid by
another drawn with the sword . . . the judgments of
the Lord are true and righteous altogether." God
knows best. With a fatalism about God's purposes

that matched his skepticism about knowing God's mind, Lincoln, as the Civil War continued, told the Baltimore Presbyterian Synod that he reposed "reliance in God, knowing . . . that He would decide for the right."[37] Somewhere in the universe there was a script, and while Lincoln never claimed to know its content, he firmly believed it existed.

Religion towers above narrow and selfish human purposes. It speaks for a spiritual order that stands outside and beyond politics. Reinhold Niebuhr wrote during the presidential election of 1952,

> Nothing that is worth doing can be achieved in our lifetime. Therefore, we must be saved by hope. Nothing which is true or beautiful or good makes complete sense in any immediate context of history. Therefore, we must be saved by faith. Nothing we do, however virtuous, can be accomplished alone. Therefore we are saved by love. No virtuous act is quite as virtuous from the standpoint of our friend or foe as it is from our own standpoint. Therefore, we must be saved by the final form of love, which is forgiveness."[38]

If those who relate religion to politics could capture some of the serenity in Niebuhr's words, they might help restore the balance between church and state.

Another lesson to be drawn is that any too-simple version of the relation between religion and politics can prompt in reaction more thoughtful and considered judgments. One such response was that of Cardinal Joseph L. Bernardin. On 26 October 1984, in an address at Georgetown University, he warned that there was no place for single-issue politics in the church's quest for a consistent moral vision. He reasoned that "the civil law must be rooted in the moral law, but it may not at times incorporate the full range of moral law." The "question is not whether the deepest personal convictions of politicians should influence their public choices, but how the two should be related." He added that "the development of public policy requires a wider consensus than the personal conviction of any individual—even a public figure." Without condemning fellow bishops, the Chicago prelate explained that the present world situation "resists a 'one-issue' focus by the church, even when the urgent issue is abortion or nuclear arms."[39]

Another reconsideration of the challenge to church-state relations comes from the political side of the spectrum, from Governor Cuomo, speaking on 14 September 1984 at the University of Notre Dame. He found some of the challenges to traditional thought about church and state simplistic, most of them fragmentary, and "a few spoken with purely political intent, demagogic." He relayed a lesson in practical politics, saying, in language reminiscent of Reinhold Niebuhr and Walter Lippmann, "There is no church teaching that mandates the best political course for making our belief everyone's rule, for spreading this part of our Catholicism. There is neither an encyclical nor a catechism that spells out a political strategy for achieving legislative goals." Cuomo reminded church politicians that "most of us are offended when we see religion being trivialized by its appearance in political throwaway pamphlets. The American people need no course in philosophy of political science or church history to know that God should not be made into a celestial party chairman."[40]

Finally, those who seek the proper role for religion in politics must learn to discriminate between shallow propaganda and carefully thought-out positions. The pastoral letter on war and peace of the National Conference of Catholic Bishops is a stunning achievement. It represents the labor of hundreds of able leaders grappling for more than two years under collective discipline "to develop and perfect" a theology of peace suited to a civilization poised on the brink of self-destruction. The letter was revised through a succession of drafts. Consultations were held with past and present government officials. The Vatican sponsored several international ecclesiastical sessions especially for European leaders. Looking back on the process and product, Ambassador George Kennan, a non-Catholic, could say, "This paper . . . may fairly be described as the most profound and searching inquiry yet conducted by any responsible collective body into the relations of nuclear weaponry, and indeed of modern war in general, to moral philosophy, to politics and to the conscience of the national state."[41] As a Protestant, I wish the denominations I know had made a comparable effort. To compare such an effort with off-the-cuff statements by politically ambitious, sometimes church-related politicians is little short of blasphemy.

If the present conflict over church-state relations is to be resolved, a return to the American tradition of constitutionalism and an even more respected 2,000-year tradition of studying morality and politics is needed. Church-state relations are too important to leave to the politicians, whether they presume to speak for church or state.

Kenneth W. Thompson

ENDNOTES

1. Don K. Price, *America's Unwritten Constitution: Science, Religion and Political Responsibility* (Baton Rouge: Louisiana State University Press, 1983).

2. Last article of the Kentucky Resolutions of 1798.

3. Ibid.

4. See, for example, Nikolay Berdyayev (*sic*), *Solitude and Society*, trans. George Reavey (1938; repr. ed., Westport, CT: Greenwood Press, 1976).

5. See Paul Tillich, "Reinhold Niebuhr's Doctrine of Knowledge," in *Reinhold Niebuhr: His Religious, Social and Political Thought*, ed. Charles W. Kegley and Robert W. Bretall (New York: Macmillan, 1956), pp. 35-43; see also idem, *Systematic Theology* (Chicago: University of Chicago Press, 1967).

6. Rom. 14:5-12.

7. See John Dewey, *Philosophy and Civilization* (Magnolia, MA: Peter Smith, n.d.); Hans J. Morgenthau, *The Purpose of American Politics* (1960; repr. ed., Washington, DC: University Press of America, 1982).

8. See Paul A. Freund, *On Law and Justice* (Cambridge, MA: Harvard University Press, 1968); see also Oliver Wendell Holmes, *The Common Law*, ed. Mark DeWolfe Howe (Cambridge, MA: Harvard University Press, 1963).

9. This concept appears in many of Niebuhr's writings; see, for example, his *Justice and Mercy*, ed. Ursula M. Niebuhr (New York: Harper & Row, 1974).

10. Harold Nicolson, *Diplomacy* (1939; repr. ed., London: Oxford University Press, 1955), p. 50.

11. Ed Briggs, "Fundamentalist-Moderate Showdown Drawing Near," *Richmond Times-Dispatch*, 1 Sept. 1984.

12. Ibid.

13. Kenneth A. Briggs, "Political Activism Reflects Churches' Search for a Role in Secular Society," *New York Times*, 9 Sept. 1984. Reprinted by permission.

14. Ibid.

15. Ibid.

16. *Daily Progress* (Charlottesville, VA), 11 Nov. 1984.

17. Ibid., 10 Nov. 1984.

18. *New York Times*, 6 Aug. 1984.

19. *Washington Post*, 14 Aug. 1984.

20. Ibid.

21. "Interfaith Group Sees Church-State Peril," *Richmond Times-Dispatch*, 6 Sept. 1984.

22. Ibid.

23. Ibid.

24. Ibid.

25. Ibid.

26. *Washington Post*, 24 Aug. 1984.

27. Lou Cannon, "Reagan & Company," *Washington Post*, 16 Apr. 1984.

28. Ibid.

29. Ibid.

30. Ibid.

31. Ibid.

32. Ibid.

33. Ibid.

34. *Washington Post*, 3 Sept. 1984.

35. *Daily Progress* (Charlottesville, VA), 6 Sept. 1984.

36. Quoted in Hans J. Morgenthau and David Hein, *Essays on Lincoln's Faith and Politics* (Lanham, MD: University Press of America, 1983), p. 9.

37. Ibid.

38. Niebuhr, *Justice and Mercy*.

39. "Cardinal Bernardin Urges Rejection of Single-Issue Politics," *Washington Post*, 26 Oct. 1984.

40. Quoted in the *New York Times*, 15 Sept. 1984.

41. George F. Kennan, "The Bishop's Letter," *New York Times*, 1 May 1983.